D1590123

Vices of the Mind

Vices of the Mind

*From the Intellectual
to the Political*

Quassim Cassam

OXFORD
UNIVERSITY PRESS

OXFORD
UNIVERSITY PRESS

Great Clarendon Street, Oxford, OX2 6DP,
United Kingdom

Oxford University Press is a department of the University of Oxford.
It furthers the University's objective of excellence in research, scholarship,
and education by publishing worldwide. Oxford is a registered trade mark of
Oxford University Press in the UK and in certain other countries

Published in the United States of America by Oxford University Press
198 Madison Avenue, New York, NY 10016, United States of America

British Library Cataloguing in Publication Data

Data available

Library of Congress Control Number: 2018957720

ISBN 978-0-19-882690-3

Printed and bound in Great Britain by
Clays Ltd, Elcograf S.p.A.

For Deborah

Preface

In her book *Thinking to Some Purpose*, published in 1939, Susan Stebbing wrote, 'There is an urgent need today for the citizens of a democracy to think well. It is not enough to have freedom of the press and parliamentary institutions.' Our difficulties, she suggested, 'are due partly to our own stupidity, partly to the exploitation of that stupidity, and partly to our own prejudices and personal desires'. Perhaps it didn't need saying in 1939 which difficulties she was referring to. Her book is an attempt to encourage her readers to improve their thinking by alerting them to some of the varieties of flawed thinking to which we are prone. For example, there is what Stebbing calls 'twisted thinking'. My thinking is twisted 'when I believe I am thinking effectively and have discovered sound reasons for my conclusion but am mistaken in this belief'. Stebbing's technique is to illustrate this and other types of flawed thinking with examples taken from the political debates of her day, and this gives her book a practical focus to which she obviously attached great importance.

It isn't hard to understand why, writing on the eve of a world war, Stebbing thought it was important to identify the intellectual vices that contributed to the disasters of the 1930s. It would be naïve to suppose that improved thinking would have been enough to avert the rise of fascism but the idea that 'our difficulties' at that time were partly due to our intellectual defects and partly to the exploitation of those defects is one that will resonate with many readers today. It certainly resonated with me when I sat down to write this book in 2016. It would be fatuous to compare the historical significance of 2016 with that of 1939, though one might also take the view that it's too early to tell. Nevertheless, from my perspective and I suspect the perspective of many readers of this book, 2016 was a very bad year, a true *annus horribilis* which saw the rise of extremism in Europe and America, the political disintegration of parts of the Middle East, the Brexit vote in the UK, and the election of Donald J. Trump as the 45th president of the United States.

Readers who are unconcerned about these developments will probably see no reason why they should be of any great philosophical, as distinct from political, interest. If, like me, you view these developments with dismay there is a pressing and obvious question: how on earth could such things have happened? The answer to this question is no doubt complex but—and this is in the spirit of Stebbing—it's hard not to think that stupidity and the exploitation of that stupidity have something to do with it. Stupidity in this context means foolishness, not lack of intelligence. It is one of the intellectual vices that Stebbing identifies. Others include prejudice and closed-mindedness. Prejudice is an attitude whereas closed-mindedness is most naturally understood as a character trait. Intellectual vices come in several different varieties and are not confined to flawed thinking. The relationship between thinking styles, attitudes, and character traits will come up several times in this book.

Intellectual vices or, as I prefer to call them, 'epistemic' vices are systematically harmful ways of thinking, attitudes, or character traits. Epistemic vices are, first and foremost, *epistemically* harmful and the other harms they cause—including political harms—are a consequence of their epistemic harms. Epistemic vices get in the way of knowledge. They obstruct the gaining, keeping, and sharing of knowledge and it's because they do that that they can have disastrous consequences in the political realm. The eight chapters that follow give examples of some of these consequences. Each chapter begins with a detailed description of a significant event or development—often a politically significant event or development—in the unfolding of which epistemic vices of one type or another appear to have played a not insignificant role. Like Stebbing, I use real-world events to build an understanding of the nature of epistemic vices. Vice epistemology is the philosophical study of the nature, identity, and epistemological significance of epistemic vices. In these terms, this book is an exercise in vice epistemology, but not a purely abstract philosophical exercise. Understanding epistemic vices helps us to understand our world and ourselves.

Indeed, it was an interest in self-knowledge, rather than an interest in politics, that got me going on the topic of epistemic vice. In my last book, *Self-Knowledge for Humans* (2014), I made the point that we don't always know why we believe the things we believe. I gave the example of Oliver, a believer in outlandish conspiracy theories, who thinks he believes his conspiracy theories because he has good reasons to believe them. In reality, his bizarre beliefs are more a reflection of his intellectual vices, his gullibility for example, than the evidence. I quoted Linda

Zagzebski's list of intellectual vices: 'intellectual pride, negligence, idleness, cowardice, conformity, carelessness, rigidity, prejudice, wishful thinking, closed-mindedness, insensitivity to detail, obtuseness, and lack of thoroughness'. I knew the study of intellectual or epistemic *virtues* was a thriving philosophical cottage industry and I assumed that those who had written so much about virtues of the mind would have quite a bit to say about vices of the mind. Not so. In comparison to the vast literature on epistemic virtue the philosophical literature on epistemic vice is miniscule, though it does include some excellent contributions by Jason Baehr, Heather Battaly, Miranda Fricker, Ian James Kidd, and Alessandra Tanesini, among others.

The relative unpopularity of epistemic vice as a topic in philosophy came as a surprise as it seemed obvious to me that without a proper understanding of our epistemic vices there is little hope of a realistic understanding of how most humans actually think, reason, and inquire. For example, finding answers to questions is a fundamental human activity that goes more or less well depending on the extent to which how we go about doing this is influenced by our epistemic vices. In Chapter 1 I give the example of the disastrous attempts by senior members of the Bush administration to figure out how many troops would be needed after the invasion of Iraq in 2003. Arrogance and overconfidence were two of the factors that caused Donald Rumsfeld and his colleagues to go so badly wrong in their thinking and planning. Arrogance and overconfidence are epistemic vices and the Iraq fiasco is an object lesson in how vices of the mind can obstruct our attempts to know things.

I call my view of epistemic vice 'obstructivism' to emphasize the fact that epistemic vices get in the way of knowledge. But not everything that gets in the way of knowledge is an epistemic vice. Epistemic vices are *intellectual* defects that get in the way of knowledge, and the point of calling them *vices* is to suggest that they are blameworthy or in some other sense reprehensible. In these terms, the intellectual arrogance that contributed to the Iraq fiasco was an epistemic vice but insomnia is not even if chronic lack of sleep makes us worse at gaining or retaining knowledge. Insomnia is neither an intellectual defect nor, at least in most cases, blameworthy. Even in the case of epistemic vices for which blame doesn't seem appropriate, there must be room for criticism. Intellectual flaws for which a person can be neither blamed nor criticized are mere defects rather than *vices*.

One of the dangers of using political examples to illustrate philosophical points is that it doesn't take long for these examples to become
outdated. One of Stebbing's early examples is a speech given by the then
British foreign secretary Austen Chamberlain in 1925. Reading Stebbing's account today, she might as well have been describing events on
Mars. Politics is best avoided if one is writing for posterity but I'm not
doing that any more than Stebbing was. Another concern about trying to
explain political or historical events by reference to the epistemic vices
of particular individuals is that such explanations are too personal and
neglect more important structural factors. Structuralists think that
people occupy places in complex networks of social relations and that
this, rather than personal factors, explains their conduct. Another view
is that flawed thinking has more to do with 'sub-personal' cognitive
biases—the sort of thing described by Daniel Kahneman in his book
Thinking, Fast and Slow—than with so-called epistemic vices.

I certainly don't want to downplay the explanatory significance of
structural factors or cognitive biases. Nor is it my intention to suggest
that the events described in this book can be adequately understood just
by reference to epistemic vices. Satisfying explanations of our intellectual
conduct are usually multidimensional, and structural and sub-personal
factors are often a part of the explanatory story. But so, in many cases, are
epistemic vices. There is more about this at the end of Chapter 1. As
I argue there, when our thinking goes wrong or our inquiries fail to
uncover obvious truths the explanation *is* sometimes personal. Having
said that, I should also say that the examples I give are for illustrative
purposes only, and that readers who disagree with my reading of them
should still be able to see their philosophical point. I can well imagine
some readers detecting in my discussion some of the very same vices that
I attribute to others. I don't claim to be free of the epistemic vices
described below.

The plan for this book is very simple. Chapter 1 sketches the fundamental tenets of obstructivism. Chapter 2 is a study of the vice of closed-
mindedness. I take this to be a character vice—an epistemic vice that
takes the form of a character trait—and the example I give is the closed-
mindedness that led intelligence officers in Israel to dismiss evidence of
an impending attack by Egypt and Syria in 1973. Chapter 3 is about
thinking vices, as illustrated by some judicial thinking in the case of the
Birmingham Six, who were wrongly convicted for terrorist outrages in

the 1970s. Chapter 4 focuses on epistemic vices that are attitudes rather than character traits. One such attitude, which was on display in the run-up to Brexit, is epistemic insouciance, which is a kind of indifference to truth. Chapter 5 gives an account of knowledge and how epistemic vices get in the way of knowledge. A key question here is whether epistemic vices like dogmatism can protect our knowledge when it is under attack. I found it helpful to think about Holocaust denial in this connection. Chapter 6 asks whether our epistemic vices are blameworthy or otherwise reprehensible. Chapter 7 is about stealthy vices, epistemic vices that are inherently hard to detect. This stealthiness is what accounts for the difficulty that most of us have in knowing our epistemic vices. Finally, in Chapter 8, I conclude with a moderately optimistic account of the prospects of self-improvement in respect of our epistemic vices.

Material from Chapter 4 has appeared previously in my paper 'Epistemic Insouciance', published in the *Journal of Philosophical Research*, volume 43 (2018). Chapter 7 is based on my paper 'Stealthy Vices', published in *Social Epistemology Review and Reply Collective*, volume 4 (2015). I thank the editors of both journals for permission to reuse this material. The paper that got me started on vice epistemology was my article 'Vice Epistemology', which came out in *The Monist*, volume 99 (2016).

A Leadership Fellowship awarded by the Arts and Humanities Research Council gave me the time to write this book. I thank the AHRC for its generous support. I also thank the University of Warwick for some extra study leave that made all the difference. For helpful discussions and comments I thank Mark Alfano, Heather Battaly, Naomi Eilan, Jonathan Freedland, Fleur Jongepier, Ian James Kidd, Brent Madison, and Fabienne Peter. I also thank Alessandra Tanesini and an anonymous second reviewer for reading and commenting on the typescript on behalf of Oxford University Press. This is my fifth book for Oxford. My first book came out in 1997, and it has been a pleasure working with Peter Momtchiloff for over two decades.

Contents

Contents

1

The Anatomy of Vice

At a press conference after the US invasion of Iraq in 2003, defense secretary Donald Rumsfeld was questioned about the scenes of chaos and looting in Baghdad. 'Stuff happens' was his response to indications that things weren't exactly going according to plan. As events unfolded it was becoming increasingly clear that the architects of the invasion—Rumsfeld, President George W. Bush, Vice-President Dick Cheney, and deputy defense secretary Paul Wolfowitz—had seriously underestimated the potential for an Iraqi insurgency and the troop numbers needed to contain it.

How could they have been so wrong? One study suggests there was little planning for maintaining order and stability after the invasion because it was thought that the task would be easy.[1] The Bush administration assumed that Iraq 2003 would be a cakewalk but the reality was different.[2] Senior administration figures believed that American soldiers would be welcomed with open arms by the Iraqis and that local security forces would willingly assist the occupation of their own country by a foreign power.[3] Even at the time these assumptions seemed a barely credible exercise in wishful thinking, and their naïvety was demonstrated by the disaster that unfolded after the invasion. How could Rumsfeld and other members of the administration have believed that things would be so easy? What were they thinking?

In his account, Thomas E. Ricks points out that senior figures in the military, including army chief of staff General Eric Shinseki, had argued

---

[1] This was a study by the Rand Corporation quoted in Ricks 2007: 78–9. I've drawn extensively on Ricks' book in this chapter. I'm aware that not all readers will agree with Ricks about Iraq.

[2] The administration's attitude was well expressed by a 2002 *Washington Post* column by Kenneth Adelman. The title of the column was 'Cakewalk in Iraq'.

[3] See Ricks 2007: 110–11.

that at least 300,000 troops would be needed to pacify Iraq.[4] Wolfowitz
and Rumsfeld thought they knew better and insisted on a much lower
number, below 40,000.[5] They didn't just ignore Shinseki's advice, they
derided it. According to Wolfowitz, claims that several hundred thou-
sand US troops would be needed were 'wildly off the mark', and it wasn't
credible that more soldiers would be needed to keep order after the
invasion than to invade Iraq in the first place.[6] He got his way, and
when the looting in Baghdad started the US military lacked the resources
to do anything about it. It seems obvious in retrospect that Wolfowitz
and Rumsfeld should have listened to Shinseki. Why didn't they?

This is where, in Ricks' account, things start to get personal. The story,
as he tells it, is that Bush, Cheney, Rumsfeld, and Wolfowitz, the four
horsemen of the Iraqi apocalypse, acted as they did because they were
'arrogant', 'impervious to evidence', and 'unable to deal with mistakes'.[7]
The president was incompetent, Wolfowitz was a know-it-all who didn't
know it all, and Rumsfeld's 'Stuff happens' remark was one among many
indications of his hubris and arrogance. Ricks also mentions what he
calls 'systemic' factors, but the overall impression is that the Iraq fiasco
was due in large part to the *personal* failings of President Bush and some
of his senior colleagues.

My concern here isn't with whether Ricks' analysis is correct—this
isn't a book about the Iraq war—but the nature of the personal
failings he draws on to explain the Iraq fiasco. So-called 'virtues of the
mind'—open-mindedness, thoroughness, humility, and so on—have
been extensively discussed by philosophers.[8] Arrogance, imperviousness
to evidence, and an inability to deal with mistakes are vices of the mind.
The dictionary definition of 'vice' is 'evil or grossly immoral conduct'.
This isn't the sense in which vices of the mind are vices. 'Vice' is from the
Latin *vitium*, which is a fault or a defect. Vices of the mind are personal
intellectual failings that have a negative impact on our intellectual conduct.[9] If Ricks is right then arrogance, imperviousness to evidence, and

[4] Ricks 2007.
[5] See Ricks 2007: 68–74 and also chapter 8 of Andrew Cockburn 2007.
[6] See the account in Ricks 2007: 97–8.
[7] These descriptions are all from Ricks 2007.
[8] Book-length discussions of intellectual virtues include Kvanvig 1992, Montmarquet
1993, Zagzebski 1996, Roberts and Wood 2007, Baehr 2011, and Battaly 2015.
[9] See the discussion below on why I prefer 'failing' to 'defect'.

an inability to deal with mistakes were among the intellectual failings that prevented Rumsfeld from coming to know the answers to certain rather pertinent questions, such as: how many American troops will be needed after the invasion? Rumsfeld's vices prevented him from listening to military advisors who knew the answer to this question better than he did. As a result he got it wrong.

I'm using this example not in order to make a political point but because it perfectly illustrates how vices of the mind are obstacles to knowledge or how, as José Medina puts it, they 'get in the way of knowledge' (2013: 30). There was knowledge to be had but Rumsfeld missed out on it because of his attitude towards those who had it. Suppose that Shinseki knew what he was talking about and tried to share his knowledge with Rumsfeld. He was prevented from doing so by Rumsfeld's unwillingness to listen and his unfounded conviction that he knew better. For Rumsfeld, 'military dissent about Iraq had to be considered the result of ignorance' (Ricks 2007: 42) and he showed his disdain for Shinseki by naming his successor fourteen months prior to his retirement. This is the kind of behaviour that led John Batiste, who turned down the position of commander of US forces in Iraq, to comment: 'The trouble with Don Rumsfeld is that he's contemptuous, he's dismissive, he's arrogant and he doesn't listen' (Cockburn 2007: 215). A list of the intellectual vices that contributed to the Iraq fiasco would also include dogmatism, closed-mindedness, prejudice, wishful thinking, overconfidence, and gullibility. It's easy to detect overconfidence and wishful thinking in the assumption that Iraq could be subjugated with just 40,000 soldiers.[10] Rumsfeld's unwillingness to tolerate dissent is evidence of closed-mindedness and dogmatism. Senior members of the administration were gullible if they believed reports of Iraqi weapons of mass destruction (WMD). And so on.

Intellectual vices are obstacles to knowledge, but not all obstacles to knowledge are intellectual vices. For example, suppose that acute insomnia makes people who suffer from it forgetful and inattentive during waking hours. That would be a reason to classify insomnia as an obstacle to knowledge, but not as an intellectual vice unless one is prepared to

---

[10]   On the role of overconfidence in promoting war, see Johnson 2004. As Johnson points out, 'overconfidence contributes to causing war' (2004: 5). The 2003 Iraq War is a textbook example of this phenomenon.

view it as an *intellectual* defect. The distinction between intellectual and other defects is hard to define but, at an intuitive level, conditions like insomnia aren't conditions of the intellect even though they undoubtedly have intellectual consequences.[11] Forgetfulness and inattentiveness sound more like intellectual defects but they aren't intellectual vices for a different reason: they aren't defects for which a person can reasonably be criticized, at least where they are caused by insomnia. Defects that don't merit criticism aren't intellectual *vices* regardless of whether they get in the way of knowledge. Some intellectual vices are severely criticized. Others are seen as only mildly reprehensible, but there is no such thing as an intellectual vice that merits no criticism at all.[12]

Sometimes it's difficult to know whether a trait is a vice or not because it is difficult to know whether it gets in the way of knowledge. For example, the classification of closed-mindedness as an epistemic vice can be challenged on the grounds that this trait can protect a person's knowledge by making them less susceptible to being misled by people who know less than they do. This sort of worry can be dealt with by stipulating that the classification of closed-mindedness as a vice of the mind depends on whether it *normally* or *systematically* gets in the way of knowledge, not on whether it invariably does so.[13] In the case of stupidity, another defect that was on prominent display in Ricks' story, the question is not whether it gets in the way of knowledge—it obviously does—but whether it is genuinely reprehensible. Is a person's stupidity something for which they can reasonably be criticized? Not if stupidity is understood as lack of intelligence, but it can also be understood as foolishness or lack of common sense.[14] Stupidity in this sense is a reprehensible obstacle to knowledge, a genuine intellectual *vice*.

---

[11] The point I'm making here is similar to one that Casey Swank makes in a helpful discussion. What I have so far been calling intellectual virtues and vices Swank calls 'epistemic' virtues and vices. Swank points out that 'it has always just gone without saying that (whatever else they might be) epistemic virtues and vices are, to begin with, epistemic traits' (2000: 197). However, although the distinction is often clear, in practice it's probably a fool's errand trying to come up with necessary and sufficient conditions for a trait or defect to be specifically epistemic or intellectual.

[12] 'Reprehensible' is sometimes defined as 'deserving of strong criticism'. I take it to mean 'deserving of some criticism'. 'Mildly reprehensible' is not an oxymoron.

[13] See Driver 2001: 82 on the importance of the qualification 'systematically'. However, she is mainly concerned with moral rather than intellectual virtues and vices.

[14] On the distinction between these two kinds of stupidity see Mulligan 2014.

Another label for intellectual vice is 'epistemic vice'. I prefer this label because it highlights the fact that these vices get in the way of knowledge. In effect, Ricks attributes a bunch of epistemic vices to Rumsfeld and his colleagues and explains their intellectual and other conduct partly by reference to these vices. Such 'vice explanations' are familiar enough in politics and history, and in later chapters I'll give other examples that cast light on the notion of an epistemic vice. An objection to vice explanations is that they are too personal and ignore more important factors, including the systemic factors that Ricks mentions. It's hard to assess this suggestion without greater clarity about the nature of systemic and other alternatives to vice explanations. Plainly, a convincing account of the events described by Ricks needs to be multidimensional. From a vice perspective the important point is not that Rumsfeld's decisions can be explained by reference to any single factor but that, if Ricks is to be believed, epistemic vices are among the factors that help us to make sense of his thinking and his decisions.

Because of its emphasis on the role of epistemic vices in obstructing knowledge I call my account *obstructivism*. The emphasis in obstructivism is on the *consequences* of epistemic vices for our knowledge rather than on their *motives*. The contrast is with motivational accounts of epistemic vice, which are based on motivational accounts of epistemic virtue. These see the epistemic virtues as 'rooted in a deep and abiding desire for knowledge' (Baehr 2011: 4). Whether or not this view of epistemic virtue has anything going for it, epistemic vices aren't rooted in a desire for ignorance and needn't have epistemic motives that account for their badness. For obstructivism, epistemic vices don't have to have bad motives and aren't vices because they have bad motives. For example, closed-mindedness is motivated by a desire for firm answers rather than confusion or ambiguity, but it is far from obvious that such a desire is a bad motive or one that accounts for the badness of closed-mindedness.

It's hard to talk about epistemic or other vices without mentioning Aristotle. As will soon become apparent, there are many disagreements between obstructivism and accounts of epistemic vice inspired by Aristotle, but there are a couple of points on which agreement is possible. One is that vices are harmful. Aristotelian accounts emphasize the harmfulness of vices for their possessor.[15] For obstructivism epistemic vices are

---

[15] Taylor 2006 is a good example of this approach.

epistemically harmful to their possessor. That is, they are harmful to us as *knowers* and this is the sense in which, like vices generally, they are 'destructive of the self and prevent its flourishing' (Taylor 2006: 1). Reading Ricks it might seem strange to put the emphasis on the ways in which Rumsfeld's epistemic vices were harmful to *him*, but the point is not to deny that a person's vices can be harmful to others. The ways in which Rumsfeld and his colleagues were harmed by their epistemic vices resulted in policies that were immensely harmful (and not just epistemically) to others, but the question one keeps coming back to is: how could their judgement have been so poor? This is the question to which obstructivism offers an answer.

Aristotelian views and obstructivism also agree that epistemic vices are reprehensible to some degree. One suggestion is that 'merely to use the labels "virtue" and "vice" indicates candidates for praise and blame' (Taylor 2006: 6). Some have questioned whether we have the kind of responsibility for our epistemic vices that is required for them to be blameworthy. However, blame is not the only form of criticism, and it is possible to be *critical* of a person's epistemic vices without *blaming* them.[16] Whether or not a deeply arrogant person deserves blame for being that way, they can certainly be criticized for their arrogance. One issue in such cases is whether what is being criticized is the vice itself or— if there is a difference—the person whose vice it is. Regardless, it does seem that some form of appropriately targeted censure must be in order where vice is concerned.

Obstructivism raises many questions. Here are the most pressing ones:

1. I've said that epistemic vices are obstacles to knowledge, but how exactly do they get in the way of knowledge? What is the mechanism, and what is the significance of the concession that they don't *invariably* get in the way of knowledge? For that matter, what is obstructivism's conception of knowledge?
2. What kind of *thing* are epistemic vices? The examples I have given are a mixed bag. Some, such as closed-mindedness, are character traits. However, others might better be described as attitudes. It was Rumsfeld's arrogant *attitude* that was his undoing, and this raises a more general question about the relationship between character

---

[16] On the distinction between blaming and criticizing see Driver 2000: 132.

traits and attitudes. To make things even more complicated, some epistemic vices are neither character traits nor attitudes but ways of thinking. One such epistemic vice is wishful thinking. Are there any more varieties of epistemic vice? Which type of vice, if any, is the most fundamental?

3. Is it plausible that epistemic vices don't need a motivational component? Even if it isn't their motivational component that accounts for their badness, must each vice have a specific motivation that makes it the vice it is?

4. In what sense are epistemic vices reprehensible? Are they blameworthy or merely open to criticism? What are the conditions under which a character trait, attitude, or way of thinking is blameworthy, and do epistemic vices satisfy these conditions?

5. What are the strengths and limitations of vice explanations? What are 'systemic' or other alternatives and how do these alternatives relate to vice explanations? In what sense might vice explanations be 'too personal'?

The rest of this chapter will briefly address each of these questions in order to set the stage for the more detailed discussion of later chapters.

Knowledge is something that we can acquire, retain, and transmit. Put more simply, it is something that we can gain, keep, and share. So one way to see how epistemic vices get in the way of knowledge is to see how they obstruct the acquisition, retention, and transmission of knowledge. For example, an important source of knowledge is *inquiry*, defined as the attempt to find things out, to 'extend our knowledge by carrying out investigations directed at answering questions, and to refine our knowledge by considering questions about things we currently hold true' (Hookway 1994: 211). Inquiry is an activity in which we are all engaged at least some of the time. It is by inquiring that we look for answers to our questions, ranging from the trivial ('Where are my socks?') to the momentous ('What are the causes of global warming?'). Inquiry can be more or less effective, that is to say, more or less knowledge-conducive. Could it be, then, that epistemic vices obstruct the acquisition of knowledge by impeding effective inquiry?

To get a sense of how an epistemic vice might do this, consider once again the vice of arrogance. An arrogant person has an intellectual superiority complex and is dismissive of the views and perspectives of other people. It is easy to see why that is so bad for one's ability to acquire knowledge by inquiry. In the real world inquiry is rarely a solitary activity, at least in relation to complex questions. There is usually the need to learn from others and to rely on their expertise. This means being willing to defer to others and acknowledge that one doesn't know it all. These are all different ways of saying that effective inquiry requires a degree of intellectual humility. Effective inquirers are good listeners; they can own up to their mistakes and learn from them. Arrogance is a problem for effective inquiry because it tends to make one a poor listener and unwilling to learn from others or from one's own mistakes. This was Rumsfeld's problem, and his arrogance did him no good at all in his inquiries.[17]

Inquiry is, of course, not the only source of knowledge. It is also possible to acquire knowledge by perception, and in these cases it is less obvious how epistemic vices can get in the way of knowledge. For example, if I look out of the window and see that it is raining, how can I be prevented by an epistemic vice from knowing that it is raining? What epistemic vice would that be? It is true that epistemic vices are less of a threat to knowledge by perception than knowledge by inquiry, but even when it comes to perceptual knowledge epistemic vices can make their presence felt. For example, a person witnesses a crime but misidentifies the perpetrator as a result of prejudice. They literally can't believe their eyes and so are deprived of the knowledge they would otherwise have had. What one sees is affected by one's beliefs and background assumptions. It isn't just a matter of taking in what is in front of one's eyes, and this creates an opening for vices like prejudice to obstruct the acquisition of knowledge by perception. As long as the intellect plays a role in knowledge-acquisition, whether by the senses or other means, intellectual vices can get in the way.

When it comes to understanding the role of epistemic vices in obstructing the sharing of knowledge, Ricks provides some useful illustrations. I've already mentioned Shinseki's failed attempts to share his knowledge with Rumsfeld, where the failure was due to the latter's unwillingness to listen. Sometimes, not being willing to listen is not an

---

[17] As Tiberius and Walker point out, a 'dismissive attitude towards the views and perspectives of others' is 'at the heart of arrogance' (1998: 382). Tanesini 2016 argues convincingly that arrogance produces ignorance by silencing others.

epistemic vice. There is no obligation to listen to those who are plainly ill-informed about the topic at hand and don't know what they are talking about. In such cases epistemic vices don't impede the sharing of knowledge because there is no knowledge to be shared. The problematic case is where epistemic vices prevent a person who knows from sharing their knowledge with a person who doesn't. The epistemic vices that obstruct the sharing of knowledge might be the vices of the putative recipient of knowledge, the vices of the knowledge transmitter, or both. In one scenario the person trying to share their knowledge is an expert who isn't believed because what they have to say is at odds with the prejudices of their audience. In another case the problem is that the expert's dogmatism and arrogance are so off-putting that they make non-experts unwilling to listen. The sharing of knowledge requires both sides in the exchange to be virtuous at least to some degree.[18]

An epistemic vice that threatens the retention or preservation of pre-existing knowledge is gullibility. Imagine an intelligence analyst who believes, with justification, that Iraq doesn't possess WMD. Assuming his belief is true, he can be credited with knowing that Iraq doesn't possess WMD.[19] He is then informed by a patently untrustworthy source that Iraq has WMD. Because the analyst is gullible he changes his mind and is now of the opinion that Iraq has WMD. He has gone from knowing something (that Iraq doesn't have WMD) to not knowing it, and his loss of knowledge is due to his gullibility. If he had been less gullible he would have ignored the source and continued to know the truth. What is more, the analyst can reasonably be criticized for his gullibility: he should have known better than to trust that source.

It's instructive to compare this scenario with one in which a person fails to retain an important piece of knowledge as a result of forgetful-ness. The difference is that forgetfulness is not, as such, an epistemic vice. A person can't reasonably be criticized for being forgetful unless their forgetfulness is taken as an indication of carelessness or ill will.[20] That can happen, but in these cases it is the carelessness or ill will that is criticized. Forgetfulness, per se, isn't reprehensible even though individual instances

---

[18] Fricker 2007 is the classic account of how the epistemic vice of prejudice can prevent the sharing of knowledge.
[19] This is not the place to be worrying about Gettier cases.
[20] See Smith 2005.

of forgetting can be. It isn't clear, in any case, that all things considered, forgetfulness is an obstacle to knowledge. Knowledge can be lost by forgetting, but without forgetting there would be no room for new knowledge. In this sense forgetting *abets* knowledge by making room for new knowledge. It's worth adding that much of the knowledge that is lost by forgetting is useless knowledge. Forgetting is only problematic in cases where a person forgets what they really need to remember or ought to remember.

Obstructivism is compatible with more than one view of knowledge. My view assumes that knowledge requires true belief: if P is the proposition that only a small number of troops would be needed to subjugate Iraq then Rumsfeld knew that P only if P was true, which it wasn't, and he believed that P, which he did. More controversially, I take it that in order to know that P one must be reasonably confident that P.[21] It may be, as Timothy Williamson notes, that 'modest people know many things without being especially confident of them' (2009b: 297). Still, without an appropriate degree of confidence that P one doesn't know that P. One also doesn't know P if one's confidence is unjustified or misplaced. Rumsfeld was confident that P but his confidence was unjustified. To put it another way, he didn't have the right to be confident.[22]

What level of confidence is required for knowledge and how that level of confidence can be justified are difficult questions. For my purposes here the following observations will suffice: the degree of confidence required for knowledge is less than certainty but a person who knows, and so believes, that P must be prepared to rely on P in their practical reasoning. Rumsfeld evidently satisfied this condition: in his practical reasoning about Iraq he took it for granted that only a small number of

---

[21] How confident is 'reasonably confident'? At least confident enough to count as believing that P. However, the 'reasonably' in 'reasonably confident' doesn't just refer to one's degree of confidence. It also indicates that one's confidence must itself be reasonable (as opposed to unreasonable). Miranda Fricker notes that 'many conceptions of knowledge cast some sort of epistemic confidence condition as a condition of knowledge' (2007: 49). On the notion that in order to know that P one must be 'reasonably confident' that P see Williamson 2000: 97.

[22] Adapting an example from A. J. Ayer, a superstitious person who inadvertently walks under a ladder might be confident that he was about to suffer a misfortune. Even if he *is* about to suffer a misfortune, he didn't know that this was going to be so because he didn't have the *right* to be confident. In Ayer's terminology, he didn't have 'the right to be sure'. One reason is that 'he arrived at his belief by a process of reasoning which would not be generally reliable' (1956: 31). For a discussion of Ayer's view see Foster 1985: 85–125.

troops would be needed to get the job done. What it takes for one's confidence to be justified is partly an objective and partly a subjective matter. If one arrives at the belief that P using an unreliable method then one's confidence that P is *de facto* unjustified. This is the 'objective' dimension of justified confidence. If the method is reliable but one has no rational basis for relying on it then one's confidence is still unjustified. What is needed for knowledge is both that one's confidence is reliably based and reasonable.

This account of knowledge means that there are several different ways for epistemic vices to get in the way of knowledge. One is by reducing the likelihood that the affected individual's beliefs will be true. An arrogant and closed-minded inquirer is much more likely to end up with false beliefs than a humble and open-minded inquirer, and that is one reason for categorizing the former pair as epistemic vices and the latter pair as epistemic virtues. Alternatively, or additionally, an epistemic vice can get in the way of knowledge by getting in the way of belief. For example, the rarely recognized vice of underconfidence disposes one to abandon one's beliefs far too easily, even beliefs that are true, rational, and reliably based. To this extent underconfidence has at least as good a claim to be classified as an epistemic vice as Rumsfeldian overconfidence. A third possibility is that epistemic vices get in the way of knowledge by undermining one's right to be confident in one's beliefs. A person whose arrogance and closed-mindedness led him to believe that P, or whose belief is sustained by these vices, might be very confident that P but their confidence is unjustified.

Obstructivism is a form of consequentialism. The consequentialism I have in mind is similar to consequentialism about moral virtues and vices.[23] This view says that 'a virtue is a character trait that produces more good (in the actual world) than not *systematically*' (Driver 2001: 82).[24] Moral vices systematically produce bad states of affairs. Worlds in which benevolence systematically has bad consequences would be ones in which benevolence isn't a moral virtue, but in the

---

[23] See, for example, Driver 2001. Obstructivism is, in many respects, the epistemic analogue of Driver's consequentialism about moral virtues and vices.

[24] So, for example, 'for justice to be a virtue it must systematically lead to good, or lead to good on balance and nonaccidentally' (Driver 2001: xviii). This quotation helps to clarify what Driver means by 'systematically'.

actual world benevolence is a virtue. The point of 'systematically' is to allow us to ascribe moral virtue in the actual world to people who, as a result of bad luck, aren't able to produce good: 'if they possessed a character trait that systematically produces good in that context (though not in their particular case) they still have the relevant moral virtues' (2001: 82–3).

Obstructivism doesn't restrict epistemic virtues and vices to character traits but the idea is similar. The 'good' in the epistemic case is knowledge. Epistemic vices systematically obstruct the gaining, keeping, or sharing of knowledge in the actual world. Epistemic virtues are conducive to knowledge. The point of the 'systematically' is to allow for cases in which an epistemic virtue has bad epistemic effects or an epistemic vice had good epistemic effects. Luck comes into it, as in the moral case, but there would be no justification for classifying closed-mindedness or arrogance as epistemic vices if they didn't *systematically* get in the way of knowledge.[25] The point of distinguishing between 'systematically' and 'invariably' is to make room for the possibility that epistemic vices can have unexpected effects in particular cases.

The next question is: what kind of things are epistemic vices? It is surprising how often it is taken for granted in philosophy that epistemic vices are character traits. It is even more surprising given that philosophers who take this for granted often go on to give examples of epistemic vices that clearly aren't character traits. There is much more about character in Chapter 2, but for the moment character traits can be defined as stable dispositions to act, think, and feel in particular ways. For example, an arrogant person has the stable disposition to (a) behave arrogantly, that is to say, in ways that are aggressively assertive, overbearing, or presumptuous, (b) think of themselves as superior to others, and (c) feel superior. Intellectual arrogance pertains to one's intellectual conduct and sense of

[25] What about possible worlds in which closed-mindedness, say, doesn't systematically get in the way of knowledge or is even conducive to the gaining, sharing, or keeping of knowledge? And what if, in such worlds, open-mindedness normally gets in the way of knowledge? If such a thing is possible—and it's not clear that it is—then the obstructivist should accept that these are scenarios in which closed-mindedness would be an epistemic virtue and open-mindedness an epistemic vice. Whether closed-mindedness would, in these circumstances, be morally virtuous is a further question. For further discussion of such 'role-reversal' scenarios see Montmarquet 1987, Driver 2001: 78–83, Cassam 2016, and Madison 2017. My concern in this book is with character traits, attitudes, and ways of thinking that *actually* get in the way of knowledge and are *actually* epistemic vices.

intellectual superiority. A person who is arrogant in this sense has what Medina calls a 'cognitive superiority complex' (2013: 31).

In these terms, wishful thinking isn't a character trait even though there is a good case for regarding it as an epistemic vice. It is a way of thinking rather than the disposition to act, think, and feel in particular ways. It gets in the way of knowledge because it is thinking in which the thinker's desires have a greater influence than logical or evidential considerations. Wishful thinking is what a person does rather than what a person is like. A person's character is, of course, partly a function of how they think, but this is not a good reason to classify ways of thinking themselves as character traits. For example, to attribute Rumsfeld's views about the number of troops needed in Iraq to wishful thinking is to make a comment about the nature and the quality of the thinking that led to a particular conclusion. The fact that a person is guilty of wishful thinking on a particular occasion or topic says something about them, but how much it says depends on whether their thinking was in character. A person who is prone to wishful thinking might be described as a 'wishful thinker', but one doesn't have to be a fully fledged wishful thinker to engage in the occasional spot of wishful thinking.

An example of an epistemic vice that is neither a character trait nor a way of thinking is prejudice. To describe someone as prejudiced against something or someone is to describe their *attitude*. I will have more to say about attitudes in Chapter 4, but the basic idea is that attitudes are orientations or postures towards something. Examples of attitudes in the pre-theoretical sense are contempt and hostility. To be contemptuous of someone is to adopt a scornful posture towards them, where this isn't just a matter of what one believes about them but also of how one feels. There is such a thing as *feeling* hostile or contemptuous. These attitudes are affective postures but needn't be character traits. One can be contemptuous towards a particular person without being a contemptuous person, someone who is generally disposed to be contemptuous. In the same way, one can have a prejudice about something in particular without being a prejudiced person, a person with numerous strong prejudices.

Some epistemic vices can be understood as character traits or as attitudes. Arrogance is a case in point: a person's attitude towards others can be arrogant, and a person can also be arrogant. Although arrogance as an attitude and as a character trait are closely related, they are still distinct insofar as the presence of the attitude in a particular case does not entail the presence of the character trait. It is possible to be arrogant in certain respects without being an arrogant person. Arrogance in particular respects is compatible with humility in others. One might be hard pushed to say in such cases whether a person who combines arrogance with humility is an arrogant person, but it might still be quite clear that some of their attitudes are arrogant.

Once character traits, ways of thinking, and attitudes are recognized as different kinds of epistemic vice, certain obvious follow-up questions suggest themselves. One which is best left open is whether these are the only three types of epistemic vice. Although there might be others, the most widely recognized epistemic vices fall into one or other of these categories.[26] Here, for example, is Linda Zagzebski's list: 'intellectual pride, negligence, idleness, cowardice, conformity, carelessness, rigidity, prejudice, wishful thinking, closed-mindedness, insensitivity to detail, obtuseness, and lack of thoroughness' (1996: 152). There is nothing here that isn't a character trait, attitude, or way of thinking, and this leads naturally on to the next question: is there one type of epistemic vice that is in any sense the most basic or fundamental?

A trait X is more basic than another trait Y if X can be explained without reference to Y, but Y can't be explained without reference to X. In this case, X is *explanatorily* more basic than Y. In this framework, some ways of thinking are more basic than their corresponding character traits. If being a wishful thinker is a character trait then the only way to explain it is by reference to wishful thinking—a wishful thinker is one who is disposed to engage in wishful thinking but the reverse isn't true. The characterization of wishful thinking as thinking that is more heavily influenced by the thinker's desires than by logical or evidential consid-erations makes no reference to 'wishful thinkers'. However, this might be a reflection of the fact that 'wishful thinker' is a manufactured trait that is defined by reference to wishful thinking and nothing else. Other traits aren't like that. For example, as will become apparent in Chapter 2, one can say a lot about what it is to be closed-minded without saying

---

[26] In comments on an earlier draft of this chapter an anonymous referee suggested that on my account there is no reason not to classify certain feelings as epistemic vices. I don't deny this.

anything about closed-minded thinking. What it is to *be* closed-minded is prior to what it is to think closed-mindedly: to think in this way is just to think as a closed-minded person would think. This suggests that there is no general rule about whether epistemically vicious character traits or epistemically vicious ways of thinking are more basic. It depends on the trait and the way of thinking.

As for the relationship between character traits and attitudes, consider prejudice again. A prejudice isn't just an attitude towards something, someone, or some group, but an attitude formed and sustained without any proper inquiry into the merits or demerits of the object of prejudice. Prejudices can either be positive or negative, and it is in the nature of prejudice not to be based on evidence. There is nothing in this explanation about prejudice as a character trait. There doesn't even have to be such a trait. However, if prejudice is a trait then there is certainly no hope of understanding it without reference to the corresponding attitude. In this case the attitude is explanatorily prior to the character trait. Whether this is generally the case remains to be seen.[27]

The next question concerns the supposed motivational component of epistemic vices. As I've noted, motivational accounts of epistemic vice are inspired by motivational accounts of epistemic virtue. Zagzebski sees motives as emotions and argues that a person who has a virtue V has motives associated with V. For example, 'an open-minded person is motivated out of a delight in discovering new truths, a delight that is strong enough to outweigh the attachment to old beliefs' (1996: 131). A *motive*, for Zagzebski, occurs at a particular time or period of time. A *motivation* is the persistent tendency to be moved by a motive of a certain kind. In these terms, every virtue can be defined in terms of a particular motivation, and the goodness of the virtue is at least partly a function of the goodness of its particular motivation. Underpinning the specific motivational component of each intellectual virtue is a general motivation which Zagzebski calls 'the motivation for knowledge' or for 'cognitive contact with reality' (1996: 167). In this sense 'all the intellectual virtues have the same foundational motivation' (1996: 166).

---

[27] Someone who thinks that attitudes are primary is Alessandra Tanesini. On her account attitudes are primary since character traits are clusters of attitudes and ways of thinking flow from attitudes.

If this account of intellectual virtue is used to model epistemic vices then one would suppose that the latter can be defined in terms of particular motivations that partly explain their badness and that all epistemic vices have the same foundational motivation. What could that foundational motivation be? As I've noted, there is no reason to suppose that epistemic vices are rooted in a desire for ignorance. Epistemic vices may *result* in ignorance but that is not the same as being motivated by a desire for ignorance. In that case, could it be that the epistemic vices are grounded not in a desire for ignorance but in an inadequate or excessively weak desire for knowledge?[28] That doesn't seem right either. The closed-minded person can be as passionate about knowledge as the open-minded person. The closed-minded needn't lack a healthy desire for knowledge but their approach to inquiry isn't conducive to knowledge. There is a mismatch between what they seek—cognitive contact with reality—and how they go about achieving it. I'll say more about this in Chapter 2.

Even if epistemic vices lack a common motivational foundation, it could still be true that individual vices can be defined in terms of particular desires or motivations. This is more plausible in some cases than others. Take the vice of stupidity, understood as foolishness. What is the component of motivation that is specific to stupidity in this sense? It's not clear that there is one. If one is committed to the motivational conception one might see this as a reason for denying that stupidity is an epistemic vice, but obstructivism turns this argument on its head: stupidity is an epistemic vice, it can't be defined in terms of particular motivations, so it isn't true that epistemic vices generally can be defined in these terms. In the case of epistemic vices that are not definable by their motives, vices are distinguished from another not by their motivational components but by the dispositions with which they are associated and the particular way they get in the way of knowledge. It isn't as if, without reference to motive, we have difficulty grasping the difference between stupidity and other epistemic vices.

Even in the case of epistemic vices that can be partly defined by their motivational components it is a further question whether they have motives that are bad in themselves or that account for the overall badness

---

[28] Zagzebski 1996: 208.

of the vice. In his useful study of closed-mindedness Arie Kruglanski argues that 'the tendency to become closed or open minded is intimately tied to one's epistemic motivations, that is, to (implicit or explicit) goals one possesses with respect to knowledge' (2004: 5). In the case of closed-mindedness one of the motivations is the need for closure, that is, 'the individual's desire for a firm answer to a question, any firm answer as compared to confusion and/or ambiguity' (2004: 6). This doesn't seem an inherently bad motive and even has potential benefits. The point at which it becomes problematic is the point at which it gets in the way of knowledge.

The next question is: in what sense are epistemic vices reprehensible? The simplest view is that epistemic vices are blameworthy. When a vice V is described as blameworthy it isn't V that is blameworthy but the person whose vice V is. If the Iraq fiasco is blamed on Rumsfeld's arrogance then this is 'blame' in a purely causal sense.[29] When Rumsfeld himself is blamed for his arrogance this is 'blame' in a different sense. One view is that the blame in this case is moral blame.[30] Another is that it is what is sometimes called 'epistemic blame'. Epistemic blame is blame directed at a person on account of specifically *epistemic* failings that cause specifically *epistemic* harms. Imperviousness to evidence, which is one of the vices that Ricks attributes to Rumsfeld, is an example of an epistemic failing. Getting in the way of knowledge is an epistemic harm. Epistemic failings can also cause moral harms, such as the killing of civilians in Iraq, but epistemic failings are not, as such, moral failings. Some epistemic vices might be moral as well as epistemic failings, and be morally as well as epistemically blameworthy, but being morally blameworthy isn't what makes them *epistemic* vices.[31] They are epistemic vices because they are epistemically blameworthy.

Some have questioned the distinction between moral and epistemic blame. They argue that epistemic blame is really a form of moral blame and that epistemic vices are a sub-class of moral vices.[32] On this view, the assertion that Rumsfeld was arrogant in the run-up to the 2003 Iraq War is an epistemic evaluation of him, but 'epistemic evaluation is a form of

---

[29] It is in this sense of blame that a dead battery might be blamed for a car's failure to start. See Beardsley 1969.

[30] See Coates and Tognazzini 2013 for an excellent survey of different accounts of moral blame. For my purposes here it isn't necessary to decide which is the correct account.

[31] Perhaps arrogance is both a moral and an epistemic vice.

[32] See Zagzebski 1996 and Dougherty 2012.

moral evaluation' (Zagzebski 1996: 6).[33] This might be a reasonable thing to think if one is willing to regard all epistemic failings as moral failings and all epistemic harms as moral harms. On the face of it, though, there is a world of difference between genuine moral failings such as cruelty and mundane intellectual failings such as gullibility and wishful thinking. It would be excessively moralistic to regard all such failings as moral. A person's wishful thinking might in some cases be morally culpable because of the non-epistemic harms it causes but epistemic and moral culpability are not the same thing.

To complicate matters even further, there are epistemic vices that aren't blameworthy in *any* sense, and therefore not morally blameworthy. To see how this can be, more needs to be said about the conditions under which a person is blameworthy for an epistemic vice V. In general, for a person S to be blameworthy for V it must be the case that V is *harmful*. This is the harm condition on blameworthiness.[34] Accordingly, if V is an epistemic vice for which S is epistemically blameworthy then V must be epistemically harmful, to S or to others. A second condition on blameworthiness is the responsibility condition: S is blameworthy for V only if V is a character trait, attitude, or way of thinking for which S is *responsible*. Neither condition is straightforward but the responsibility condition is my immediate concern here.

One kind of responsibility is *acquisition responsibility*: a person is responsible in this sense for a vice V just if they are responsible for acquiring or developing it. One way for that to be true is if the person made choices in the past that led them to develop V.[35] The implication is that they are responsible and blameworthy for V because they acquired it voluntarily. This is the Aristotelian view defended by Linda Zagzebski.[36] For her, a vice is an acquired defect, just as a virtue is an acquired excellence. It takes time to develop virtues and vices, and 'this feature is connected with the fact that we hold persons responsible for these traits' (1996: 116). How are virtues acquired? By training, habituation, and imitation. For example, one might acquire the virtue of open-mindedness

---

[33] Zagzebski worries that her stance might be seen as 'excessively moralistic' (1996: 257). I think she is right to worry about this.

[34] In general, 'we judge a person to be blameworthy when they are responsible for harm, and have no excuse' (Pickard 2013: 1142).

[35] See Smith 2005: 238–9.

[36] And also by Jonathan Jacobs in Jacobs 2001. On Aristotle, see Broadie 1991: 159–78.

by imitating open-minded people in one's thinking, practising open-minded thinking so that it becomes an entrenched habit, and training oneself to be open to diverse perspectives. It takes time and effort to become open-minded and that is why one is responsible for being that way. Virtues aren't innate and they can't be acquired 'at the flip of a switch' (1996: 120).

Whatever one makes of this account of virtue acquisition, it does not offer a plausible picture of vice acquisition. It isn't as if becoming arrogant or closed-minded requires time and effort, or that vice acquisition requires training. One doesn't normally acquire epistemic vices by practising or by imitating other people who already have them. Closed-minded and arrogant people typically don't have to work at being that way. For some it comes naturally; vices can be cultivated but don't have to be. For Aristotle vice is voluntary but that doesn't seem plausible in many cases. Heather Battaly gives the example of a young man in the Swat valley whose dogmatism is largely the result of bad luck, 'including the bad luck of being indoctrinated by the Taliban' (2016: 100). There isn't much sense in which the young man's dogmatism is voluntary but it's surely still a vice. Furthermore, it's possible to criticize his dogmatism without holding him responsible for becoming that way.

More generally, suppose that we aren't usually responsible for our initial possession of epistemic vices, for becoming dogmatic or closed-minded or whatever. But even if we lack acquisition responsibility for a vice we might be responsible in other ways or in other senses. A person who is not responsible for *becoming* dogmatic might still be responsible for *being* that way. Acquisition responsibility is backward-looking: it is concerned with the actual or imagined origin of one's vices. However, apart from the question of how one came to be a certain way there is also the question of what one can now do about it. Intuitively, there is a distinction between attributes that, however one got them, one is stuck with, and attributes that are malleable, that is, open to revision or modification through one's own efforts. If a person has the ability to modify their character traits, attitudes, or ways of thinking then they still have control over them and, because of that, can be responsible for them.[37] This form of responsibility is *revision responsibility* since the

---

[37] In her discussion of how we can be responsible for our own attitudes, Angela Smith compares what she calls the 'voluntary control view' with her own preferred 'rational

focus is on what the subject can and can't change or revise. In principle, one can be revision responsible for a vice for which one is not acquisition responsible.

There is more than one way of understanding the notion of revision responsibility and there is also the question whether, when an epistemic vice is said to be open to revision, what matters is whether it is open to revision *in principle* or *in practice*. These questions will come into sharper focus in Chapter 6, but the important point for the moment is that what it takes for one to be responsible for an epistemic vice is that one has control over it, the type of control to which the notion of revision responsibility gives expression. If there are reasons for thinking that character traits aren't malleable then that would be a reason for thinking that one lacks revision responsibility for those epistemic vices that are character traits. This is not my view. On my view epistemic vices, including intellectual character traits, are malleable enough for revision responsibility. *Personality* traits such as agreeableness, extraversion, and neuroticism might not be malleable, but when it comes to character traits there is, as Gabriele Taylor puts it, 'normally something we can do about what we are given' and 'we need not be wholly in the grip of what dispositions we may find in ourselves' (2006: 16).[38] It is only if and because this is so that we are revision responsible for our character traits.

How does this help with Battaly's example? The problem with the Taliban recruit is not just that he isn't acquisition responsible for his dogmatism. It's also doubtful whether he is revision responsible. Given his circumstances, changing his dogmatic outlook might not be a

relations' view. The former says that what is essential for attributions of responsibility is that a person have the ability to control or modify their attitudes 'through her own voluntary efforts' (2005: 240). The latter says that in order for a creature to be responsible for an attitude, 'it must be the kind of state that is open, in principle, to revision or modification through that creature's own process of rational reflection' (2005: 256). Either way, what counts for responsibility is revisability. There is more on the relationship between voluntary control and rational revisability in Chapter 6.

[38] The 'Big Five' personality dimensions are extraversion, neuroticism, conscientiousness, agreeableness, and openness. These are determined partly by genetic factors and partly by environmental factors. To the extent that one's personality traits can't be changed through one's own efforts one lacks revision responsibility for them. This would also be a reason for adopting Taylor's distinction between personality traits and character traits. The latter label should be reserved for traits for which one is at least partly revision responsible. Some personality psychologists use 'character' and 'personality' interchangeably, but it's better not to do that. An excellent introduction to personality psychology is Nettle 2007.

practical possibility for him. For a start, he may be unable to recognize his dogmatism for what it is or see it as an epistemic vice that needs correcting. Even if he does manage to see it as a problem he may lack practical strategies for tackling it in an environment in which the vice is constantly being reinforced. If he isn't revision responsible for his dogmatism he isn't blameworthy for it, and if he isn't blameworthy then why call it a 'vice'? Aren't epistemic *vices*, as distinct from mere defects, supposed to be blameworthy? Or do such examples show that vice doesn't *require* something for which we can be blamed even if people are often blamed for their vices?

What Battaly's example shows is that it is possible for people to have epistemic vices for which they aren't blameworthy.[39] In that case, in what sense is the young Taliban recruit's dogmatism still a *vice*? It is epistemically harmful but so are mere defects. One way to justify talk of vices in such cases is to argue that even if the Taliban recruit isn't revision responsible for his dogmatism it isn't in the nature of dogmatism to be unrevisable. From the fact that *his* dogmatism is unrevisable and so not blameworthy it doesn't follow that nobody's dogmatism is revisable or blameworthy. There can be individual variations in blameworthiness for the same epistemic vice. Indeed, even if one thought that dogmatism is an incurable condition for which blame is *never* appropriate this would still leave it open that those who have this vice are open to criticism on account of it. There is no such thing as an epistemic vice that merits no criticism, and the Taliban recruit is not immune to criticism for his epistemic and other vices—his attitude towards women, for example—just because they are the result of environmental factors over which he has no control.

This suggests the following taxonomy: to begin with, there are cognitive defects for which neither blame nor criticism is appropriate. These are 'mere' cognitive defects rather than epistemic vices. For example, although being blind from birth is certainly an obstacle to some kinds of knowledge—for example, knowledge of how things look—it would be wildly inappropriate to criticize a person's blindness, let alone regard them as blameworthy for being blind. Secondly, there are intellectual failings that are certainly open to criticism, and in this sense reprehensible, but for one reason or another not blameworthy. Perhaps, like the Taliban

---

[39] As Battaly puts it, 'it seems *possible* for us to have virtues and vices for whose possession we are neither praiseworthy nor blameworthy' (2016: 107).

recruit's dogmatism, they fail the responsibility test for blameworthiness. Lastly, there are intellectual failings that are not just reprehensible (open to criticism) but also blameworthy, in the epistemic sense of 'blameworthy'. Since revision responsibility for an epistemic vice can vary from person to person, one and the same epistemic vice can be blameworthy in some cases without being blameworthy in every case.

Suppose, then, that a person S has an epistemic vice V, and that one is prepared to criticize S on account of this, but not blame S for V because S lacks responsibility for V. In that case, why not regard V as a mere cognitive defect rather than an epistemic vice? What is the point of positing epistemic *vices* that aren't blameworthy? One response to this question is to note that people are criticized for traits that reflect badly on them but that not every trait that reflects badly on a person is one for which he is strictly responsible and so blameworthy.[40] It is one thing to judge that the Taliban recruit is not blameworthy for his dogmatism but his dogmatism nevertheless reflects badly on him. In the same way, a person's stupidity reflects badly on him regardless of whether he is blameworthy for his stupidity. It is instructive that in these cases we talk about people's *failings* rather than their defects, and this way of putting things suggests that their failings cast a negative shadow over them. Failings that reflect badly on a person make him liable to criticism on account of them, even if talk of blameworthiness is not appropriate.

Still, one might wonder how a character trait, attitude, or thinking style for which a person is not blameworthy can reflect badly on him. Why think that the conditions for a person's dogmatism or stupidity to be reprehensible are less stringent than the conditions for him to be blameworthy for these failings? Consider this mundane example: S is a student with a bad attitude. He is lazy, indifferent, and insolent. A teacher can criticize S's attitude while acknowledging that his attitude is understandable and excusable given certain facts about his upbringing. To criticize someone is to find fault with them, but fault finding and

---

[40] George Sher takes it to be a truism that 'no one can deserve blame for anything that does not stand in a close enough relation *to* him to reflect badly *on* him' (2006: 57). Unlike Sher, I don't want to say that people can properly be blamed for traits over which they have no control. They can, however, be properly *criticized* for such traits. There are certain traits as well as certain attitudes that, in Sher's terminology, cast a 'negative shadow' (2006: 58) over people who have them, regardless of whether the people in question have control over these traits and attitudes or are revision responsible for them. Racist attitudes are an example.

blaming are not the same thing. It is possible for the teacher to find fault with her student's attitude without supposing that this attitude is the student's fault in a sense that would make it appropriate to blame him for it. It might be tempting in such cases to say that it is S's attitude that the teacher criticizes rather than S himself, but this distinction is hard to justify. For if S's attitude is in character, an expression of the kind of person that S is, then his bad attitude can hardly fail to reflect badly on him. Criticizing his *attitude* is a way of criticizing *him* since attitude is not something separate from him. In much the same way, criticizing the Taliban recruit's dogmatic attitude is a way of criticizing him. It is not just a matter of finding fault with his dogmatism but of finding fault with *him* on an account of a bad attitude that is truly his and so reflects badly on him. In this context it doesn't matter whether his dogmatism is also blameworthy. It is still reprehensible and an epistemic vice.

Here, then, is how obstructivism conceives of epistemic vices: epistemic vices are blameworthy or otherwise reprehensible intellectual failings that systematically get in the way of knowledge. More fully:

(OBS)   An epistemic vice is a blameworthy or otherwise reprehensible character trait, attitude, or way of thinking that systematically obstructs the gaining, keeping, or sharing of knowledge.

(OBS) only talks about character traits, attitudes, and ways of thinking because the most commonly cited epistemic vices fall into one or other of these three categories. If there are other blameworthy or reprehensible personal failings that systematically get in the way of knowledge then one should be relaxed about admitting them as epistemic vices.

The remaining question is whether vice explanations are too personal. This question arises because epistemic vices are *personal* failings and part of the point of attributing such failings to people is to explain their conduct. A worry about this approach is that it neglects other more pertinent but less personal factors. Two alternatives to vice explanations are of particular interest. One draws attention to the role of *structural* factors in the explanation of human conduct. The other focuses on the role of *cognitive biases*. Sally Haslanger explains the first alternative as follows:

Individuals exist within social structures; we are part of social structures. We work for organizations, we play on sports teams, we raise children in families. In the case of structured wholes, the behavior of their parts is constrained by their position in the whole, and such constraints are relevant to explaining the behavior of the parts.   (2015: 4)

On this view, if one is serious about explaining Rumsfeld's conduct one needs to focus not on his individual psychology or personal epistemic vices but on the social and organizational structures within which he operated and by which his conduct would have been constrained. For example, there is the fact that he occupied a key role in the Department of Defense, with its own traditions and links to arms manufacturers. He didn't operate in a social and political vacuum in which everything turned on his personal outlook or character. He represented a set of interests that he would have taken into account in his planning and decision-making and that limited his room for manoeuvre. By focusing on Rumsfeld the man, one risks losing sight of all these highly pertinent factors.

'Structuralism', as Haslanger's view might be called, offers important insights, but the way to take account of them is not to say that the epistemic vices identified by Ricks played no part in explaining Rumsfeld's conduct.[41] The sensible view is that personal and structural factors were both relevant. It's easy to speak vaguely about the structural constraints on Rumsfeld's conduct but once one gets down to specifics it's hard to see vice explanations as irrelevant. For example, what were the structural constraints that explain Rumsfeld's view that military dissent about Iraq had to be deemed the result of ignorance? Given his position as defense secretary one might have expected him to take the military's advice more seriously and it's not plausible that he behaved as anyone else in his position would have behaved. No doubt he wasn't free to do anything he liked but what he actually did and how he did it was an expression of his character. Structural explanations can be illuminating but they also have their limits.[42] Sometimes an individual's character traits, attitudes, or ways of thinking are what make the difference.

Cognitive biases are 'mental errors caused by our simplified information processing strategies' (Heuer 1999: 111).[43] We are hard-wired to

[41] I'm not suggesting that this would be Haslanger's view. Unlike more extreme structuralists, such as Louis Althusser, she isn't proclaiming what Jackson and Pettit describe as the 'abolition of the subject' (1992: 111). See Althusser and Balibar 1979, Jackson and Pettit 1992, Thompson 1995, and Haslanger 2016.

[42] There is more about this in Chapter 2.

[43] This is Heuer's summary of the conception of cognitive biases developed in the 1970s by Daniel Kahneman and Amos Tversky. See Kahneman 2011 for an overview. Like

use simple rules of thumb ('heuristics') to make judgements based on incomplete or ambiguous information, and while these rules of thumb are generally quite useful, they sometimes lead to systematic errors. These errors are, or are the result of, cognitive *biases*. An example is confirmation bias, the tendency to search for evidence that confirms one's pre-existing beliefs and interpret any evidence one finds as confirming what one already thinks. Cognitive biases are predictable, universal, and mostly unconscious. It has also been argued by some notable theorists that cognitive biases can't be controlled because they stem from what Timothy H. Wilson and Nancy Brekke describe as 'uncontrollable mental processes' (1994: 118). If true this would make it difficult to think of cognitive biases as blameworthy since it would leave no room for revision responsibility. In addition, hard-wired biases that are built into the way our minds work aren't person-specific—we all have them—and they aren't personal failings in the way that ordinary epistemic vices are personal failings. And yet, cognitive biases offer powerful explanations of our intellectual conduct. Whereas vice explanations are 'personal', explanations in terms of cognitive biases are 'sub-personal'.[44]

Consider this example: the stated rationale for the US invasion of Iraq was a National Intelligence Estimate (NIE) which asserted that Iraq had WMD. WMD were never found and by 2004 it was widely accepted that most of the major judgements in the NIE were wrong. What is the explanation of these errors? According to a Senate Intelligence Committee report the problem was that the intelligence community 'had a tendency to accept information which supported the presumption that Iraq had . . . WMD programs more readily than information that contradicted it'.[45] Ambiguous evidence was interpreted as 'conclusively indicative' of a WMD programme while evidence that Iraq didn't have

Kahneman (e.g. Kahneman 2011: 3–4), Heuer writes as if cognitive biases *are* systematic errors. It would be more accurate to describe them as the *cause* of various systematic errors in our thinking.

[44] In sub-personal explanations, 'the person, qua person, does not figure' (Elton 2000: 2). Their concern is not with what *people* do but with how their brains operate. The sub-personal level is, as Dennett puts it, the explanatory level of 'brains and events in the nervous system' (2010: 105).

[45] All the quotations in this and the next paragraph are from the 2004 *Report on the U.S. Intelligence Community's Prewar Intelligence Assessments on Iraq* by the Select Committee on Intelligence. As well as confirmation bias, the report also makes much of the extent to which intelligence analysts were affected by 'groupthink', the phenomenon described in Janis 1982.

such a programme was ignored. When United Nations inspectors failed to find evidence of active Iraqi WMD programmes many intelligence analysts 'did not regard this information as significant'. In effect, the view that Iraq had WMD became 'a hypothesis in search of evidence'.

This reads like a textbook illustration of confirmation bias in action. According to the Senate Report the intelligence community struggled with the need for intelligence analysts to 'overcome analytic biases', such as 'the tendency to see what they would expect to see in the intelligence reporting'. Even if this is interpreted as a sub-personal explanation of the conduct of those responsible for the NIE this would still leave it open that there are *other* cases in which personal vice explanations work better. For example, Ricks' vice explanation of Rumsfeld's conduct is still in play and can't be replaced by a better sub-personal explanation. Rumsfeld's conduct was presumably influenced in various ways by his cognitive biases but there is no sub-personal cognitive bias that provides a more convincing explanation of his handling of Shinseki than Ricks' vice explanation. Arrogance is not a cognitive bias but a character trait or attitude. Sometimes there is no better explanation of a person's conduct than one in personal terms: getting personal in the way that Ricks does can be appropriate.

It's also not absolutely clear, in any case, that cognitive biases shouldn't be regarded as epistemic vices. Cognitive biases are universal, but so are some epistemic vices such as wishful thinking. If cognitive biases are hard-wired, so are some epistemic vices. Wishful thinking is again a case in point. People vary in the extent to which they engage in wishful thinking, but they also vary in the extent of their susceptibility to confirmation bias. Cognitive biases are mostly unconscious but so are epistemic vices: people are rarely conscious of their own epistemic vices and often don't know they have them. If the intelligence analysts lacked control over their cognitive biases this might count against regarding them as blameworthy, but being susceptible to blatant cognitive biases still doesn't reflect well on them. In addition, we will see in later chapters that there might be effective strategies for 'cognitive debiasing' (Croskerry et al. 2013: ii66). If this is right then the analysts responsible for the NIE are blameworthy for their cognitive biases not only because they had terrible consequences but because cognitive biases can be overcome to some extent. Revision responsibility for obvious and extreme confirmation bias is not impossible. The intelligence analysts would have known about the existence and dangers of cognitive bias and could have done much more than they did to guard against their own biases.[46]

If cognitive biases are genuine epistemic vices what kind of epistemic vice are they? The tendency to search for evidence that confirms one's pre-existing beliefs can be thought of as an attitude towards new evidence. Alternatively, it is a way of thinking. It's harder to think of cognitive biases as character traits though they may underpin some character traits such as closed-mindedness. There is no decisive reason for regarding cognitive biases as a category of epistemic vice that is fundamentally different from the ones listed in (OBS), but it wouldn't particularly matter anyway if cognitive biases are different. I've already said that (OBS) should be relaxed about admitting additional varieties of epistemic vice as long as they satisfy the criteria.

Where does this leave the suggestion that vice explanations are 'too personal'? It's easy to see the force of this objection if proponents of vice explanations are trying to promote the notion that structural and sub-personal factors don't play an important role in explaining our intellectual and other conduct. There is, of course, no need for them to do that or to deny that satisfying explanations of our intellectual conduct are almost certainly going to have to be multidimensional. As well as structural and sub-personal explanations account also needs to be taken of the force of *situational* explanations of human behaviour generally: sometimes our conduct has much more to do with the situations in which we find ourselves than with our supposed virtues or vices.[47] All of this should certainly be acknowledged by obstructivism. However, there are cases where structural, sub-personal, and situational explanations don't do the job and where it is difficult to understand a person's intellectual conduct other than by reference to their epistemic vices. I've given one example in this chapter and will give others in later chapters. Sometimes when our thinking goes wrong or our inquiries fail to discover seemingly obvious truths the explanation *is* personal. The role of epistemic vices shouldn't be exaggerated but nor should it be underestimated.

---

[46] They would have known all about cognitive bias thanks to the work of Richards Heuer, who wrote excellent survey articles about this subject for the benefit of intelligence analysts at the CIA. Some of this work is reproduced in Heuer 1999. According to Heuer, his aim was to translate the psychological literature on cognitive bias 'into language that intelligence analysts can understand' (1999: vii). There is little evidence that the intelligence analysts criticized by the Senate Report took on board Heuer's insights.

[47] See Ross and Nisbett 2011.

2

A Question of Character

The first Egyptian tanks crossed the Suez Canal soon after 2 pm on Saturday 6 October 1973. Israel's much vaunted Bar-Lev defensive line across the canal was quickly overrun and within hours some 90,000 Egyptian soldiers and 850 tanks were on the Israeli side of the canal. At the same time, Syrian forces were advancing on the Golan Heights. In the end Israel prevailed but at huge cost in lives and equipment. Many of these losses have been attributed to the fact that 6 October 1973 was Yom Kippur and that the Israeli Defence Force was taken by surprise. Yet Israel had excellent information about Egyptian and Syrian plans to attack. The problem wasn't lack of credible intelligence but the reluctance of senior figures in Israel's Directorate of Military Intelligence (AMAN) to take indications of an impending attack at face value. How could this have happened? What went wrong?

These questions are addressed in Uri Bar-Joseph's study of the Yom Kippur war, *The Watchman Fell Asleep* (2005), and other work on the psychology of the Yom Kippur surprise by Bar-Joseph and Arie Kruglanski.[1] Instead of explaining AMAN's failure by reference to generic cognitive biases Bar-Joseph and Kruglanski focus on what they see as the closed-mindedness of two intelligence officers, the Director of Military Intelligence Major-General Eli Zeira and AMAN's senior Egyptian affairs specialist Lieutenant-Colonel Yona Bandman. Relying on interviews and documentary evidence, Bar-Joseph and Kruglanski

---

[1] See Bar-Joseph and Kruglanski 2003. Other famous surprise attacks include the Nazi attack on the Soviet Union in June 1941, the Japanese attack on Pearl Harbor in December 1941, and the attack on New York's World Trade Center on 11 September 2001. For a discussion of the similarities and differences between these events and the Yom Kippur surprise see the opening pages of Bar-Joseph and Kruglanski's article. There is an extensive literature on surprise attacks. The classic work on Pearl Harbor is Wohlstetter 1962. For an overview see Dahl 2013.

conclude that these two individuals had a particularly high need for cognitive closure and that this led them to provide policy-makers with a distorted intelligence picture.

The need for closure comes in two forms, non-specific and specific. The non-specific need for closure is the desire for a confident judgement on an issue as compared to confusion and ambiguity.[2] A need for specific closure is the desire for a particular answer to a question. The need for closure is associated with the following general tendencies:

1. Reluctance to consider novel information once a given conception has been adopted or 'frozen upon'.
2. Denial or reinterpretation of information that is inconsistent with one's prior conception.
3. Placing a particular premium on clarity, order, and coherence.
4. Having a poor appreciation of perspectives different from one's own.
5. Displaying high levels of self-confidence and self-assuredness.
6. Being intolerant of others whose opinions contradict one's own.
7. Having an authoritarian style of leadership and decision-making.[3]

Open-minded individuals have a lower need for closure. Time pressure and other situational factors can elevate a person's need for closure but differences in different people's need for closure can't be accounted for in purely situational terms.

According to Bar-Joseph and Kruglanski, Zeira and Bandman 'froze' upon the view that Egypt was unlikely to attack. This view prevailed partly because of Zeira and Bandman's 'closed-mindedness to alternative possibility' (2003: 82) and partly as a result of their high prestige within AMAN. They had highly authoritarian managerial styles, didn't tolerate dissent, and displayed all the other tendencies of individuals with a high need for closure. For Zeira it was a dogma that Egypt's President Sadat would not attack. If he did attack 'it would be Sadat's mistake, not his' (2003: 88). An especially revealing episode was when news came that the Soviet Union, an ally of Egypt and Syria, was carrying out emergency evacuations of its personnel from both countries. Was this not evidence that war was imminent? Not according to Zeira, who advised Israeli

---

[2] Kruglanski 2004: 6–7.   [3] This list is from Bar-Joseph 2005: 251.

Prime Minister Golda Meir that while the Soviets might have believed that Egypt and Syria were about to attack Israel, this only proved that they didn't know the Arabs as well as he did. Bar-Joseph's comment about this episode is that it reflected a 'Weltanschauung of intellectual megalomania and hubris, and a pretension to know and understand, better than anyone else, what really happens in these two states' (2005: 172). In other words, Zeira was led astray by an epistemologically lethal combination of closed-mindedness, overconfidence, arrogance, and dogmatism.

In describing Zeira's closed-mindedness Bar-Joseph and Kruglanski are describing an intellectual character trait that gets in the way of knowledge. Zeira was prevented by his closed-mindedness from knowing that an attack on Israel was imminent, despite having at his disposal ample evidence of an impending attack. The way that closed-mindedness got in the way of knowledge in this case suggests that it is an obstacle to knowledge more generally: the intellectual dispositions that Bar-Joseph and Kruglanski attribute to Zeira are obstacles to effective inquiry, to attempts to extend our knowledge by carrying out investigations aimed at answering questions. As an intellectual character trait that obstructs effective inquiry closed-mindedness also looks like a trait that gets in the way of knowledge *systematically*. Assuming that closed-mindedness is also reprehensible, it satisfies the conditions for being an epistemic vice: it is a reprehensible character trait that systematically obstructs the gaining, keeping, or sharing of knowledge.

Closed-mindedness is usually at the top of philosophical lists of epistemic vices. Even if not all epistemic vices are character traits it does seem plausible that closed-mindedness is a character vice, an epistemic vice that is also a character trait. Unlike most other epistemic vices, this vice has been studied in some detail by philosophers and psychologists. So if it is representative of character vices generally then taking a closer look at closed-mindedness is potentially a way of arriving at a better understanding of character vices more generally. That is the mission of this chapter: to build an account of character traits and character vices that shows how closed-mindedness can be a character vice that explains the intellectual conduct of people like Zeira and Bandman. The extent to which closed-mindedness is representative of character vices more generally remains to be seen.

In order to carry out the mission of this chapter, answers are needed to the following questions:

1. What is a character trait and in what sense is closed-mindedness a character trait?
2. What is the impact of closed-mindedness on the gaining, keeping, or sharing of knowledge?
3. How representative is closed-mindedness of character vices generally?
4. In what sense, if any, is closed-mindedness reprehensible?
5. Is it plausible to explain a person's intellectual or other conduct by reference to character traits like closed-mindedness? Are there better explanations?

What is a character trait? Discussion of this topic has tended to concentrate on moral character traits. Given their greater familiarity it's worth pausing briefly to take a look at their nature and structure before plunging into a discussion of intellectual traits. I have described character traits as stable dispositions to act, think, and feel in particular ways. Moral traits like courage, honesty, and cruelty have three dimensions: behavioural, psychological, and ethical.[4] With regard to the behavioural dimension it is generally assumed that moral character traits require behavioural consistency.[5] For example, the dispositions of an honest person are such that they are consistently honest in a range of situations in which their honesty is put to the test. They won't just be honest when it is convenient or easy to be honest but also when it is inconvenient and difficult.[6] This behavioural consistency must in turn be grounded in their motives, desires, and values. They are consistently honest not for pragmatic reasons but because they have the proper desires and motives: they have the desires and motives of an honest person. Finally, what accounts for their desires and motives are their values: they want to do the right thing because they value honesty.

---

[4] As John Doris puts it, 'attributing a quality of character invokes a depiction of behavior and psychology: The brave person acts distinctively, with distinctive motive, affects and cognitions' (2002: 5). This is one sense in which character traits are 'intelligent dispositions' (17). Here is how Doris tries, not very satisfactorily, to capture the evaluative dimension of character traits: the honest person 'presumably behaves as she does because she values forthrightness' (19).

[5] See Doris 2002, chapter 2, and many other philosophical discussions of character, as described in Merritt et al. 2010.

[6] In Doris' terminology this makes honesty a *robust* trait: 'if a person has a robust trait, they can be confidently expected to display trait-relevant behavior across a wide variety of trait-relevant situations, even where some or all of these situations are not optimally conducive to such behavior' (2002: 18).

On this account, traits like honesty aren't mere behavioural dispositions but behavioural dispositions that have the appropriate ethical and psychological foundations.[7]

How much behavioural consistency do character traits require? The usual assumption is that a high degree of consistency is required but this overlooks some important differences. Mark Alfano distinguishes between high-fidelity and low-fidelity traits.[8] High-fidelity virtues require near-perfect consistency. For example, a person who steals but only very occasionally isn't honest, any more than someone who cheats on their spouse, but only very occasionally, is faithful. In contrast, although low-fidelity virtues such as generosity require a higher level of consistency than one would expect without them, they don't require near-perfect consistency. A person who gives money to charity, tips well, and helps friends in need might be viewed as generous even if their generosity is far from unfailing.

Ordinary vices such as dishonesty and cruelty are low fidelity.[9] Dishonesty doesn't require that one is consistently dishonest; occasional dishonest acts are enough. For a person to be cruel they don't have to be consistently cruel. Sporadic cruelty is enough. In the case of these traits the focus is on what those who have them are *capable* of doing rather than on what they consistently do. 'Capable' in this context means morally rather than physically capable.[10] Moral capacities and incapacities are, as Bernard Williams puts it, 'expressive of, and grounded in, the agent's character' (1993: 60). There are certain things a truly honest person just can't do and that is why he never does them. These are things that a dishonest person is capable of doing, but that doesn't mean that he will consistently do them. When people are dishonest it can be difficult to

---

[7] Williams 1985: 8–11 is an excellent though pithy discussion of some of the issues here.

[8] Alfano 2013: 31–2.

[9] Cruelty is one of Montaigne's 'ordinary vices'. Ordinary vices, as Judith Shklar sees them, are 'the sort of conduct we all expect, nothing spectacular or unusual' (1984: 1).

[10] This is how Bernard Williams (1993: 62) explains the distinction between physical and moral incapacity: 'if I am (physically) incapable of lifting a 500 lb weight then I will not lift it, period. If I were to try to lift it I would fail. In the case of a moral incapacity it isn't necessarily true that if I tried to do the thing in question I would fail. It isn't true, for example, that if an honest person tried to fiddle his taxes he would fail. If he tried he might well succeed but it wouldn't occur to him to try. Or if it did occur to him it's not just that he *wouldn't* do it but that, in a certain sense, he *couldn't* do it. In contrast, the dishonest person *could* do it even if he chooses not to.'

predict when and how their dishonesty will manifest itself but when they *do* behave dishonestly they do so because they *are* dishonest.

Turning now to closed-mindedness, the behavioural dimension of this trait is apparent from Bar-Joseph and Kruglanski's account: a closed-minded individual is disposed to freeze on a given conception, to be reluctant to consider new information, to be intolerant of opinions that contradict their own, and so on. These can be seen as 'behavioural' dispositions but only if 'behaviour' is understood broadly enough to include a person's intellectual conduct. What makes closed-mindedness an *intellectual* trait is that many of the dispositions with which it is closely associated are intellectual dispositions—dispositions to think, reason, and respond to new information in certain ways. A closed-minded person is a person who has these and other relevant dispositions. Whether these dispositions are only necessary for closed-mindedness or both necessary and sufficient depends on whether closed-mindedness also requires specific motives and values.

In most cases a person will have the dispositions associated with closed-mindedness because they have a high need for closure, but what if they don't?[11] What if they have the dispositions without the need? Would they still count as closed-minded or is a high need for closure necessary for closed-mindedness? On the one hand, one might think that a person with the dispositions described by Bar-Joseph and Kruglanski is *de facto* closed-minded regardless of their motives or need for closure. On this view, closed-mindedness is entirely a matter of one's disposi-tions. On the other hand, if a person really has the dispositions that Bar-Joseph and Kruglanski attribute to Zeira then it would seem to follow that they have a high need for closure. This suggests that although this need is indeed a component and not just a cause of closed-mindedness it isn't an *independent* component. The need for closure, which is the 'psychological' component of closed-mindedness, is constituted by one's dispositions, the very dispositions that define the trait.

What are the values with which closed-mindedness is associated? The explicit values and motives of a closed-minded person might not be different from those of an open-minded person. Zeira sought cognitive

---

[11] Suppose that a person's arrogance causes them to be closed-minded even if they lack any independently identifiable need for closure. I thank an anonymous referee for this suggestion.

contact with reality, with the reality of Egypt and Syria's intentions, and would presumably have seen knowledge of their intentions as more important than the avoidance of confusion and ambiguity. In theory he valued knowledge as much as any open-minded person but his implicit values were different. Given the conduct described by Bar-Joseph it's hard to avoid the conclusion that in practice Zeira placed greater value on the avoidance of confusion and ambiguity than on knowledge. However, the basis of this claim about Zeira's implicit values is his intellectual dispositions. Just as his need for closure was constituted by the dispositions that define closed-mindedness, the value he placed on the avoidance of confusion and ambiguity is constituted by the same dispositions. The implication is that closed-mindedness is fundamentally dispositional: to be closed-minded is to have certain intellectual and other dispositions, and a person who has these dispositions can also be described as having certain motives and values. These motives and values are, however, a reflection of their dispositions.

Understood in this way, is closed-mindedness high fidelity or low fidelity? Imagine a person who is not generally reluctant to consider novel information or to give credit to views that are different from their own. However, on one subject they are immovable: the merits of their children. No amount of evidence of their son's bad behaviour can induce them to view him as anything other than a paragon of virtue. They aren't usually disposed to be intolerant of views that contradict their own but they are highly intolerant of negative assessments of their son. Intuitively, they aren't closed-minded since their intellectual conduct in this case is out of character. The most one can say is that they are *capable* of being closed-minded but that isn't enough for them to be closed-minded in the way that being capable of cruelty is sufficient for cruelty. Indeed, it's not even clear that their defensiveness about their children is strictly an example of closed-mindedness, as distinct from blind love. Regardless, closed-mindedness is unlike many moral vices in being high fidelity rather than low fidelity. There is a consistency requirement on closed-mindedness that is like the consistency requirement on moral virtues. The dispositions of an honest person are such that they are consistently honest, and the dispositions of a closed-minded person are such that they are consistently closed-minded. Closed-mindedness, then, is an intellectual character trait constituted by intellectual dispositions that aren't subject-specific.

Next, what is the impact of closed-mindedness on the gaining, sharing, and keeping of knowledge? I've briefly described the impact of closed-mindedness on inquiry and suggested that closed-mindedness gets in the way of knowledge by obstructing effective inquiry. This is a way for closed-mindedness to stymie the gaining of knowledge. A way for it to obstruct the sharing of knowledge is to make those who have this trait less inclined to listen. Zeira was in possession of plenty of raw intelligence indicating an impending attack on Israel. Those who supplied this intelligence can be seen as attempting to share their knowledge of an impending attack with Zeira and others at AMAN. They were prevented from doing so by the fact that Zeira wouldn't listen, and his unwillingness to listen was the result of his closed-mindedness. If he had been less closed-minded he might have learned something, and this is an illustration of the point that the sharing of knowledge depends on the open-mindedness of the putative recipient.

The negative impact of closed-mindedness on the pursuit of knowledge seems so clear and obvious as to hardly need saying. Knowledge is based on evidence, and so depends on a willingness to go where the evidence leads regardless of whether where it leads is compatible with one's prior views. Since closed-mindedness implies an *un*willingness to go wherever the evidence leads it's hard to see how it can be anything but an obstacle to knowledge, whether to its acquisition, its transmission, or its retention. And yet it is sometimes suggested that closed-mindedness has substantial epistemological benefits, and that it can and does abet knowledge in some circumstances. Those who say this don't have to deny that closed-mindedness *sometimes* gets in the way of knowledge. The issue is whether it does so *systematically*. If not then it isn't an epistemic vice.

What are the supposed epistemological benefits of closed-mindedness? This quotation from Arie Kruglanski is a good place to start for anyone with an interest in displaying the epistemological upside of a supposed epistemic vice:

As highly sentient creatures, we hardly budge without at least a degree of forethought, aimed at equipping us with a reliable knowledge base from which to launch intelligible conduct. However, objectively speaking such a process has no natural or unique point of termination. It could be carried on indefinitely as we seek ever more information relevant to a given judgement or opinion. Yet our time is finite, and hence the search must be terminated at some point . . . It seems that Mother Nature . . . came to our rescue with a simple solution: the capacity to occasionally shut our minds, that is, develop the sense of secure knowledge that obviates our felt need for further agonizing deliberation . . . [O]ur capacity for closed-mindedness allows us to get on with our lives, rather than remain in indefinite cognitive limbo, perennially buried in thought, as it were.   (2004: 1–2)

There is a slight element of exaggeration in what Kruglanski says here. Many investigations do have natural and unique points of termination. For example, an investigation into whether Egypt would attack Israel in 1973 would naturally have terminated when Egyptian tanks started to cross the Suez Canal. What is true is that our investigations *can* be open-ended and there is often, though not always, scope for further investigation. At some point in such cases there may be strong practical reasons for coming to a conclusion and sticking with it. A good investigator has a sense of when enough is enough and diminishing returns are setting in. But the decision to call a halt at that point isn't properly described as closed-minded. What allows us to 'get on with our lives' isn't closed-mindedness but the ability to judge when no further research into the question at hand is necessary. We could go on indefinitely but shouldn't do so if there is no need. Even after the decision to call a halt has been taken there is no question of shutting our minds to new information that bears on the issue. That really would be closed-minded but it is neither necessary nor appropriate to shut our minds in this sense.

What Kruglanski's discussion establishes, therefore, is not that *closed-mindedness* has a legitimate role in inquiry but that something else with which closed-mindedness is all too easily confused has such a role. This something else is a proper sense of closure, a sense that one has done all that *needs* to be done in order to answer the question at hand even if one hasn't done *everything* that can be done. Hence a doctor who calls for a barrage of tests to diagnose a patient may be aware that there are further tests that could be done. However, if the existing test results establish with near certainty that the patient has a particular condition it isn't closed-minded not to go on requesting more tests. What would be closed-minded is failing to request additional tests when there is a significant chance that they will turn up something new. Failing to request additional tests in such circumstances is a threat to knowledge in two ways: first, it increases the likelihood that one's diagnosis will be false. Second, even if one's initial diagnosis is correct, one doesn't have the right to believe it if one has closed-mindedly failed to eliminate other live possibilities.

Another dubious argument for closed-mindedness is that it can help to protect one's knowledge. For example, if I already know that Neil Armstrong stepped on the moon in 1969 then there is surely nothing to be gained by listening to conspiracy theorists who tell me that the moon landing was faked. If I listen to them long enough I might change my mind and lose the knowledge that I already have. So if I want to retain my knowledge that Neil Armstrong set foot on the moon then I should simply shut my mind to moon landing conspiracy theories. I should do everything possible to avoid or ignore them, and that looks like a way of saying that the way to protect my knowledge is to be closed-minded.[12] However, the real reason I am entitled not to listen to the conspiracy theorists is not that their views are inconsistent with my prior conception but that they are unlikely to be correct given the available evidence. Only the evidence can justify a policy of non-engagement, not the fear of having my mind changed by conspiracy theories. Given the evidence I have no such fear.

I'll have more to say in Chapter 5 about the notion that epistemic vices can protect our knowledge. The discussion so far doesn't support this notion and the case for viewing closed-mindedness as an obstacle to knowledge is solid and straightforward: on the one hand there is the impact of closed-mindedness on the truth of our beliefs. To the extent that closed-minded inquirers are unreceptive to certain types of evidence—evidence that is inconsistent with their prior conception— they are significantly more likely to miss or ignore key information and to end up with false beliefs as a result. If their prior conception is correct then being unreceptive to evidence that is inconsistent with it won't result in false beliefs but it can still make it the case that one no longer has the right to one's prior conception. If the Egyptians and Syrians had unexpectedly called off their attack at the last minute then Zeira would have been right that they wouldn't attack but he wouldn't have had the right to his confident belief that they wouldn't attack. He wouldn't have had this right, and wouldn't have known they wouldn't attack, because his confidence had more to do with his closed-mindedness than with the evidence. These impacts of closed-mindedness on know-ledge are generalizable rather than a reflection of the specifics of one

---

[12] Kripke (2011) describes a similar view of the role of dogmatism in protecting our knowledge. There is more about this in Chapter 5.

example. On that basis, it is reasonable to conclude that closed-mindedness *systematically* obstructs knowledge both in virtue of the nature of closed-mindedness and the nature of knowledge.

The next question was whether closed-mindedness is representative of character vices generally. One issue is whether character vices generally are high fidelity. It might seem that they aren't. Consider the epistemic vice of gullibility.[13] A person who has this vice need not be one who is constantly being duped. What matters is that they are susceptible to being duped in circumstances in which a non-gullible person would be safe. Viewed from this perspective one or two striking displays of gullibility, especially ones with dire consequences, might be enough for a person to qualify as gullible, just as one or two striking displays of cruelty are enough for them to count as cruel. A gullible person doesn't have to be consistently gullible any more than a cruel person has to be consistently cruel. The implication is that gullibility is low fidelity, and therefore that closed-mindedness, which I've argued is high fidelity, isn't representative of character vices generally. Some vices require a great deal of behavioural consistency while others do not.

In fact there is less to this distinction than meets the eye. When a person is taken in by a seemingly obvious scam this does raise questions about their intellectual character, and they might be accused of being gullible. However, there is a difference between judging that their *conduct* in this instance was gullible and judging that *they* are gullible. They may have reacted to the scam as a gullible person would react but that doesn't make them a gullible person unless their reaction on this occasion is taken as indicative of an underlying disposition. That is hard to know without looking at their conduct more generally. What one is looking for to justify accusations of gullibility is a *pattern* of gullible conduct. In this sense there is little difference between gullibility and closed-mindedness. Bar-Joseph and Kruglanski are only justified in accusing Zeira of closed-mindedness on the basis that his intellectual conduct in relation to Yom Kippur 1973 was not out of character but rather indicative of a more general tendency. The significance of this will become much clearer in Chapter 3 but in the meantime it remains plausible that character vices generally are high fidelity. It is always a

[13] As David Owens notes, gullibility is a 'distinctively epistemic vice' (2000: 124).

delicate matter how much consistency they require but it is plausible that they all require greater consistency than low-fidelity moral vices.

Another issue concerns the psychological component of character vices. The question is not whether they have the same psychological component as closed-mindedness (a need for closure) but whether every character vice has *a* psychological component that makes it the particular vice it is. That is not so. In Chapter 1 I gave the example of stupidity, defined as foolishness rather than lack of intelligence, and suggested that there is no desire or motive that is specific to it. There is no motive or desire that relates to stupidity in the way that the need for closure relates to closed-mindedness. Obscurity is another example of an epistemic vice with no easily identifiable psychological component. In contrast, gullibility does appear to be tied to one's epistemic motivations, including the need or desire to believe what one is being told. However, what makes a person gullible isn't just that they have this desire but their inability to restrain it in cases where what they are being told is obviously suspect. So the psychological component of gullibility isn't just the desire to believe but the unrestrained desire to believe.

This suggests that character vices are something of a mixed bag and that there are some respects in which closed-mindedness isn't representative of all other character vices. But for the most part the structure of closed-mindedness provides a reasonably accurate guide to the structure of character vices generally. If reflection on closed-mindedness leads one to view character vices generally as relatively high-fidelity intellectual dispositions with both a behavioural and a psychological component one won't go too far wrong. What really would be a good reason for not treating closed-mindedness as a guide to character vices generally is if closed-mindedness is not a vice at all. Philosophical discussions of epistemic vice tend to assume that closed-mindedness is not just an epistemic vice but the archetypical epistemic vice. That is why it is at the top of philosophical lists of epistemic vices and why it seems perfectly sensible to allow one's understanding of epistemic vices, or at least character vices, to be shaped by one's understanding of closed-mindedness. But what if closed-mindedness is not the archetypal character vice and doesn't deserve its elevated position in philosophical thinking about epistemic vices?

To see the force of this question it's worth considering the following issue: 'epistemic vice' is a term of art and, as with many other terms of art, the best way of explaining what is at issue is by example. So one begins one's explanation of the notion of an epistemic vice by identifying a few exemplary vices and saying that epistemic vices are *that* kind of thing. But on what basis are traits like closed-mindedness identified as exemplary or archetypal vices? One view is that the identification of exemplary vices is partly a matter of *ideology*, and that the identification of closed-mindedness as an exemplary epistemic vice says more about the ideological commitments of those responsible for the identification than about the nature of epistemic vice. For example, from a liberal perspective it is completely obvious that closed-mindedness is a vice and open-mindedness a virtue but there are other ideological standpoints from which this is far from obvious. For Mill, open-mindedness is 'part of the way of life of a developed individual' (Ryan 1974: 139) and a person whose judgement is deserving of confidence is one who whose practice is to 'listen to all that could be said against him' (2006: 27).[14] However, for the Islamist ideologue Sayyid Qutb open-mindedness is the enemy of knowledge and the best protection against being led astray in one's thinking is to be closed-minded about certain fundamental matters.[15] Open-mindedness opens the door to corruption and apostasy whereas closed-mindedness keeps the door firmly closed. From this standpoint, closed-mindedness isn't even an epistemic vice, let alone an exemplary vice.

It is true that open-mindedness is a 'liberal virtue', in the sense that it is an epistemic virtue that is associated with and endorsed by liberal thinkers such as Mill, whereas closed-mindedness is a 'liberal vice'. However, the fact that liberals endorse open-mindedness while condemning closed-mindedness doesn't show that the identification of exemplary virtues and vices is simply a matter of ideology. The other hypothesis is that liberals like Mill are actually on to something and adopt their particular stance because they see that closed-mindedness *is* an obstacle to knowledge whereas open-mindedness is an aid. Mill is quite clear about this in *On Liberty* where he argues that the only way we

[14] On the role of open-mindedness in liberalism see Hare 1983.
[15] Here is how Paul Berman describes Qutb's view: 'He wanted Muslims to understand that, if tolerance and open-mindedness were accepted as social values, the new habits of mind would crowd out the divine' (2004: 78). For more on Qutb, see Amis 2008: 56–82, Bergesen 2008, and Wright 2011: 9–37.

can approach knowledge of a subject is by 'hearing what can be said about it by persons of every variety of opinion, and studying all modes in which it can be looked at by every character of mind' (2006: 27). This is an *argument* for open-mindedness and against closed-mindedness. In the same way, Qutb argues against open-mindedness. These arguments have to be assessed on their merits rather than on the basis of their admittedly strong ideological and theological associations. Viewed from this perspective the irresistible verdict is that Mill's argument is better than Qutb's, and there is no reason to revise the assumption that closed-mindedness is an exemplary epistemic vice. If closed-mindedness is at the top of most philosophers' lists of epistemic vices the reason is that it belongs there.

In what sense is closed-mindedness reprehensible? Is it merely deserving of criticism or is it also blameworthy? The first thing to say is that closed-mindedness is very often seen as reprehensible and people are in fact criticized for it. There isn't much doubt, for example, that Bar-Joseph and Kruglanski are critical of what they regard as Zeira's closed-mindedness. If pressed to say why closed-mindedness merits criticism the obvious first step is to draw attention to its consequences, and the story of Zeira and Bandman is helpful in that regard as it makes plain the adverse epistemological and non-epistemological consequences of closed-mindedness. In their case one might be doubly critical of their closed-mindedness because of the position they occupied. For those whose job it is to estimate the threat of an attack by a foreign power, closed-mindedness to evidence of such an attack is, and certainly was in this case, utterly disastrous. There are occupations that can tolerate a degree of closed-mindedness but intelligence analyst isn't one of them.[16]

However, while it might seem fair to criticize Zeira and Bandman for their closed-mindedness, and so to regard their closed-mindedness as 'reprehensible' in this sense, it's less obvious that this is a trait for which they deserved *blame*. The connotations of 'blame' are different from those of 'criticize' and it could be argued that blame isn't really appropriate in this case. Their closed-mindedness was *to* blame for a very serious intelligence failure, but it doesn't follow that Zeira and Bandman were 'blameworthy' for their closed-mindedness, for being that way. The

---

[16] The impact of closed-mindedness on intelligence analysis is discussed in Wastell et al. 2013.

latter implies that they were responsible for their closed-mindedness, and then the question is: is closed-mindedness a trait for which anyone can be held responsible? One issue is whether it is either usual or possible for a person to be *acquisition responsible* for their closed-mindedness, that is, responsible for acquiring this trait. Another is whether there is room for *revision responsibility* for closed-mindedness, that is, whether this is a trait that can be modified through one's own efforts.

With regard to acquisition responsibility, it is certainly conceivable that someone like Qutb might actively cultivate their closed-mindedness but this isn't the normal case and not usually the basis on which people are held responsible for being closed-minded. A person who actively cultivates a trait has what might be called *positive* acquisition responsibility for it. They have *negative* acquisition responsibility if they fail to take steps to avert its growth. This assumes that they are able to tell that they are becoming closed-minded and can do something about it. It can only be a matter of speculation to what extent this is possible. However, to regard Zeira and Bandman as responsible for their closed-mindedness one doesn't have to suppose that they were negatively or positively responsible for acquiring this trait. Of greater relevance is whether they were revision responsible for being closed-minded. That depends on whether, in general, this trait is susceptible to regulation and management.[17] If not then Zeira and Bandman shouldn't be regarded as blameworthy even though they can still be criticized for their closed-mindedness.

This is where the distinction between character and personality comes into its own.[18] Character traits are malleable enough for revision responsibility. When it comes to character there is normally something we can do about what we are given. This isn't true of personality traits. Given this way of distinguishing between character and personality, it's an empirical question where a trait like closed-mindedness falls. Bar-Joseph and Kruglanski don't talk much about character in their discussion, and describe Zeira and Bandman's high need for closure as reflecting a shared 'personality structure' (2003: 82). This formulation and others like it

---

[17] See Jacobs 2001: 26.

[18] For Doris the difference is that character traits have an evaluative dimension that personality traits may lack. The honest person values honesty but the introvert may not value retiring behaviour in social situations. See Doris 2002: 19.

might be seen as implying that closed-mindedness is a fixed personality trait, though Bar-Joseph and Kruglanski don't actually say this. Whatever their view, what matters is whether closed-mindedness is susceptible to regulation and management. If not then one should refrain from blaming people for being closed-minded. I'll come back to this issue in later chapters but the case for regarding closed-mindedness as blameworthy has yet to be made.

The remaining question is whether a person's intellectual or other conduct can be plausibly explained by reference to traits like closed-mindedness or whether there are other explanations that work better. As John Doris observes, 'character and personality traits are invoked to explain what people do and how they live' (2002: 15). How well do they do that? Not very, according to Doris and other 'situationists' who argue that 'situational factors are often better predictors of behavior than personal factors' (Doris 2002: 2). Situationism started out as an attempt to call into question the reality of moral character traits but it has also been taken to call into question the extent to which our *intellectual* conduct can be explained by our *intellectual* character traits. However, reflection on Zeira and Bandman, and the nature of character vices, brings out the limitations of situationism. Situationism's insights, such as they are, can be easily and straightforwardly accommodated within the framework I've been developing in this chapter.

What is the evidence that situational factors are often better predictors of behaviour than personal factors such as character? In one study students at a theological seminary were asked to lecture on the parable of the Good Samaritan on the other side of campus.[19] Some were told that they had time to spare, others that they were running late. On their way they encountered someone who was clearly in need of help. Only one of several variables seemed to make a difference to their willingness to stop and help: how much of a hurry they were in. The influence of such situational factors on our behaviour has been seen as a major problem for the existence of *robust* character traits. If a person has such a trait 'they can be confidently expected to display trait-relevant behavior in a wide variety of trait-relevant situations, even where some or all of these situations are not optimally conducive to such

---

[19] Darley and Batson 1973.

behavior' (Doris 2002: 18). For example, if compassion is a robust trait then a trait-relevant situation in which a person might confidently be expected to display it is encountering someone on the ground who is clearly in need of help. Robust traits require consistency, and if people have robust moral traits then insubstantial and morally irrelevant situational factors, such as being a few minutes late for a lecture, would not have substantial effects on what people do in a highly trait-relevant situation. However, the Good Samaritan study and others like it seem to show that trivial situational factors have a major impact on what people do. Situationists conclude that people don't have robust character traits like compassion and courage, and that how they behave is often better explained by other factors.[20]

These considerations don't directly call into question the existence of intellectual as distinct from moral traits, but there is a version of situationism ('epistemic situationism') that does target intellectual character traits.[21] Whereas moral character traits are highly sensitive to *morally* irrelevant situational influences, intellectual or epistemic traits are highly sensitive to *epistemically* irrelevant situational influences. For example, one would think that curiosity, creativity, and flexibility are intellectual virtues, yet studies suggest that people are more likely to reason creatively, flexibly, and curiously 'when their moods have been elevated by such seemingly trivial and epistemically irrelevant situational influences as candy, success at anagrams, and comedy films' (Alfano 2013: 124). A conclusion one might draw from this is that these people lack creativity, flexibility, and curiosity 'as such'.[22] At best, they only have 'local' traits like *curiosity-while-in-a-good-mood*. In that case, why is it any more plausible to think that people are closed-minded or dogmatic as such, or that explanations of their conduct by reference to their supposed intellectual character *vices* fare any better than explanations by reference

---

[20] In its most extreme form situationism says that 'there is no reason at all to believe in character traits as ordinarily conceived' (Harman 2000: 223). See also Harman 1999. Harman 2003 is more circumspect: 'the evidence indicates that people may differ in certain relatively narrow traits but do not have broad and stable dispositions corresponding to the sorts of character and personality traits we normally suppose that people have' (2003: 92). For moderate situationists like Doris the issue is not whether there are character traits but whether there are robust character traits. See Doris 2002: 178, note 36.

[21] Alfano 2013.   [22] Alfano 2013: 124.

to their supposed intellectual *virtues*? In both cases, it might seem that it's better to concentrate on situational factors.

Among the many questions raised by situationism the most pertinent in the present context is whether its arguments have any bearing on attempts to explain human conduct by reference to moral or intellectual *vices*. Situationists concentrate their fire on the virtues and there is a very good reason for that: their arguments are far less effective in relation to vices than in relation to virtues.[23] When it comes to moral vices the problem for situationism is that these are typically low-fidelity rather than high-fidelity or robust traits. Since they don't require behavioural consistency the absence of such consistency wouldn't call their existence into question in the way that, for situationism, the absence of behavioural consistency does call into question the existence of moral virtues. Given that dishonest people don't have to be consistently dishonest, one might ask what triggers their sporadic displays of dishonesty. It wouldn't be particularly surprising if the triggers include situational factors but dishonesty is nevertheless a trait that some people have and others lack. Or so it would seem.

Is closed-mindedness a trait that some people have and others lack? If, as I've argued, closed-mindedness is high fidelity then the issue of consistency can't be dodged. A genuinely closed-minded person is more or less consistently closed-minded but it's hard to read about Zeira and Bandman without concluding that some people *are* consistently closed-minded, just as it is hard to read Ricks on Rumsfeld without concluding that some people *are* consistently arrogant. The studies quoted by Alfano certainly don't threaten the idea that some people are closed-minded as such, and there is no evidence that Zeira was only closed-minded-when-in-a-bad-mood. It seems, rather, that closed-mindedness is a personal trait that, in some people, runs deep. The depth of this trait, and its role in explaining the conduct of those who have it, couldn't really be any clearer than it is in Bar-Joseph's account of the Yom Kippur surprise. He is careful not to claim that situational variables play no part in producing a high need for closure but his account as a whole is hard to reconcile with the notion that a

---

[23] As Doris recognizes when he points out that 'attribution of negatively valenced traits may require very little in the way of behavioral consistency; perhaps one doesn't have to reliably falter, but only sporadically falter, to be counted a coward' (2002: 20).

predominantly situational explanation of the surprise is feasible.[24] At the end of his book he speculates that if certain other individuals had been in charge of AMAN at the crucial time the surprise might have been averted.[25] This is just a vivid way of making the point that people and their personal traits matter when it comes to explaining historical events like the Yom Kippur surprise; it is not just a matter of situation.

Yet, for all their apparent plausibility, one might still wonder whether accounts such as Bar-Joseph's are quite as compelling as I have been making out. Bar-Joseph's account is, above all, a *story*. It isn't of course a work of fiction but it is nevertheless an example of what Charles Tilly calls a 'standard story'.[26] The problem with standard stories, it might be argued, isn't that they ignore trivial situational influences on human conduct but that they ignore very far from trivial *structural* influences. This is the 'structuralist' critique of vice explanations of thought and action. The point is not to suggest, as some situationists like to say, that there is no reason to believe in character traits as ordinarily conceived but to suggest instead that vice explanations exaggerate the importance of epistemic vices and other such personal factors in explanations of our conduct. By the same token, they seriously underestimate the importance of structural factors. Strictly speaking, an obstructivist could agree that structural explanations are often better than vice explanations since obstructivism is mainly a view about the nature of epistemic vices rather than their importance. But why devote so much time and attention to epistemic vices if they don't play a major role in explaining our conduct? By questioning the merits of vice explanations structuralism is at least an indirect challenge to obstructivism, and this challenge needs to be faced.

Tilly introduces the notion of a standard story with the following observation:

For reasons that lie deep in childhood learning, cultural immersion, or perhaps even in the structure of human brains, people usually recount, analyse, judge, remember, and reorganize social experiences as *standard stories* in which a small number of self-motivated entities interact within a contiguous time and space. Although prior and externally imposed conditions enter standard stories as

---

[24] The situational variables he mentions are 'high levels of time pressure, noise, fatigue, and dullness of the information-processing task' (2005: 250).

[25] Bar-Joseph 2005: 251.

[26] Tilly 2002: 26–7 and Haslanger 2015. It was Haslanger who put me on to Tilly's work. Also highly relevant is Haslanger 2016.

accidents, facilities and constraints, all meaningful action occurs as a consequence of the designated actors' deliberations and impulses. (2002: 8)

There is nothing in this passage about character traits but it would certainly be in the spirit of Tilly's view to regard standard stories as ones in which all meaningful action occurs as a consequence of designated actors' deliberations, impulses, *and character traits*. On this basis, a recipe for constructing a standard story might look something like this: start with a limited number of independent characters with specific motives, capacities, resources, and, one might add, virtues and vices.[27] Set the characters in motion and 'make sure everything that happens results directly from your characters' actions' (2002: 26). If this is what a standard story is like then Bar-Joseph's account of the Yom Kippur surprise is a standard story, as is Ricks' (2007) account of the Iraq fiasco. Bar-Joseph attributes a huge intelligence failure to the actions of a limited number of self-motivated individuals, represents their actions as a direct consequence of their deliberations, impulses, and character traits, and suggests that different people in the same position would have acted differently and produced a different outcome. Ricks' account of the Iraq fiasco has a similar structure.

Is there anything wrong with standard stories? That depends on one's view of their two most striking theoretical commitments, *individualism* and their *psychologism*:[28] they focus on a small number of individuals ('designated actors') and attribute the outcomes they want to explain to the psychology of these individuals. For present purposes character traits are 'psychological' and play a crucial explanatory role in standard stories. Standard stories are, in this sense, *personal* and they have plots like those of a novel or a play.[29] According to structuralism that is the fundamental problem. Because of their focus on individuals and their idiosyncratic psychologies standard stories forget that individuals only exist within complex social structures. They are 'nodes in a structure' (Haslanger 2016: 128) and their behaviour is constrained by their position in a network of social relations. What that means is that in many cases it isn't individuals'

---

[27] See Tilly 2002: 26 and Haslanger 2015.
[28] These commitments are noted in Haslanger 2015: 9. There is a different perspective on the relationship between structural and psychological explanation in Jackson and Pettit 1992.
[29] See Tilly 2002: 27.

psychologies that explain their actions but the constraints imposed by the structures within which they operate.[30]

For an example of a structural explanation consider the following question: why do women continue to be economically disadvantaged relative to men?[31] Given that women earn significantly less than men, it isn't surprising that when couples have children it is more often than not the woman who takes time off to look after the children. It might be true that women who quit their jobs in these circumstances or work part time do so because they want what is best for their families but this is a superficial explanation of their choice. A deeper explanation is that 'their behavior is constrained by the fact that they are constitutive parts of a family system, and that system exists with a broader structure' (Haslanger 2015: 4). As long as this structure disadvantages them by paying them less their options are limited and their decision-making is constrained. What is more, the structure that disadvantages women is self-perpetuating because the more women take on childcare responsibilities, the greater the income disparity with men.

This, then, is a structural explanation of gender inequality: women are economically disadvantaged relative to men because they are 'positioned in a self-perpetuating economic structure that systematically disadvantages them' (Haslanger 2016: 122). Notice that there is nothing here about the psychology (or biology) of men or women, or about their characters or vices.[32] The explanation is impersonal and brings home the point that social structures impose constraints on our choices. In Tilly's terminology, Haslanger's explanation of inequality is a 'non-story' explanation that gets away from the individualism and psychologism of standard stories.[33] It is important to see, though, that non-story explanations don't abolish the individual or individual psychology. They don't deny that people make the choices they make because they have particular beliefs and desires. For example, it's still true on a structuralist reading

---

[30] This line of thinking is developed in Haslanger 2016.

[31] This is Haslanger's example. See her 2016: 122.

[32] This is what Tilly is getting at when he says that 'standard storytelling provides an execrable guide to social explanation' (2002: 35). Like Haslanger he focuses on the inability of standard storytelling to account for inequality.

[33] According to Tilly most significant social processes fall into 'non-story' mode because 'at least some crucial causes within them are indirect, incremental, interactive, unintended, collective, and/or mediated by the nonhuman environment' (2002: 32).

that many women quit their jobs because they want what is best for their families and believe that quitting will be best. But the further question is: why is quitting best for their families? The answer to *this* question is not psychological but structural.

What is the relevance of all this for vice explanations of our conduct? One might be tempted to argue as follows: vice explanations are individualistic and psychologistic, and the lesson of structuralism is that such explanations are, in a certain sense, deeply unsatisfactory. So, for example, if we are serious about understanding how the Yom Kippur surprise came about it would be much more to the point to look at the structural constraints on Zeira than at his supposed closed-mindedness. If we are serious about understanding what went wrong in Iraq we would be well advised to think about Rumsfeld's position as a node in a structure, in what used to be called the 'military-industrial complex', than at his supposed arrogance. As in Haslanger's example, Ricks' standard story about the Iraq fiasco and Bar-Joseph's standard story about the Yom Kippur surprise need to be replaced by non-story explanations. Perhaps Zeira *was* closed-minded. Perhaps Rumsfeld *was* arrogant. But to suppose that this is the crux of the matter in either case is the height of naivety.

The obvious response to this line of argument is that it confuses two different sorts of case. There are, of course, processes or outcomes that can't be properly explained by standard stories but the important question is: *which* types of process and *which* type of outcome? For structuralism it is *social* processes that call for a structural explanation, and writers like Tilly are mainly concerned to argue that *social* explanation is structural explanation. What counts as a social process then? That's a difficult question but all the examples given are macro-level social phenomena such as social inequality. Nobody in their right mind would want to give a vice explanation of social inequality but it doesn't follow that particular historical events like the Yom Kippur surprise can't be given a vice explanation or that such events can be made sense of in structural terms. In the case of the Yom Kippur surprise the intellectual character vices of specific individuals really did make all the difference. If someone other than Zeira had been in charge, AMAN might not have delivered such poor-quality strategic warnings to Israel's political leaders. Of course one can then ask whether there is a structural explanation of the fact that someone like Zeira was appointed Director of Military

Intelligence. Could it be that it is in the nature of organizations like AMAN to promote people like Zeira? That is far-fetched. The fact that a person like Zeira was calling the shots in the run-up to the Yom Kippur surprise was just bad luck.[34]

It doesn't follow that particular historical events can never be understood in structural terms or that vice explanations are always appropriate. The claim is only that it is sometimes appropriate to explain such events in vice rather than structural terms. However, this gives rise to a boundary problem: given the relative obscurity of the notion of a social process, where and how do we draw the line between cases where vice explanations are in order and ones that call for a structuralist response? It might help to make the problem vivid to have a few more examples to work with, so consider the following list.

1. Why did the Department of Defense underestimate the number of US troops that would be needed in Iraq after the invasion in 2003?
2. Why was there such a wide gap between the excellent information available to AMAN on the eve of the Yom Kippur war and the poor quality of the strategic warning it produced?
3. Why do women continue to be economically disadvantaged relative to men?
4. Why do people believe conspiracy theories?
5. What are the causes of diagnostic errors in medicine?

I've suggested that vice explanations are appropriate in relation to the first two questions, but not the third. What about the two new questions at the end of the list? What kind of response is appropriate for them? Some responses have focused on character vices. In my own earlier work I attributed belief in conspiracy theories to the vice of gullibility.[35] A number of social psychologists have posited a 'conspiracy mentality' that some people have and that disposes them to believe in conspiracy theories.[36] Although this isn't how social psychologists see it, the conspiracy mentality is akin to a character vice if not actually a

---

[34] Bar-Joseph 2005: 251.   [35] Cassam 2015b.
[36] See Bruder et al. 2013: a conspiracy mentality is 'the general propensity to subscribe to theories blaming a conspiracy of ill-intending individuals or groups for important societal phenomena' (2).

character vice.[37] In relation to the last question there is an interesting literature in the medical journals in support of the notion that physician overconfidence is a major cause of diagnostic error.[38] Assuming that over-confidence is an epistemic vice then this amounts to a relatively straight-forward vice explanation of diagnostic error.[39]

Not everyone is convinced, however. For example, there is the view that conspiracy thinking has more to do with poverty and marginaliza-tion than with gullibility or a conspiracy mentality.[40] This is a social rather than a vice explanation of the intellectual conduct and beliefs of so-called 'conspiracy theorists'. This doesn't mean that people who believe in outlandish conspiracy theories aren't gullible or that they don't have a conspiracy mentality. The point is that these vices them-selves, like many other epistemic vices, have a deeper explanation in the social circumstances of their possessors.[41] On the issue of diagnostic error, doctors work in complex systems, and it has been argued that medical errors have their origins not so much in the foibles of individual doctors as in systemic factors.[42] It could still be true on this account that some doctors *are* overconfident but to explain what is actually a systemic or structural phenomenon—medical error—in such personal terms is to be guilty of what might be called a 'level confusion'.[43]

This discussion brings out just how difficult it can be to decide whether a particular outcome is best explained in personal or structural terms. Having said that, it is also true that the personal and the structural are often intertwined, and that one and the same phenomenon can sometimes be explained at both levels. The question in such cases is whether primacy should be accorded to one or other level, and there is

[37] Social psychologists tend to see the conspiracy mentality more as a personal trait than a character trait.

[38] For example, Berner and Graber 2008.

[39] This isn't the only possible interpretation of overconfidence and its role in causing diagnostic error. Other interpretations are discussed in Cassam 2017.

[40] This is the line taken in Freeman and Bentall 2017.

[41] The idea that epistemic vices can (sometimes) be explained by the social circumstances of their possessors is developed by Medina. He sees closed-mindedness, epistemic laziness, and epistemic arrogance as 'epistemic vices of the privileged', that is, as epistemic vices that 'the better-off of society can (or even tend to) develop' (2013: 30). These epistemic vices are *structural and systematic* (31).

[42] Reason 2000.

[43] 'Level confusion' is borrowed from Alston 1980, where it is used in a very different sense.

no simple formula for answering this question. At the same time, the intermingling of structural and personal factors points to the possibility of a limited rapprochement between vice explanations and structural or systemic explanations. The idea would be to recognize a sliding scale of outcomes. At one end are outcomes that can only adequately be understood in structural terms. Social inequality is an excellent example. At the other extreme are outcomes that can only be adequately understood in vice terms. In the middle are many outcomes that have to be understood partly in structural terms and partly by reference to the epistemic vices and other personal qualities of designated actors. A level confusion occurs when an outcome that should be explained at one level is explained at the other. The level at which a particular outcome 'should' be explained can be controversial but what should not be controversial is that there are some outcomes that can't be explained and understood without reference to the epistemic vices of specified individuals. This is one way the idea of an epistemic vice earns its keep. Epistemic vices are obstacles to knowledge that can in appropriate cases explain how people think and what they do. Sometimes, though, structural or systemic explanations are better.

That more or less completes the mission of this chapter, which was to answer five fundamental questions about closed-mindedness and character vices generally. Before closing there is one more concern about vice explanations that I want to mention since it leads on to Chapter 3. I've suggested that character vices are high-fidelity dispositions and that it can be difficult to tell whether a person is, say, closed-minded or gullible without considering their intellectual conduct generally. What if it turns out that Zeira wasn't generally closed-minded in his thinking and that his conduct in relation to the Yom Kippur surprise was out of character? As I've noted, his *thinking* in this single case would still qualify as closed-minded even if one is reluctant on that basis to describe *him* as closed-minded. This suggests that terms like 'closed-minded', which I've taken to refer to character vices, actually have a dual use: they can be used to characterize a *person* or they can be used to describe their *thinking*, either in general or in a particular case. No doubt these two uses are closely related but they are still distinct. Closed-minded thinking is an epistemically vicious way of thinking, and this points to the existence of *thinking vices* as distinct from character vices. The next challenge is to develop an account of thinking vices and their relationship to character vices.

3

Vicious Thinking

At 8.18 pm on the evening of 21 November 1974 a bomb exploded in the Mulberry Bush pub in Birmingham, England. Minutes later, a second bomb exploded at the nearby Tavern in the Town. In all, twenty-one people were killed that evening and many more were seriously injured. The bombings were the work of the 'Provisional' wing of the IRA (Irish Republican Army), which saw itself as waging an anti-colonial war against British rule in the north of Ireland.[1]

At around 7 pm that same evening six Irishmen gathered at Birmingham's New Street station. Five of them were on their way to Belfast to attend the funeral of James McDade, who had blown himself up the previous week while attempting to plant a bomb in Coventry. The sixth man was there to see the others off. After the Birmingham bombs went off, the booking clerk at New Street station informed the police that a group of men with Irish accents had earlier that evening bought train tickets to Belfast. It wasn't long before all six men were under arrest and charged with murder.

At their trial in 1975 the prosecution case rested on two main pillars: that two of the men had been in recent contact with nitro-glycerine and that all six had confessed. The defence argued that the forensic evidence was unreliable and that the confessions had been beaten out of the defendants. In his summing-up the judge, Mr Justice Bridge, made it as clear as possible that he thought the defendants were guilty and that the defence case had no merit.[2] If the men were innocent, Bridge contended, then the police had been involved in a conspiracy 'unprecedented in the

---

[1] For a fascinating and influential account of the events of 21 November 1974, the role of the IRA in those events, and the response of the criminal justice system see Mullin 1990.

[2] As James Wood observes, Bridge 'brought his authority to bear upon the jury so as to ensure the outcome he clearly desired' (1999: 226).

annals of British criminal history'.[3] He found this incredible and the jury agreed with him. All six defendants were found guilty and each was sentenced to twenty-one life sentences.

A year later the Birmingham Six, as they came to be called, appealed unsuccessfully against their convictions. They also took out a civil action against the police for injuries they claimed to have sustained in police custody. This was also unsuccessful. One of the three judges who ruled on the civil action was Lord Denning. He declared:

If the six men win, it will mean that the police were guilty of perjury, that they were guilty of violence and threats, that the confessions were involuntary and were improperly admitted in evidence and that the convictions were erroneous... This is such an appalling vista that every sensible person in the land would say: it cannot be right that these actions should go any further.[4]

By the time Lord Denning made his pronouncement the case of the Birmingham Six had already become a *cause célèbre* thanks in large part to the efforts of journalist Chris Mullin, who had become convinced that the Six were victims of a miscarriage of justice. Mullin's TV programmes and his book *Error of Judgement* dismantled the police case against the Six. But when the matter was considered again by the Court of Appeal in 1988 the Lord Chief Justice, Lord Lane, concluded: 'The longer this hearing has gone on, the more convinced this court has become that the verdict of the jury was correct'.[5] At last, in 1991 the Court of Appeal ruled that the original convictions were unsafe and unsatisfactory, and that the forensic evidence at the first trial had been demonstrably wrong even judged by the state of forensic science in 1974. The Birmingham Six were released.

The case of the Birmingham Six was one of several notorious and widely publicized miscarriages of justice.[6] In retrospect, the case against the Six seems so obviously flawed as to raise an obvious question: how could the judiciary have been so gravely mistaken over such a long period of time? The answer to this question is complex but in 1991 Mullin, who was by now a member of parliament, said this in his evidence to the Royal Commission on Criminal Justice:

---

[3] See Mullin 1990: 201 and Wood 1999.   [4] Quoted in Mullin 1990: 216.
[5] Quoted in Mullin 1990: 267.
[6] See the essays on miscarriages of justice in Walker and Starmer 1999.

It is my view that, with honourable exceptions, most of those who preside over our criminal justice system are congenitally incapable of owning up to mistakes, let alone taking the steps to prevent a recurrence. I have had the opportunity of studying at close quarters the demeanour of many of those responsible for the administration of justice and, despite what has happened, I detect little evidence of the humility that will be necessary if the tragedies of the last two decades are not to be repeated. On the contrary, despite all that has happened, there exists within the legal profession a degree of complacency and self-satisfaction that is not in my experience to be found in any other walk of life, with the possible exception of the police force.   (1991: 8)[7]

Commenting on another notorious miscarriage of justice, the case of the Guildford Four, Mullin wryly observed: 'What is one to make of the judgment of Lord Roskill and his colleagues at the Guildford appeal in 1976? . . . The most generous interpretation is that it displayed extreme gullibility, not to say stupidity—and I have never heard it suggested that Lord Roskill is stupid' (1991: 51).

Lack of humility, complacency, self-satisfaction, stupidity, and gullibility all sound like vices, and some of these vices are epistemic. Other judicial epistemic vices that are detectable in the conduct of Lord Denning and others include closed-mindedness and dogmatism. Their minds were closed to the possibility that the Six were innocent and they proceeded on the basis that they, and not the police, were lying. Mullin gives a vice explanation of the judicial conduct that led to miscarriages of justice, and it is hard to argue with his analysis.

Hard, but not impossible. Lord Denning's remarks about the Birmingham Six were a low point in a distinguished career, but it was the same Lord Denning who was responsible for some notably open-minded and progressive judgments on other subjects. For example, he ruled that in case of divorce the wife is entitled to an equal share of her husband's wealth, and that cohabiting as well as married couples have rights to each other's property. These are not the views of a closed-minded stick-in-the-mud.[8] Lord Lane was no less iconoclastic in some of his judgments. Only a year after his ruling in the Birmingham Six appeal he freed the Guildford Four on the grounds that the police had lied in order to secure their convictions. Critics often accused Lord Lane of being conservative, blinkered, and behind the times. Yet in quashing

<hr />

[7] References are to paragraph numbers rather than page numbers of Mullin's evidence.
[8] For more on Lord Denning see Freeman 1993, Burrell 1999, and Dyer 1999.

the convictions of the Guildford Four he said that the police's interview notes must have been 'the invention of some fertile constabulary mind'. This is not the attitude of a blinkered conservative who thought that the police could do no wrong.

These examples illustrate the need to distinguish between the qualities of a *thinker* and qualities of a person's *thinking* on a given occasion or in a particular case.[9] The thinking that led to the Birmingham Six spending seventeen years in jail may well have been closed-minded but it doesn't follow that the individual judges who did the thinking were themselves closed-minded. Closed-mindedness is a 'high-fidelity' vice, which means that only thinkers whose thinking is *consistently* closed-minded qualify as closed-minded. With Lord Lane and Lord Denning there is no clear evidence of a consistent pattern of closed-minded thinking and some evidence that points the other way. This calls into question a vice explanation of their conduct in the case of the Birmingham Six *if* the implication of such an explanation is that their conduct in the case was representative of their judicial and epistemic conduct generally. It wasn't.

Closed-mindedness is usually conceived of as a *character vice*, an epistemic vice that is also a character trait. Closed-mindedness as a quality of a particular piece of thinking is a *thinking vice*, an epistemically vicious way of thinking or 'thinking style'. It is one thing to *be* closed-minded and another to *think* closed-mindedly. The two are related but not identical. A closed-minded thinker thinks closed-mindedly but closed-minded thinking isn't the exclusive preserve of closed-minded thinkers. When closed-minded thinkers think closed-mindedly about a particular topic their thinking is in character. When otherwise open-minded thinkers think closed-mindedly in a given case their thinking is out of character. Without a distinction between thinking vices and character vices it is difficult to do justice to the epistemic conduct of Lord Denning and Lord Lane. The evidence of their vicious thinking in relation to the Birmingham Six is contained in the reasoning that led to their flawed judgments. The evidence that this style of thinking might not have been typical for them is contained in their reasoning in other cases, including ones where the honesty of the police was at issue.

---

[9] Interestingly, some such distinction is implicit in Chris Mullin's comment on Lord Roskill—his judgment in relation to the Guildford Four might have been stupid but *he* wasn't: 'I have never heard it suggested that Lord Roskill is stupid'.

In John Doris' terminology, a *robust* character trait is one that is reliably and consistently manifested in trait-relevant behaviour in a wide variety of trait-relevant eliciting conditions, including situations that aren't conducive to such behaviour. In contrast, what John Doris calls 'local traits' are fine-grained and situation-specific. For example, courage is a robust trait. 'Sailing-in-rough-weather-with-friends courageous' is a local trait.[10] A person with the robust trait is expected to show courage in any relevant situation. A person with the local trait can only be expected to show courage when they are sailing in rough weather with friends. They may not behave courageously even in quite similar situations.

Can Lord Denning's conduct in respect of the Birmingham Six be attributed to a local trait? He may not have been closed-minded *simpliciter* but was he 'closed-minded-in-cases-where-police-honesty-was-at-issue'? Possibly, but this clearly won't do for Lord Lane, given his judgment in the case of the Guildford Four. In his case the local trait would need to be even more fine-grained, something along the lines of: 'closed-minded-in-cases-concerning-the-guilt-or-innocence-of-the-Birmingham-Six'. This is hardly recognizable as a character trait and sounds, if anything, like a needlessly cumbersome way of capturing the viciousness of his thinking about the Birmingham Six. Whether, as the local trait attribution suggests, he would have thought the same way about other cases involving the Birmingham Six is hard to say but that doesn't alter the fact that his thinking in the 1988 trial was defective.

This might give the impression that thinking vices only need to be distinguished from character vices if the latter are high fidelity rather than low fidelity. It's important to correct this impression. Suppose that closed-mindedness is a low-fidelity character vice and that even just a few instances of closed-minded thinking are enough for one to count as closed-minded. In that case, despite his open-minded thinking on other issues, Lord Denning might still come out as closed-minded. This doesn't alter the fact that being closed-minded is not the same as thinking closed-mindedly. The distinction at issue here is the distinction between traits and actions. For example, being a smoker is a trait that some people have. Smoking is an action; it is something that some people do. Regardless of how much or how little smoking it takes to be a smoker, smoking

---

[10] Doris 2002: 115.

and being a smoker are different kinds of thing; they belong in diverse ontological categories. Exactly the same goes for the relationship between dangerous driving and being a dangerous driver. Perhaps driving dangerously once or twice is sufficient to make one a dangerous driver. Or maybe an extended pattern of dangerous driving is needed. Either way, driving dangerously is what a person *does* whereas a dangerous driver is what a person *is*.

If the distinction between being closed-minded and thinking closed-mindedly is the distinction between a trait and an action the next question concerns the relationship between the two. In the driving case the relationship is straightforward. A dangerous driver is basically a driver who drives dangerously, and an understanding of what it is to be a dangerous driver depends on a prior understanding of what it is to drive dangerously. The reverse is not true: an understanding of what it is to drive dangerously doesn't depend on a prior understanding of what it is to be a dangerous driver. Driving dangerously is what dangerous drivers do but this hardly explains what dangerous driving *is*. To drive dangerously is to drive aggressively or too fast, to jump traffic lights, to overtake risk-takingly, and so on. A dangerous driver is one who drives like *that*.

An analogous account of the relationship between being closed-minded and thinking closed-mindedly would say that a closed-minded thinker is one who thinks closed-mindedly, and that an understanding of what it is to *be* closed-minded relies on a prior understanding of what it is to *think* closed-mindedly. The reverse isn't true. Thinking closed-mindedly is what closed-minded thinkers do but that hardly explains what closed-minded thinking is. Closed-minded thinking is thinking that is inflexible and unreceptive to evidence that conflicts with one's pre-existing views, regardless of its merits. This explains the thinking vice (thinking closed-mindedly) without any reference to the matching character vice (closed-mindedness), but there is no prospect of explaining the character vice without any reference to the thinking vice. There is more to being closed-minded than thinking in a particular way.[11] To be closed-minded is to be intolerant of others whose opinions contradict one's own and to place a particular premium on clarity, order, and coherence. These are not thinking styles but attitudes or values. Still, at

---

[11] See the discussion and references in Chapter 2.

least part of what it is to be closed-minded is to think closed-mindedly, and an explanation of what it is to have the character vice must refer to the thinking vice.

One way of putting this would be to say that the thinking vice is more basic than the character vice. There are many senses in which one thing might be more basic than another. One kind of basicness is explanatory basicness: X is explanatorily more basic than Y just if X can be explained without reference to Y but Y can't be explained without reference to X.[12] In these terms, the implication of what I have just been saying is that when it comes to closed-mindedness the thinking vice is explanatorily more basic than the character vice. This can be made vivid by imagining a scenario in which one has no conception of the character vice. It would still be possible in these circumstances to have an understanding of the thinking vice, and use this understanding to develop an understanding of the character vice. In contrast, not having a grasp of the thinking vice entails not having a grasp of the character vice.

The idea that thinking vices are more basic than character vices also comes out in other ways. We have a rich and fine-grained vocabulary to describe thinking vices. Thinking can be wishful, dogmatic, illogical, biased, irrational, confused, perverse, blinkered, muddled, careless, or superstitious. *People* can also be some of these things, but in each case the character vice is defined by reference to the thinking vice rather than vice versa. For example, a wishful thinker, if there is such a thing, is one who is prone to wishful thinking. This type of thinking can be defined as thinking in which one's wishes are more influential than logical or evidential considerations. Having defined wishful thinking in this way, without any mention of wishful thinkers, it is then open to us to stipulate that to be a wishful thinker is to be prone to wishful thinking. In the order of explanation the thinking vice comes first.

To summarize, my claims in this chapter so far are that:

a. Thinking vices are distinct from character vices.
b. Thinking that is epistemically vicious in some respect or other isn't the exclusive preserve of thinkers who have the corresponding character vice.

---

[12] This is the account of explanatory basicness I give in Cassam 2009: 23. See Williamson 2009a for further discussion and refinements.

c. There is a straightforward sense in which thinking vices are explanatorily more basic than character vices.[13]

For the rest of this chapter I'm going to ignore worries about the relationship between the two different kinds of vice and concentrate on thinking vices. I introduced thinking vices by using a series of examples but examples only get one so far. For a deeper understanding of what thinking vices are supposed to be it would be helpful to have a deeper understanding of what thinking is supposed to be.

Work by Daniel Kahneman and others suggests that there is a distinction between fast and slow thinking, and this raises the question whether thinking vices are vices of fast thinking, of slow thinking, or both.[14] Another question concerns the status of thinking vices as vices. Epistemic vices get in the way of knowledge but how do thinking vices do that? This leads on to a third question: do thinking vices only get in the way of knowledge given certain assumptions about how the world works? For example, Lord Bridge's thinking about the Birmingham Six went wrong because it assumed, falsely, that the police aren't in the business of framing people in the manner alleged by the defence. What if the police really were incorruptible? In that case would there have been anything wrong with Lord Bridge's way of thinking? The issue here is whether thinking vices are, so to speak, *unconditionally* or only *conditionally* vicious.

To begin at the beginning, what is thinking? Imagine being confronted by a complex question ('How could the judiciary have been so wrong in the case of the Birmingham Six?'). The goal is to answer this question. The first step is to identify a range of possibilities, that is, a range of possible explanations of the target event or phenomenon. For example, possible explanations in this case include bias, incompetence, and the quality of the forensic evidence. Next, one looks for evidence for

---

[13] If one were inclined to resist this conclusion, one way to do so would be to argue that just because a thinking vice X can be explained without any explicit reference to a character vice Y it doesn't follow that our *understanding* of X isn't shaped by our *understanding* of Y. For example, inflexibility and a negative attitude towards contrary evidence are the distinguishing marks of closed-minded thinking, but why these marks in particular? Could it be that what enables us to identify, organize, and prioritize the distinguishing marks of X is a background understanding of Y? If so then X would not be explanatorily more basic than Y.

[14] See, for example, Kahneman 2011.

each explanation. For each piece of evidence there is also the task of deciding on its strength and the appropriate weight to attach to it. This might require more thinking and the search for more evidence. For example, in order to decide how much weight to attach to the quality of the forensic evidence at the Birmingham Six trials one needs to decide on its quality and whether it was bad enough to explain the miscarriages of justice. Suppose, finally, that one identifies what one takes to be the best explanation of what went wrong in the Birmingham Six trials. This preferred explanation might represent a single factor as crucial or, much more likely, a cluster of factors. Either way, there is still the issue of whether the preferred explanation is strong enough to endorse. That depends not just on *its* strength but the likelihood that there are other, better explanations that one hasn't thought of. If that seems likely then one might hesitate to draw a firm conclusion from one's reflections. Otherwise the thinking concludes with an endorsement or judgement.[15]

What is striking about this idealized but hopefully not completely unrealistic example is that it represents thinking as sequential, as involving the making of a succession of *moves* in thought. The different stages or phases of thinking in the example correspond to the different phases of thinking described by Jonathan Baron. He breaks thinking down into a number of distinct phases or functions.[16] These include the identification of goals, the consideration of possibilities, and the seeking and weighing of evidence. The *goal* is to find an acceptable answer to a question, the *possibilities* are answers to the question implicit in the goal, and the *evidence* is used to evaluate possibilities. Thinking is a 'method of choosing among potential possibilities' (Baron 1985: 90), and *ways* of thinking are particular *ways* of doing that. They are ways of including or excluding possibilities, of evaluating evidence, or drawing conclusions. Ways of doing these things that get in the way of knowledge are potential thinking vices and I'll give some examples of thinking vices below. As will become apparent, these vices aren't idiosyncratic or unusual. They are perfectly ordinary and easy to recognize, at least in other people's thinking. They are cognitive *styles* that different episodes of thinking can have in common. For example, if two individuals are

---

[15] The account of thinking in this paragraph owes a lot to Baron 1985. See also Cassam 2010.

[16] See Baron 1985, chapter 3.

prone to superstitious thinking then they have the same thinking style at least in this respect even if their individual superstitions are different.[17]

To sum up, thinking as I have just described it is:

i. Goal-directed.
ii. Sequential.
iii. Effortful.
iv. An intentional action or series of actions: it is something that a person does.
v. Conscious.

Thinking that has these features is slow thinking. The contrast is with a type of thinking that is goal-directed but not sequential, effortful, or conscious. It isn't an intentional action and it isn't something that a person does. This is fast thinking.

The following is a simple though slightly fanciful example that brings out some of the features of fast thinking: a mathematically gifted subject is asked what is 21,582 divided by 11 and they immediately give the correct answer: '1962'. Keith Frankish, whose example this is, comments that although *answering* the question was an intentional action, *working out* the answer was not: 'the subject did not *do* anything to work it out; the operations involved were entirely subpersonal' (2009: 92). The personal/sub-personal distinction came up in Chapter 1. With this distinction in place it's clear why fast thinking isn't something that a person does. It is a process rather than an action, and if it is really sub-personal then by definition it isn't done by a person.

In that case, why regard fast thinking as a form of thinking? Frankish describes the process leading to the answer '1962' as 'subpersonal reasoning', but is it really reasoning any more than it is thinking? Cases where a person answers a question instantaneously are ones where the *person* doesn't have to think about it, but it doesn't follow that no *thinking* was involved unless it is stipulated that only personal-level thinking is thinking. Given how useful the notion of sub-personal reasoning or 'thinking' has proved in cognitive science that would not be an especially sensible stipulation. From an ordinary language perspective sub-personal processing isn't 'thinking', but this point is only of very limited significance.

[17] There is more about 'cognitive styles' or 'thinking styles' in Stanovich and West 1997 and Sternberg 1997.

In these matters, ordinary language isn't decisive. I'll assume, in any case, that fast thinking is thinking. It has only one of the five features I listed— (i)—whereas slow thinking has all five. Assuming that this account of the distinction between fast and slow thinking is correct, the question whether thinking vices are vices of slow thinking, fast thinking, or both can now be tackled.

An argument for seeing thinking vices as vices of slow rather than fast thinking might start from the premise that thinking vices are first and foremost vices that affect the selection of possibilities, the weighing of evidence, and the drawing of conclusions. Since these are the component parts of slow rather than fast thinking, thinking vices must be vices of slow rather than fast thinking. How can they be vices of fast thinking if fast thinking doesn't involve the selection of possibilities, the weighing of evidence, or the drawing of conclusions? A possible response to this question would be to insist that fast thinking *does* involve these things, or something like them, at the sub-personal level. Another would be to argue that fast thinking has its own distinctive thinking vices. Perhaps there are vices of slow thinking and (different) vices of fast thinking. There is something to be said for both responses but before going into this any further it would be helpful to have some illustrations of the ways that different thinking vices affect the different phases of slow thinking.

Mr Justice Bridge's summing-up in the Birmingham Six trial is as good an illustration as any of how the consideration of possibilities in slow thinking can be epistemically vicious. The possibility that the defence had invited him to consider was that the Six had been set up by the police. Bridge refused to consider this possibility not because he had an adequate reason not to take it seriously but because it went against his prior conviction that the police were blameless. In closed-minded slow thinking, only possibilities that do not conflict with one's prior views are seen as genuine, and the slowness of the thinking is no guarantee that relevant possibilities won't be ignored or excluded.

For an illustration of the ways in which the weighing of evidence in slow thinking can be epistemically vicious there is Mr Justice Bridge's response to the prison doctor's evidence that the Birmingham Six's visible injuries had probably been inflicted by the police.[18] Bridge

---

[18] Bridge invited the jury to consider whether they could believe a single word of what Dr Harwood, the prison doctor, had said in court. Just for good measure Bridge added:

attached little weight to this evidence and suggested that the injuries had probably been self-inflicted. Why was he so dismissive of the prison doctor's evidence? Because if the doctor's evidence was accepted then the police were guilty. Assuming that the police were innocent, the doctor had to be lying. There is no denying that if the police's innocence had already been settled at this point then Bridge's reasoning would have been impeccable. However, since their innocence hadn't been settled, the way he reasoned that the doctor must be lying was question-begging and dogmatic: evidence that pointed to police misconduct was rejected for no better reason than that it pointed to police misconduct.

As well as thinking vices that have to do with the identification of possibilities and the weighing of evidence, there are also thinking vices that relate to the transition from evidence or premises to conclusions. In the simplest case, it is thinking in which the conclusions drawn aren't entailed or supported by the thinker's premises or by their evidence. This is illogical or confused thinking. The transition from premise to conclusion in such cases can be the result of several different factors, including other thinking vices. So as not to give the impression of an obsession with Mr Justice Bridge, here is a different example: a gambler who sees a succession of coin tosses coming down heads thinks that the next toss will be tails because a tails is now 'due'. This is an example of superstitious or magical thinking, thinking that posits a causal link between unconnected events, namely, previous coin tosses and the next toss. The positing of such a link leads the gambler to a conclusion that doesn't follow from his premises. Superstitious thinking is epistemically vicious thinking.[19]

Although it's natural to suppose that the thinking in these examples is slow rather than fast, not much turns on this assumption. Suppose that the exclusion of relevant possibilities from consideration is something that happens instantaneously and automatically rather than as a result of conscious reflection. Imagine that Mr Justice Bridge's bias in favour of the police was so strong that the possibility that they might have been at fault, or that the prison doctor was telling the truth, didn't cross his mind. Perhaps all his reasoning was sub-personal but this would not have made it immune to the thinking vices that I've attributed to his slow

'There are inescapably many perjurers who have given evidence. If Dr Harwood is one of them is he not the worst?' (Wood 1999: 227).

[19]   On superstitious and magical thinking see Vyse 1997.

thinking. By the same token, the gambler's belief that the next coin toss will be tails needn't have involved the explicit drawing of a conclusion at the end of a process of conscious reasoning. When fast thinking results in judgements that only make sense if relevant possibilities were excluded or too little (or too much) weight was attached to a certain piece of evidence then it is *as if* there was a process of determining which possibilities were relevant or how seriously a certain piece of evidence should be taken. These are normally thought of as personal-level processes but perhaps something analogous can go on implicitly in fast thinking. At any rate, fast thinking isn't immune to epistemic vices like closed-mindedness, and can be just as rigid, perverse, and superstitious as slow thinking.

Fast thinking also has its own vices, though these are described as biases rather than as vices. Cognitive biases are systematic errors that result from the use of heuristics in our thinking. A heuristic is a 'simple procedure that helps find adequate, though often imperfect, answers to difficult questions' (Kahneman 2011: 98). For example, when people are asked to estimate the value of a house they are guided by the asking price. This serves as an 'anchor' around which estimates vary, even if the asking price has no clear rationale. The anchoring bias is powerful even if the anchor is a random number. The following is an illustration of the power of random anchors in the selection of possibilities:

German judges with an average of more than fifteen years of experience on the bench first read a description of a woman who had been caught shoplifting, then rolled a pair of dice that were loaded so every roll resulted in either a 3 or a 9. As soon as the dice came to a stop, the judges ... were asked to specify the exact prison sentence they would give to the shoplifter. On average, those who had rolled a 9 said they would sentence her to 8 months; those who rolled a 3 said they would sentence her to 5 months; the anchoring effect was 50%.

(Kahneman 2011: 125–6)

In fast thinking anchoring is an automatic process of adjustment. However, there is also a 'form of anchoring that occurs in a deliberate process of adjustment' (2011: 120), and there is nothing in Kahneman's account of the German judges that reveals whether their thinking was deliberate or automatic. It could have been either because both fast and slow thinking are susceptible to the effects of anchoring.[20]

---

[20] See Kahneman 2011: 120–2.

Should the cognitive biases of fast thinking be seen as epistemic *vices*? The fact that they give rise to systematic errors isn't enough to make them vices. They also need to be blameworthy or otherwise reprehensible. Blame is only appropriate for biases for which one is, in the terminology of Chapter 1, 'revision responsible', that is for biases that one can modify. I'll have more to say in later chapters about the extent to which sub-personal cognitive biases can be controlled or modified. Meanwhile, even if these biases aren't strictly blameworthy they are still open to criticism in some cases. For example, regardless of whether it is fair to *blame* the German judges who allowed their sentencing decisions to be influenced by the roll of a dice, they can be *criticized* for the thinking that underpinned their decisions. Their thinking was vicious to the extent that it was influenced by extraneous considerations in the selection of possibilities, in this case the selection of an appropriate sentence. Whether their thinking was fast or slow, it was still reprehensible and still vicious. The fact that a bias is sub-personal does not render it immune to criticism.

The question was whether thinking vices are vices of fast thinking, of slow thinking, or both. The answer is both. On the one hand, the epistemic vices commonly associated with slow thinking, with the deliberate identification of possibilities and weighing of evidence, can also affect fast thinking. On the other hand, it now appears that at least some of the cognitive biases of fast thinking are also operative in slow thinking. For example, anchoring is something that happens at both levels. The fact that thinking vices can be vices of fast and slow thinking should come as no surprise since fast and slow thinking are closely related. Much of what passes for slow thinking is grounded in sub-personal reasoning, and what is due to conscious deliberation is not easily distinguishable from what is due to non-conscious processing. In theory there could be slow-thinking vices that have no fast-thinking analogue, or fast-thinking biases that have no bearing on slow thinking, but there is nothing in the notion of a thinking vice that supports the thesis that these are specific vices of slow or of fast thinking.

The next task is to explain how thinking vices get in the way of knowledge. In one way this is perfectly straightforward: thinking vices lead to systematic errors and if they do that then it follows that they get in the way of knowledge. But is it true that thinking vices make us error prone? Wishful thinking would normally be regarded as a thinking vice but it is possible to imagine scenarios in which it doesn't lead to error. Suppose that instead of merely wishing the demise of Thomas à Becket, his 'turbulent priest', Henry II had also believed that he *was* dead, and believed Becket was dead because he wanted him dead. The knights who knew what Henry wanted thought it was their duty to ensure that their king's wishes were fulfilled and duly killed Becket. So Henry's wishful thinking didn't lead to error. However, such cases are, though possible, not typical. It isn't normally the case that wishful thinking is self-fulfilling. The straightforward case for continuing to classify wishful thinking as an epistemic vice is that more often than not it does lead to error, and so gets in the way of knowledge, because it is thinking in which the thinker's wishes count for more than the evidence. If the thinker is king or a dictator whose flunkies make sure that his wishes always come true, then wishful thinking won't be such a bad bet, epistemically speaking, but for most of us it is not a reliable pathway to true belief.

Another way to explain how thinking vices get in the way of knowledge is to focus on the confidence condition for knowing: for one to know the truth of some proposition P one must be reasonably confident that P and one must have the right to be confident. If it is wishful thinking rather than the evidence that leads a person to believe P then they don't have the right to be confident that P even if, by some chance, P turns out to be true after all. They have the right to be confident only if their belief was reasonable and formed using a reliable method.[21] A belief based on wishful thinking rather than the evidence is neither. The same goes for beliefs that are the result of superstitious thinking. Imagine a superstitious thinker who believes he will come to harm if he walks under ladders. Because he is so superstitious, walking under ladders affects his behaviour in such a way that he does come to some harm whenever he accidentally walks under a ladder. Although his superstitious thinking leads him to form a true belief about the dangers of walking under ladders, he doesn't have the right to be confident that walking under ladders is dangerous. For a start, superstitious thinking isn't a generally reliable method for forming true beliefs about the future; it won't generally lead to true beliefs because it posits causal links between unconnected events. This also means that beliefs based

---

[21] For a discussion of some of the issues here see Foster 1985: 85–125 and BonJour 2001.

on superstitious thinking aren't reasonable, and this is another way that superstitious thinking deprives thinkers of the right to be confident that things are as they take them to be. In order for superstitious thinking not to have this effect the causal links it posits would need to be real rather than imaginary. In other words, the world would need to be different from how it actually is.

This way of putting things raises a fundamental question about thinking vices: do they only qualify as vices on the basis of substantive assumptions about what the world is actually like? If so, doesn't that open up the possibility of environments or circumstances in which ways of thinking that I have identified as vicious might be virtuous? The underlying issue is whether thinking or other epistemic vices are only conditionally vicious, that is, epistemically vicious subject to the world being a certain way. A topical and at least superficially plausible example of a thinking vice or type of vicious thinking that is conditionally vicious (if it is vicious at all) is conspiracy thinking, which is related to superstitious thinking.[22] A natural thought about conspiracy thinking is that while it might indeed be epistemically vicious in environments in which large-scale conspiracies are rare, it is very far from vicious in environments in which large-scale conspiracies are commonplace. In conspiracy-rich environments it is surely *anti*-conspiracy thinking that is epistemically vicious.[23] If that is so then conspiracy and anti-conspiracy thinking are examples of thinking vices (or virtues) that are conditionally vicious (or virtuous).

An example of conspiracy thinking is the thinking that has led many Americans and others to conclude that the attack on New York's World Trade Center on 11 September 2001 was the culmination of a fiendish plot by the American government. According to the 'official' account given in the report of the 9/11 Commission, the 9/11 attacks were planned by Khalid Shaikh Mohammad and executed by nineteen mostly Saudi terrorists.[24] The plan was to hijack fully laden commercial aircraft and fly them into the twin towers of the World Trade Center, with the aim of killing as many civilians as possible. The attack was successful in its own terms and resulted in the deaths of over 3,000 people, including

[22] The label 'conspiracy thinking' is from Zonis and Joseph 1994.
[23] As Charles Pigden argues in Pigden 2017.   [24] Kean and Hamilton 2012.

the hijackers. Yet in the years since 9/11 a vociferous minority has rejected this account and claimed that the World Trade Center was destroyed not by aircraft impacts and the resulting fires but by explosives planted in advance by US government agents. According to this theory, aircraft impacts couldn't have brought down the towers and were a diversion from the main event, which was a controlled demolition. As for the government's motives in mounting an attack on its own population, one theory has it that its aim was to ensure public support for invading Iraq and Afghanistan. Other theories have also been proposed but what they all have in common is a deep scepticism about the official account, which is seen as part of the conspiracy.[25]

A conspiracy theory is 'a proposed explanation of some historical event (or events) in terms of the significant causal agency of a relatively small group of persons—the conspirators—acting in secret' (Keeley 1999: 116).[26] In these terms, the theory that the American government was responsible for the 9/11 attacks is a classic conspiracy theory. Such theories can be true and warranted but the interesting case for present purposes is where conspiracies are hypothesized to explain events when 'by any reasonable set of criteria, no conspiracy exists' (Zonis and Joseph 1994: 444). There isn't a formula for distinguishing unwarranted from warranted conspiracy theories but some conspiracy theories are clearly unwarranted. Why do people still believe such theories? The psychological literature on conspiracy theories posits a 'conspiracy mentality', that is, a general propensity to endorse conspiracy theories.[27] Individuals who endorse one conspiracy theory tend to endorse others, even ones that are mutually contradictory, and the proposed explanation

---

[25] See the essays in Fetzer 2007.

[26] Notice that this definition allows the official account of 9/11 to count as a conspiracy theory since it clearly explains the 9/11 attacks in terms of the significant causal agency of a small group of conspirators. To avoid this result, one needs to add that genuine conspiracy theories 'flip the conventional wisdom on its head' and are 'contrarian by nature' (Brotherton 2015: 68).

[27] The psychological literature on the conspiracy mentality includes Swami et al. 2011, Brotherton et al. 2013, Bruder et al. 2013, and Imhoff and Bruder 2014. In the words of one of these papers, 'there is increasing evidence that there are stable individual differences in people's tendency to believe in . . . conspiracy theories' and 'this has led some researchers to propose that the endorsement of specific conspiracy theories depends to a large extent on individual differences in the general tendency to adopt such beliefs, that is, a general *conspiracy mentality*' (Bruder et al. 2013: 1–2).

is psychological.[28] On this account, belief in a particular conspiracy theory can be explained by reference to the general propensity.

Although the conspiracy mentality is often represented as a personality trait it can also be a way of thinking or, if one prefers, a 'thinking style'. Among its other characteristics conspiracy thinking attempts to tie together seemingly unrelated events and focuses on errant data. It also presumes that we are being kept in the dark about the true nature of major events and that the conspirators are all-powerful and resourceful.[29] Studies have also found that belief in conspiracy theories is associated with superstitious and paranormal beliefs, and it has been suggested that these beliefs are associated because they are 'underpinned by similar thinking styles' (Swami et al. 2011: 458). Also relevant in this context is what Richard Hofstadter famously calls the 'paranoid style', with its associated feelings of persecution and 'grandiose theories of conspiracy' (2008: 4).[30]

These descriptions portray conspiracy thinking as vicious thinking and a source of erroneous beliefs about events such as the 9/11 attacks. Now compare the thinking that led to the uncovering of the all too real Watergate conspiracy by Bob Woodward and Carl Bernstein.[31] In 1972, the *Washington Post* reported that five men had been arrested while breaking in to the Watergate headquarters of the Democratic National Committee. One of the men was a former employee of the CIA and subsequent investigations by Woodward and Bernstein, two junior *Washington Post* reporters, uncovered an elaborate conspiracy by the Nixon administration to bug its opponents. In the course of unravelling the conspiracy, the two reporters presumably engaged in quite a bit of conspiracy thinking but their conspiracy thinking was (let's suppose) epistemically virtuous rather than vicious. In the environment in which

---

[28] See Wood et al. 2012 for evidence that the conspiracy mentality can even lead people to endorse mutually contradictory conspiracy theories. For example, the more participants in their study believed that Osama bin Laden was already dead when US Special Forces raided his compound in Pakistan, the more they believed he is still alive.

[29] There is a more extensive list of characteristics of the 'conspiracist style' in Brotherton 2015, chapter 3.

[30] The 'paranoid style' is a 'style of mind' that 'evokes the qualities of heated exaggeration, suspiciousness, and conspiratorial fantasy' (2008: 3). The paranoid style is a 'way of seeing the world and of expressing oneself' to which 'the feeling of persecution is central' (2008: 4).

[31] See Bernstein and Woodward 1974.

they operated such thinking was virtuous at least in part because it was one in which there actually were conspiracies of the kind that they postulated. Watergate was by no means the only one. It was the context that made all the difference rather than the intrinsic features of Woodward and Bernstein's thinking when compared with the thinking of, say, a 9/11 conspiracy theorist. Or so it might be argued.

Just as the context can make what would otherwise be epistemically vicious thinking epistemically virtuous, so it can also have the reverse effect. The reverse effect is illustrated by Mr Justice Bridge's approach to the Birmingham Six. He engaged in epistemically vicious anti-conspiracy thinking that, in different circumstances, might have been epistemically virtuous. In dismissing the notion that the defendants might have been telling the truth, Bridge reasoned as follows:

[C]onsider the scale of the conspiracy in terms of those involved. It ranges, does it not, from the detective constables and police constables right up through the police hierarchy to Chief Superintendent Robinson, in charge of the whole CID of the West Midlands, who has now been promoted to Assistant Chief Constable. It involved, what is more . . . close collaboration in a criminal enterprise between officers who did not know each other . . . If there had been one officer (out of) the whole lot who had said to himself, 'I cannot stomach this'. If he had reported the matter to some very senior officer, or even to some independent force. If he had even gone to the press and said 'This is what is happening', the gaffe would have been blown, would it not?   (Quoted by Mullin, 1990: 201)

Like many other examples of anti-conspiracy reasoning, Bridge's reasoning here relies on the law of parsimony: the best explanation is the simplest explanation that fits the evidence.[32] Bridge reasoned, in effect, that it was much more economical to suppose that the Six were guilty than that they had been framed by a massive police conspiracy. If there had been such a conspiracy, the chances are that it would either have failed or leaked out. Why suppose that the defence's conspiracy theory was correct when there was a simpler explanation, namely, that the Six were guilty?[33] This is a fair question, and it supports the notion that it

---

[32] Tom Nichols is someone who accuses conspiracy theories of violating the law of parsimony. See Nichols 2017: 56.

[33] Compare Bridge's reasoning with David Aaronovitch's reasoning in support of his rejection of the theory that the 1969 Apollo moon landings were faked. According to Aaronovitch, 'a hoax on such a grand scale would necessarily involve hundreds if not thousands of participants' and 'it was pretty much impossible for such an operation to be

was the context rather than the intrinsic quality of his thinking that was Bridge's undoing. His thinking was epistemically vicious because the world was quite different from how he took it to be. It was a world in which the police did conspire to frame innocents, and Bridge's true epistemic vice was naïvety. He thought the British police weren't invent-ive or resourceful enough to pull off such a complex conspiracy, but he was wrong about that.

The conclusion one might draw from all this is that there is 'nothing *inherently* vicious about believing or being disposed to believe conspiracy theories' (Pigden 2017: 121). By the same token, as Mr Justice Bridge showed, there is nothing inherently virtuous about anti-conspiracy thinking. There are environments in which either way of thinking can be epistemically virtuous or vicious, and a way to capture this context-relativity is to describe these thinking styles as *conditionally* virtuous or vicious. And then the natural next question is whether epistemic virtues and vices generally are only conditionally virtuous or vicious.[34] If there are environments in which conspiracy thinking is epistemically vicious and ones in which it is epistemically virtuous, could there not be envir-onments in which wishful thinking, arrogance, and closed-mindedness are epistemic virtues? Even in the world as it actually is, aren't there some contexts, or some roles, in which arrogance is a virtue and humility a vice? For example, a degree of arrogance or bravado might be no bad thing in a surgeon, even if there are many other fields in which it would be highly undesirable: arrogance promotes the self-confidence required to be an effective surgeon.[35]

The idea of conditional virtues and vices also makes sense of what Ian James Kidd calls the practice of 'vice-charging'.[36] Consider the debate between proponents and opponents of the view that the destruction of the twin towers on 9/11 was the work of government agents. Each side

mounted and kept secret' (2009: 2). Aaronovitch's reasoning is sound but is Bridge's reasoning any worse? Don't they both reason in the same way? Yes, at a certain level of abstraction, but once one gets down to specifics Bridge's reasoning has flaws that are not apparent in Aaronovitch's reasoning. The devil is in the detail.

[34] According to Charles Pigden, 'epistemic virtues are role relative, context relative, and end relative' (2017: 125).

[35] See Groopman 2008: 169.   [36] Kidd 2016.

accuses the other of epistemic vices such as gullibility and closed-mindedness.[37] These charges make perfect sense given their different conceptions of the way the world works. From the standpoint of someone who believes that major conspiracies by government agents are relatively common one would have to be extremely gullible to believe the official account of 9/11. Viewed from the perspective of those who have a less pessimistic view of government conduct one would have to be both gullible and foolish to believe the extravagant claims of 9/11 conspiracy theorists. It isn't possible to know, just by inspecting their thinking, which side is correct in its assessment of the other. It depends, rather, on what the world is actually like.

Seductive as this line of thinking might seem, it isn't correct. The obvious point to make is that conspiracy thinking can be vicious in a conspiracy-rich environment, just as anti-conspiracy thinking can be vicious in contexts in which conspiracies are rare. If it is really the case that the only thing wrong with Mr Justice Bridge's reasoning was that police conduct didn't match up to his estimation of it then it's not clear why this thinking should be described as vicious. Of course he was wrong about the Birmingham Six but being wrong about something isn't enough to make one's thinking vicious. It all depends on why one was wrong. What made Bridge's thinking epistemically vicious wasn't just the context. For example, the weakness of the prosecution's forensic evidence was explained to the court by the defence's forensic scientist, but Bridge swallowed the prosecution's story. Furthermore, as Mullin notes, discrepancies in the defendants' supposed confessions ought to have posed a serious problem for the prosecution's case, but this wasn't how Bridge saw things.[38] Four of the defendants admitted, independently, to planting the bombs in plastic bags even though the bombs were not left in plastic bags. How could all four have made the same mistake about such a fundamental matter? Wouldn't the simplest explanation have been that their supposed confessions were fabricated by the police, exactly as the defence alleged?

---

[37] I go in for some serious vice charging in Cassam 2015b and am taken to task for this in Pigden 2017.

[38] According to Mullin, Mr Justice Bridge tried to turn these discrepancies to the prosecution's advantage. See Mullin 1990: 200.

One obvious lesson is that the principle of parsimony is a blunt instrument when it comes to assessing the merits of hypotheses in complex cases. Viewed from one angle the defence's conspiracy theory was much less parsimonious than the theory that the Six were guilty. However, once account is taken of the weakness of the forensic evidence and the otherwise inexplicable consistencies and inconsistencies in the defendants' confessions, there is a sense in which the conspiracy theory is less complicated than the alternative to which Mr Justice Bridge subscribed. The fundamental problem, as Mullin notes, is that Bridge 'did not use his undoubtedly considerable intellect to analyse the prosecution case with a fraction of the same rigour as he applied to the defence' (1990: 202). He showed every sign of being biased against the defence and this shows up in his thinking. Regardless of whether the Six were innocent or guilty, or whether the police were in the habit of framing innocents, Bridge's anti-conspiracy thinking was biased. It wasn't bad luck or the context that was the problem but vicious thinking. In the same way, conspiracy thinking in a conspiracy-rich environment is still vicious if it isn't supported by the evidence. Just because something is the case it doesn't follow that we have good reason to believe that it is the case. When an actual conspiracy like Watergate comes to light the conspiracy theorist will no doubt say 'I told you so', but it doesn't follow that their thinking was epistemically virtuous. It all depends on what it was based on.

A way to make sense of all this is to draw a distinction between thinking vices proper and vicious thinking. So, for example, a particular piece of conspiracy thinking may or may not be vicious. When it is vicious it is because it displays thinking vices proper, such as closed-mindedness or gullibility. Thinking vices proper are generic rather than subject-specific. Thinking that displays a thinking vice proper is, to that extent, vicious, though the same thinking that displays thinking vices might also display some thinking virtues. Conspiracy thinking *as such* is neither vicious nor virtuous, and whether a given piece of thinking is virtuous or vicious isn't exclusively, or even primarily, determined by the environment in which it takes place. What it is determined by is the extent to which, like Mr Justice Bridge's thinking, it displays thinking vices proper. This is also how conspiracy thinking in a conspiracy-rich environment can still be vicious. Even in a conspiracy-rich environment conspiracy thinking can still be closed-minded or gullible or muddled.

Does this mean that it is possible, after all, to know whether a given piece of conspiracy or anti-conspiracy thinking is vicious just by inspecting the thinking itself, without reference to the environment or context? In one sense, yes. For example, it isn't necessary to know much, if anything, about a thinker's environment in order to know whether their thinking is illogical or muddled or closed-minded. These epistemic vices are, to a large extent, internal to their thinking. They have more to do with how, in the case in question, the thinker identifies possibilities, seeks and weighs evidence, and draws conclusions. If the evidence doesn't support the conclusion they draw from it then that is a flaw in their thinking that has very little to do with how the world works, as distinct from how their minds work. If they are unwilling to accept evidence that goes against what they already believe then their thinking is closed-minded regardless of whether their beliefs are true or false. Perhaps their environment determines what evidence is available to them but not what they make of the evidence.

Where does this leave the idea that epistemic vices generally are only conditionally vicious? For this to be so there would have to be possible environments in which things like wishful thinking, arrogance, and closed-mindedness are conducive to knowledge whereas open-mindedness, humility, and carefulness systematically get in the way of knowledge. Could there be such environments? If so, then it would start to look an entirely contingent matter that the character traits, attitudes, and thinking styles that we view as epistemic vices are epistemically harmful. This issue will be taken up in Chapter 5 but here are a couple of preliminary thoughts: it isn't difficult to think of scenarios in which so-called epistemic vices lead to true belief. As the case of Henry II and Thomas à Becket illustrates, wishful thinking *can* lead to true belief. With a bit of imagination it is possible to show that every supposed epistemic vice can lead to true belief in certain circumstances. What is less obvious is that epistemic vices are *reliable* pathways to true belief or that they are *systematically* conducive to true belief. Even for Henry II, wishful thinking was unlikely to have been self-fulfilling in the normal course of events.

The other point to make is that leading to true belief is not the same as being conducive to knowledge. Even in cases where an epistemic vice leads someone to believe something true that doesn't mean that they have the *right* to be confident that things are as they take them to be or that their belief is justified. Quite the contrary. If their true belief is sustained by closed-mindedness or some other epistemic vice then they don't have the right and don't know what they think they know. Knowledge isn't just true belief, and Mr Justice Bridge wouldn't have been entitled to believe that the Birmingham Six were guilty even if they were. Perhaps it isn't *logically* impossible for there to be scenarios in which 'epistemic vices' are conducive to knowledge but this is no basis for regarding genuine epistemic vices as only conditionally vicious if these scenarios are extremely far-fetched or contrived. That's the difference between thinking vices proper and conspiracy thinking. It isn't far-fetched to suppose that conspiracy thinking might be conducive to knowledge if it is evidence-based.

What about the suggestion that arrogance might be no bad thing in a surgeon or, more generally, that epistemic virtues and vices are 'role relative' (Pigden 2017: 125)? This doesn't really stand up. The self-confidence required to be an effective surgeon has little to do with the vice of intellectual arrogance. Why should a surgeon's effectiveness be improved by a tendency to regard others with disdain or by an intellectual superiority complex? Arrogance is related to overconfidence, and there is plenty of evidence that overconfidence is not a virtue in any branch of medicine.[39] It is a cause of diagnostic error and can lead surgeons to underestimate the risk of complications. It's hard to think of a single occupation in which intellectual arrogance or any other genuine epistemic vice produces better outcomes than the corresponding virtues. If this is right then epistemic vices, including thinking vices, aren't just obstacles to knowledge. They are also, and relatedly, obstacles to good practice.

The fundamental point, however, is that when a person is guilty of vicious thinking, the viciousness of their thinking is accounted for by the influence of thinking vices, and thinking vices are vices because of the way they harm our thinking. They harm our thinking by allowing it to be unduly influenced by extraneous factors such as one's wishes or preju-dices. Thinking vices are epistemically harmful as well as harmful in other ways, and I've used a whole series of examples to illustrate the harms they do. Although our thinking is undoubtedly affected in all sorts

[39] See Cassam 2017.

of ways by the environments in which we operate there is no interesting sense in which thinking vices, or epistemic vices generally, are 'relative'. Epistemically speaking, they are bad for us in just about any context in which we are likely to find ourselves, and they are certainly bad for us in the world as it is. That, in the end, is what really matters, and if we want to improve our thinking then we need to identify and tackle our thinking vices. The extent to which this type of self-improvement is possible is an interesting question which I will address in Chapter 8. In the meantime, there is another variety of epistemic vice to consider. The last two chapters have been about character and thinking vices but there are also epistemic vices that fall into neither of these categories. As noted in Chapter 1, some epistemic vices are attitudes, and getting to the bottom of attitude vices is the next challenge I want to take up.

VICES OF THE MIND

4
Epistemic Postures

In the days leading up to Britain's 2016 vote to leave the European Union (EU), a leading pro-Leave campaigner was asked by a journalist how many independent economic authorities agreed with him that Britain would be better off outside Europe. The interviewer was Faisal Islam of *Sky News* and his interviewee was Michael Gove, a government minister. Gove was pressed by Islam to admit that his views about the economic benefits of leaving the EU were not shared by most experts. In response Gove airily dismissed such concerns. 'The people of this country', he insisted, 'have had enough of experts'.[1]

Gove wasn't the only Leave campaigner who seemed to be thinking in these terms. In an interview after the vote Arron Banks, a funder of the Leave campaign, explained his side's victory on the basis that the pro-EU Remain campaign had featured 'fact, fact, fact, fact, fact' but that didn't work: 'you've got to connect with people emotionally'.[2] Facts, on this view, are boring, and politicians who rely on evidence or expert opinion in formulating their policies are likely to fail when confronted by opponents who don't feel the need to burden themselves with such matters. Many commentators detected in the posture of Gove and Banks evidence of the rise of 'post-truth politics' in the UK, a style of politics in which, in the words of the *Guardian* columnist Jonathan Freedland, 'an unhesitating liar can be king' and 'those pedants still hung up on the facts and evidence and all that boring stuff are left for dust, their boots barely laced while the lie has spread halfway around the world' (Freedland 2016).

---

[1] A full transcript of the interview is available here: https://corporate.sky.com/media-centre/media-packs/2016/eu-in-or-out-faisal-islam-interview-with-michael-gove,-30616-8pm.

[2] As reported by the *Independent*: http://www.independent.co.uk/news/uk/home-news/brexit-news-donald-trump-leave-eu-campaign-facts-dont-work-arron-banks-lies-referendum-a7111001.html.

The post-truth politicians targeted by Freedland included Boris Johnson, a former mayor of London and leading figure in the Leave campaign. In an early career as a journalist for the *Telegraph* he made his name by writing faintly comic but mendacious articles about the EU. Johnson revelled in the effect his articles seemed to be having and laughed it off when his stories were shown to bear no relation to reality. He was twice fired for lying and was described by fellow journalist Mathew Parris as 'under-prepared, jolly, sly, dishonest and unapologetic' (Parris 2016). Curiously, Johnson had a reputation for not being in favour of withdrawal from the EU. Although he wrote a pro-Leave article for the *Daily Telegraph* it later transpired that he had also written a second article arguing for the opposite point of view.[3]

It's hardly news that politicians can be cynical and dishonest but what was striking about Gove and Johnson was their sheer *insouciance*. Insouciance in the ordinary sense is lack of concern, carelessness, or indifference. The particular form of insouciance to which some politicians are prone is *epistemic* insouciance: an indifference or lack of concern with respect to whether their claims are grounded in reality or the evidence. Epistemic insouciance means not really caring much about any of this and being excessively casual and nonchalant about the challenge of finding answers to complex questions, partly as a result of a tendency to view such questions as much less complex than they really are. Epistemic insouciance is a particular form of not giving a shit. It means viewing the need to find evidence in support of one's views as a mere inconvenience, as something that is not to be taken too seriously. Finding accurate answers to complex questions can be hard work and epistemic insouciance makes that hard work seem unnecessary. The epistemically insouciant inquirer's attitude is that hard work is for suckers. Understood in this way, epistemic insouciance is an epistemic vice but one that is different from the other vices I've considered so far.

---

[3] Both articles appear as appendices in Shipman 2017. Shipman questions the view that Johnson was 'a dedicated supporter of EU membership who decided to back Leave for the simple and cynical motive of advancing his career' (2017: 171). However, according to George Osborne, who served as chancellor of the exchequer in David Cameron's administration, Johnson had repeatedly said to him before the referendum that he did not want Britain to leave the EU. See Shipman 2017: 601. It is also true that Johnson had previously argued that continued membership of the EU would be 'a boon for the world and for Europe' (https://www.theguardian.com/politics/2016/oct/16/secret-boris-johnson-column-favoured-uk-remaining-in-eu).

80   QUASSIM CASSAM

It is an *attitude* rather than a thinking style or character trait. I'll refer to epistemic vices that take the form of attitudes rather than thinking styles or character traits as *attitude vices*. The mission of this chapter is to give an account of attitude vices.

Before going any further, there is one concern about the idea of epistemic insouciance that needs to be addressed at the outset. This is the concern that it is no more than an exotic label for a perfectly familiar phenomenon: lying. For example, when Boris Johnson made claims about the EU that he knew to be false he wasn't being 'epistemically insouciant'. He was lying.[4] On this reading, calling a politician 'epistemically insouciant' is a polite way of saying, or implying, that he is a barefaced liar. In that case, why not just call him a barefaced liar? This is a reasonable question, and the best way to answer it is to relate the notion of epistemic insouciance to Harry Frankfurt's notion of bullshit. In his essay 'On Bullshit' Frankfurt gives this account of the difference between lying and bullshitting:

It is impossible for someone to lie unless he thinks he knows the truth . . . A person who lies is thereby responding to the truth and he is to that extent respectful of it. When an honest man speaks, he says only what he believes to be true; and for the liar, it is correspondingly indispensable that he considers his statements to be false. For the bullshitter, however, all these bets are off: he is neither on the side of the true nor on the side of the false. His eye is not on the facts at all, as the eyes of the honest man and of the liar are, except insofar as they may be pertinent to his interest in getting away with what he says. He does not care whether the things he says describe reality correctly.   (2005: 55–6)

It is because the bullshitter doesn't care about this that 'bullshit is a greater enemy of the truth than lies are' (2005: 61). The bullshitter doesn't *reject* the authority of truth; he pays no attention to it at all.[5]

One way to put this would be to describe the bullshitter as epistemically insouciant. Indeed, bullshit is the primary product of epistemic insouciance. Bullshit is 'produced without concern for the truth' (Frankfurt 2005: 47), and this lack of concern is the essence of epistemic insouciance. This explains why being epistemically insouciant is not the same as being a liar. Lying is something that a person *does* rather than an attitude, and the intention to conceal the truth implies that the liar is not

---

[4] This is the implication of Jonathan Freedland's description, quoted above.
[5] Frankfurt 2005: 61.

indifferent to the truth or falsity of his utterances. Epistemic insouciance is an attitude rather than something that a person does, and it does imply an indifference to the truth or falsity of one's utterances. To describe a politician as a liar rather than as epistemically insouciant is to ignore the fundamental distinction between their lies and their bullshit. Of course bullshitters can be liars, but it isn't their lying as such that makes them bullshitters, and they don't have to be liars in order to qualify as epistemically insouciant. The politicians I've accused of epistemic insouciance may or may not be liars but their political success is a testament to what James Ball aptly describes as the 'power of bullshit' (2017: 15).[6]

I've described epistemic insouciance as an attitude vice but what is an 'attitude', and in what sense are some epistemic vices attitudes? In one sense, one's attitude towards something is one's perspective on it or one's evaluation of it.[7] Attitudes require attitude objects, and an attitude object is anything towards which it is possible to have an attitude.[8] So, for example, people, political parties, and ideas are attitude objects. Attitudes can be positive or negative, weaker or stronger. A basic positive attitude is liking. A basic negative attitude is disliking. To like an idea is to have a positive attitude towards it, and liking comes in degrees. Other attitudes in this sense include contempt, indifference, disdain, suspicion, nonchalance, hostility, cynicism, and respect. These attitudes are examples of what I'll call *postures*. Later I will give examples of attitude vices that are *stances* rather than postures, but the immediate task is to explain the notion of a posture.

Two key features of postures are that they are *affective* and *involuntary*. Consider contempt as a posture towards another person. As Michelle Mason notes, contempt is a 'form of regard' that has a 'salient affective quality' (2003: 241). One element of contempt is a low regard for the object of one's contempt but contempt isn't just a matter of belief

[6] What is the relationship between epistemic insouciance and bullshit? Bullshit is not an attitude and nor, strictly speaking, is being a bullshitter, that is, being disposed to spout bullshit. Epistemic insouciance is the attitude, or an attitude, that makes one a bullshitter and thereby causes one to spout bullshit. In other words, epistemic insouciance leads to bullshit.

[7] This is roughly how psychologists conceive of attitudes. In psychology, 'most attitude theorists would argue that evaluation is *the* predominant aspect of the attitude concept. In other words, reporting an attitude involves making a decision of liking versus disliking, or favoring versus disfavoring a particular issue, object, or person' (Maio and Haddock 2015).

[8] Maio and Haddock 2015: 4.

or opinion.[9] It is something that is *felt*, and this feeling of contempt is the affective quality of the attitude. Contempt for another person is a specific posture towards them that has a range of behavioural manifestations. Examples might include refusing to shake their hand or avoiding them in social situations.[10] These behavioural manifestations of contempt are motivated by its affective quality. For Mason the affective quality of contempt is *aversion*: an object for which contempt is felt 'becomes for us a source of aversion' (2003: 241).

Another familiar affective posture is arrogance. Although this can be a character trait it can also be an attitude. At the heart of arrogance is a 'dismissive attitude towards the views and perspectives of others' (Tiberius and Walker 1998: 382). In the specific case of intellectual arrogance this attitude is grounded in a belief in one's intellectual superiority but arrogance, like contempt, isn't just a matter of belief. It also involves what Alessandra Tanesini describes as 'a feeling of superiority over others' (2016: 74). This makes intellectual arrogance another example of an *affective* posture.[11] The affective quality of arrogance, like the affective quality of contempt, is a mental presence—a feeling of superiority—but not all postures are like arrogance and contempt in this regard. For example, one might be said to *feel* indifferent about something but indifference is marked by the *absence* of certain feelings or emotions rather than by their presence. However, not even indifference is a pure

---

[9] In Mason's words, 'in taking up contempt as a form of regard I mean to justify—ultimately morally justify—a certain affective stance toward another person, not (or not merely) the adoption of a certain belief about them (e.g., that they are contemptible)' (2003: 239).

[10] These examples are from Mason 2003: 241.

[11] Is it plausible that intellectual arrogance has an affective quality? Is there really such a thing as a 'feeling of superiority' and is it essential to intellectual arrogance? On the first of these issues, there is no more reason to doubt the possibility of a person feeling superior than to doubt the possibility of their feeling smug or confident. It could be that these are all metaphorical uses of 'feeling' but there is no reason not to take appearances at face value and think of superiority, like smugness and confidence, as something that can be felt. To suppose that this feeling is not essential to arrogance is to suppose that arrogance can be totally unemotional, but I contend that arrogance with no emotional charge is not genuine arrogance. Paradoxically, intellectual arrogance is not a purely intellectual attitude, and this is the key to understanding its behavioural manifestations. All too familiar behavioural manifestations of intellectual arrogance include refusing to listen or queue-jumping in discussion. The affective quality of arrogance that motivates these behaviours is a feeling of superiority. It is as hard to conceive of affectless arrogance as it is to conceive of affectless contempt. Tanesini 2016 is an illuminating discussion of intellectual arrogance.

absence; there is something that it feels like not to care about something or to be left feeling cold about it. Like numbness, indifference is both a feeling and an absence of feeling.

I've described affective postures as involuntary. The sense in which this is so is that they aren't generally matters of choice or decision. This isn't surprising since how one feels isn't usually a matter of choice or decision. For example, if one feels contempt or respect for another person one hasn't usually chosen to be contemptuous or respectful. One can, of course, choose to *show* respect, but one can't choose to *have* respect for someone if one can see nothing about them that deserves respect. Equally, one can't decide to feel intellectually superior.[12] Even if, for some obscure reason, one decides to be dismissive of the views and perspectives of another person, one might find their views so compelling that it is impossible for one not to take them seriously.

Postures as I understand them are related to, but nevertheless different from, what Bas van Fraassen calls 'stances'. A stance, for van Fraassen, is 'an attitude adopted in relation to a particular subject' (2004: 175). A stance in this sense is 'something one can adopt or reject' (2004: 175) and serves as a *policy* or guideline.[13] It is in this sense that philo-sophical positions like empiricism are stances. For example, when empiricists declare that all factual knowledge must ultimately derive from experience they can be viewed as adopting the policy of denigrating claims to knowledge that lack any basis in experience.[14] However, stances are neither affective nor involuntary. They aren't distinguished by the presence or absence of a particular affective quality and they can be voluntarily adopted or rejected.[15] Later in this chapter I will give an example of an attitude vice that is a stance rather than a posture.

In philosophy, 'attitudes' are usually understood as 'propositional attitudes', that is, as mental states ascribed by means of a 'that' clause. Perhaps it's worth noting, therefore, that neither postures nor stances are

[12] Think of the futility of someone who is going through a crisis of intellectual self-confidence deciding to feel intellectually superior.
[13] For the idea that stances are best interpreted as policies or guidelines see Lipton 2004: 148 and Teller 2004: 161.
[14] Cf. Lipton 2004: 148: 'For example, the empirical stance includes a policy of advocat-ing scientific practices and denigrating metaphysical claims. Instead of embracing a doc-trine, the empiricist is advised to adopt such a policy.'
[15] This is the basis on which Lipton correctly interprets van Fraassen as proposing a form of 'epistemological voluntarism' (2004: 147).

propositional attitudes, though they involve propositional attitudes. The exact relationship between propositional attitudes and postures is complicated. On the one hand, it seems clear that many postures aren't propositional attitudes and many propositional attitudes aren't stances. One is contemptuous or disdainful *towards* something or someone. There is no such thing as having contempt or disdain *that* such-and-such. Also, many propositional attitudes lack an affective element.[16] To say that someone believes it is raining is to say nothing about their feelings or emotions. On the other hand, if one feels contempt for another person it is usually because one has certain beliefs about them. One's affective posture here is not a propositional attitude but is grounded in one's propositional attitudes. Stances also involve propositional attitudes even though 'having a stance can't be equated with holding particular beliefs' (van Fraassen 2004: 174). Stances are usually a reflection of what one believes.[17]

What is the case for classifying epistemic insouciance as a posture rather than a stance? One reason for not counting epistemic insouciance as a stance is that it isn't voluntary. One doesn't choose to be excessively casual and nonchalant towards the challenge of finding answers to complex questions. One just is. Epistemic insouciance is a reflection of what one cares about, and what one cares about is not typically a matter of choice or decision. It is possible not to care about what the evidence shows, or whether one's views about a particular topic have any basis in reality, without having decided not to care about these things. In addition, stances are the product of thought or reflection, but epistemic insouciance is more likely to be an unreflective attitude. To describe

[16] The contrast between attitudes and beliefs was one that Wittgenstein was drawing on when he famously wrote that one's attitude towards another person is 'an attitude towards a soul' and that one is not 'of the opinion that he has a soul'. The point of this remark is to de-intellectualize the problem of other minds. Scepticism about other minds questions whether we are justified in believing that there are minds other than our own. Wittgenstein's point is that the presumption that other people are minded is built into our interactions with them and is much more fundamental than anything that can be described as a *belief* in other minds. In my terms it is a posture or stance or orientation. We see and treat other people as sentient, minded beings, and this is our attitude *towards* them rather than a belief or opinion *about* them. The attitude involves affective reactions whose psychological depth goes beyond mere belief or opinion.

[17] As van Fraassen puts it, 'having or adopting a stance consists in having or adopting a cluster of attitudes, including a number of propositional attitudes, which will generally include some beliefs' (2004: 175).

someone as epistemically insouciant is to describe their epistemic *posture* rather than their epistemic *policy*.

If epistemic insouciance is a posture, what is its affective quality? It might seem that epistemic insouciance is marked by the absence of certain feelings or emotions rather than by their presence, but the reality is more complicated. Epistemic insouciance is not just a matter of not caring about certain things, or not caring enough. Lack of concern about what the evidence shows is one element of epistemic insouciance but another element in many cases is contempt. There is contempt for the truth, contempt for experts, and, in the case of politicians, contempt for the public. Each of these varieties of contempt is detectable in the epistemic posture of politicians who dismiss evidence that conflicts with their prejudices and promote the idea that experts are not to be trusted. The contempt of these politicians is an affective quality of epistemic insouciance and explains their indifference to matters that ought to be of concern to a conscientious truth-seeker. Furthermore, as I've noted, indifference is itself something that can be felt; it is not the pure absence of feeling.

Is contempt necessary for epistemic insouciance? In the case of some politicians one might think that the problem is not that they have contempt for the facts or evidence but that they are too lazy to seek genuine evidential support for their views. In Heather Battaly's terminology, such politicians are *slackers* who can't be bothered to do the hard intellectual work required to find accurate answers to complex questions. However, being a slacker can cause a person to be epistemically insouciant regardless of whether they feel contempt for serious inquiry or for those who engage in it. To say that a person feels contempt for something is to imply that they feel strongly about it, but slackers don't care enough about serious inquiry to feel contempt for it. As Battaly points out, a genuine slacker doesn't have the energy to feel contempt.[18]

One response to this line of thinking would be to say that whether or not a slacker is *motivated* by contempt, his epistemic insouciance and the

[18] See Battaly 2015: 99–100 for the concept of a slacker. Being a slacker in Battaly's sense means not caring about what is good or bad and failing to develop a conception of what is good or bad. It's not clear, though, that a person like Boris Johnson has no conception of what is epistemically good or bad. In his case, and the case of intellectual slackers generally, the crucial point is not that they lack a grasp of the distinction between strong and weak evidence but that they don't care enough about basing their views on strong evidence.

epistemic conduct to which it gives rise still *manifest* contempt for the facts and the evidence. On this account, however, it isn't his contempt that explains his epistemic insouciance but rather his epistemic insouciance that explains his contempt. That is, his contempt isn't an independently identifiable component of his epistemic insouciance. A slacker *displays* contempt for something for which he may not *feel* contempt; he displays his contempt by his conduct. If this is right then contempt *qua* affective posture isn't strictly necessary for epistemic insouciance even if the two often go together. What is necessary is what I have described as an indifference to the truth and to the need to base one's views on the relevant facts or evidence. It is this indifference or nonchalance that is essential to epistemic insouciance and that constitutes its affective dimension, assuming that indifference has an affective quality. Not caring about something is a negative rather than a positive affective posture.

If epistemic insouciance is an attitude what is its 'object'? Knowledge, evidence, and inquiry are *epistemic* objects, and attitudes towards epistemic objects are *epistemic attitudes*. In these terms, epistemic insouciance is an epistemic attitude. Lack of concern about what the evidence shows is one epistemic dimension of epistemic insouciance but there are others. A fundamental epistemic activity for most humans is inquiry. As noted in Chapter 1, inquiry is the means by which we search for answers to our questions, ranging from the utterly banal to the truly momentous. Inquiry is the attempt 'to find things out, to extend our knowledge by carrying out investigations directed at answering questions' (Hookway 1994: 211). Like other things we do, inquiring is something that can be done well or badly, and the quality of inquiry is partly a function of the attitude of the inquirer. To be epistemically insouciant is to have a distinctive attitude towards inquiry, to view the serious business of extending our knowledge by carrying out investigations directed at answering questions as a tedious chore that doesn't merit one's full attention. This makes epistemic insouciance an epistemic attitude, an attitude towards inquiry. However, although the objects of this attitude are primarily epistemic they aren't exclusively epistemic. Contempt for the truth isn't an epistemic attitude since truth isn't an epistemic object.

How representative is epistemic insouciance of attitude vices generally? Another striking example of an attitude vice is prejudice. According to Miranda Fricker, 'the idea of a prejudice is most basically that of a *pre-judgement'*, that is, 'a judgement made or maintained without proper regard to the evidence' (2007: 32–3). One problem with this characterization is that judgements are propositional attitudes rather than affective postures, but prejudice is an affective posture if anything is. Moreover, the objects of prejudice don't appear particularly epistemic. If one has a negative attitude towards another person on account of their race then one is certainly guilty of prejudice but races aren't epistemic objects, and racial prejudice doesn't sound much like an epistemic attitude.

These issues are brought into sharp focus by Fricker's example from Harper Lee's *To Kill a Mockingbird*.[19] In that novel, a young black man, Tom Robinson, is accused of raping a white girl, Mayella Ewell. Robinson is innocent but when evidence of his innocence comes up against the all-white jury's prejudice the latter proves decisive and he is found guilty. This verdict is a reflection of the jury's attitude towards young black men in general and Tom Robinson in particular. Its prejudice isn't just a matter of judgement. It is primarily an affect-laden posture that involves deep feelings of contempt, loathing, and superiority. Like other affective postures one's prejudices are partly a reflection of one's judgements, but this is not to say that prejudices *are* judgements. They are more visceral than that. What makes a prejudice a prejudice is that it is an *attitude* formed and sustained without any proper inquiry into the merits or demerits of its object. It is in the nature of prejudice to be resistant to counter-evidence but such resistance is not the exclusive preserve of judgements or beliefs. It can also affect affective postures.

As for whether prejudice is an *epistemic* attitude, Fricker's discussion brings out the sense in which it is. As she points out, in face-to-face testimonial exchanges the hearer must 'make some attribution of *credibility* regarding the speaker' (2007: 18). If the speaker knows something but is disbelieved by a hearer because of the hearer's prejudice against the speaker then the speaker is wronged 'specifically in their capacity as a knower' (2007: 1). This is one of the wrongs suffered by Tom Robinson, who is a victim of what Fricker calls 'testimonial injustice'. Testimonial injustice is an epistemic injustice, and a prejudice that is to blame for an epistemic injustice is, to this extent, an epistemic attitude. Prejudice counts as an epistemic attitude insofar as it is an affective posture towards

---

[19] Fricker 2007: 23–9.

another person's *epistemic* credentials. A negative attitude towards another race is not per se an epistemic attitude but it implies a negative epistemic attitude. If this is right then prejudice is not a counter-example to the view that attitude vices are epistemic postures.[20]

This is not to deny, however, that there are attitude vices that aren't postures. Earlier I introduced the distinction between postures and stances and suggested that not all attitude vices are postures. One attitude vice that is not a posture is what Jason Baehr calls 'epistemic malevolence'.[21] Moral malevolence is *'opposition to the good as such'* (2010: 190). Epistemic malevolence is 'opposition to knowledge as such' (2010: 203). Malevolence in this form is an attitude vice but a stance rather than a posture: it is a voluntarily adopted epistemic attitude that lacks an affective element.[22] If this is right then epistemic insouciance is not the model for all attitude vices. Nevertheless, epistemic insouciance and epistemic malevolence are closely related in practice. Indeed, it might be argued that at least some of the examples I've given of epistemic insouciance are actually examples of epistemic malevolence.[23] Whether this is so or not is hard to decide without a fuller understanding of the latter. Since this is Jason Baehr's notion, it is to Baehr's discussion that we need to turn.

For Baehr, the opposition to the good that is essential to malevolence, whether moral or epistemic, is robustly volitional, active, and personally deep.[24] It is volitional in the sense that it involves the will and is not the mere conviction or preference that the good should be opposed. It is active in the sense that it tends to issue in actual attempts to 'stop, diminish, undermine, destroy, speak out, or turn others against the good' (2010: 190). Finally, what makes it deep is that it reflects the malevolent person's fundamental cares and concerns. If the epistemic good is knowledge then epistemic malevolence is opposition to knowledge. In its 'impersonal' form it is opposition to knowledge 'as such', whereas personal epistemic malevolence is opposition to another person's share in knowledge or to their 'epistemic well-being as such' (2010: 203).

---

[20] 'Epistemic posture' is from Jackson 2015.
[21] If I understand him correctly, Baehr conceives of malevolence as a character trait.
[22] This is my view of epistemic malevolence rather than Baehr's.
[23] I thank Fabienne Peter for this suggestion.   [24] Baehr 2010: 190.

A rich source of examples of epistemic malevolence is research in the emerging field of *agnotology*, the study of the production and maintenance of ignorance.[25] One example is the tobacco industry's attempts to generate and maintain public ignorance concerning tobacco's impact on health. The story of this exercise in fact fighting, which is told by Naomi Oreskes and Erik Conway in their book *Merchants of Doubt*, is worth recounting if the aim is to see what real-world epistemic malevolence might look like.[26] The story begins in the 1950s with the discovery that smoking massively increases one's chances of getting cancer. The tobacco industry was thrown into panic by this discovery and reacted by hiring a public relations firm to challenge the scientific evidence. The firm recommended the creation of a Tobacco Industry Research Committee which would fund research to cast doubt on the link between smoking and cancer.

Doubt was the key. In the words of a notorious memo written by one tobacco industry executive, 'Doubt is our product since it is the best means of competing with the "body of fact" that exists in the minds of the general public'.[27] What Oreskes and Conway refer to as the 'tobacco strategy' was simple but effective. By 'cherry-picking data and focusing on unexplained or anomalous details' (2010: 18), its aim was to manufacture uncertainty about the health effects of smoking and to foster the impression of a genuine scientific debate about the link. The industry's view was that there was no proof that tobacco was bad. It promoted this view by manufacturing a debate and 'convincing the mass media that responsible journalists had an obligation to represent "both sides" of it' (2010: 16). This strategy worked, especially in court, where for many years the tobacco industry was able to defend itself by supplying expert witnesses to testify that the link between smoking and cancer was uncertain. The industry knew perfectly well that smoking was harmful but it 'conspired to suppress this knowledge . . . to fight the facts and to merchandise doubt' (2010: 33). The merchandizing of doubt about the effects of smoking was the means by which the industry tried to prevent the public from knowing what it knew. If the public doubted whether smoking was harmful, or thought it was still an open question, then they couldn't know or believe that smoking was harmful because they wouldn't be confident that this was the case.

---

[25] On 'agnotology' and the coining of this term see Proctor 2008.
[26] Oreskes and Conway 2010.   [27] Quoted in Oreskes and Conway 2010: 34.

The tobacco strategy generalizes and indeed similar methods have been used by climate change deniers, anti-vaccination campaigners, and others to sow the seeds of doubt about what is in reality overwhelming scientific evidence.[28] In every case the basic strategy is to employ scientists to denigrate the work of their mainstream colleagues and suggest that the facts are much less clear than they really are. However, Oreskes and Conway suggest that the modern era of fighting facts began with the tobacco strategy. The story they tell is 'about a group of scientists who fought the scientific evidence and spread confusion on many of the most important issues of our time' (2010: 9). An obvious question is: why would any scientist want to do that? No doubt the financial incentives were considerable but it is difficult for anyone familiar with these notions not to think that moral and epistemic malevolence were also playing a significant role. The sense in which the scientists employed by the tobacco industry were morally malevolent is that they actively undermined the physical well-being of smokers by making them less likely to kick the habit. The scientists' epistemic malevolence consisted in their opposition to the epistemic well-being of smokers by spreading knowledge-undermining doubts about the health effects of smoking. They blocked the spread of knowledge by fighting genuine facts with 'alternative facts' and relying on the inability of non-scientists and the media to tell the difference.[29] They didn't bullshit about the dangers of smoking; they lied about its dangers and about what they knew.

One worry one might have about describing the tobacco strategy as epistemically malevolent in Baehr's sense is that its target is too specific. Presumably, the tobacco industry was not opposed to knowledge as such and so didn't display epistemic malevolence in its impersonal form. Nor did it oppose the *overall* epistemic well-being of cigarette smokers. All it did was to prevent many cigarette smokers from acquiring or retaining one specific variety of knowledge—knowledge of the health consequences of cigarette smoking—and one might think that this target is too narrow for talk of epistemic malevolence to be appropriate. This is so even if it is recognized that the tobacco strategy did a lot of collateral epistemic damage. For example, its assault on scientific knowledge of the

[28] See the essays in Proctor and Schiebinger 2008.
[29] See the Wikipedia entry on 'alternative facts' for an account of the origins of this notion: https://en.wikipedia.org/wiki/Alternative_facts.

effects of smoking was also implicitly an assault on scientific knowledge more generally. Scepticism about mainstream science in one domain can easily lead to scepticism in others, but the tobacco strategy was only concerned to undermine the received scientific wisdom in one domain.

One response to this worry would be to broaden the notion of epistemic malevolence to allow even highly targeted knowledge-undermining to count as an instance of it. Even if the tobacco strategy lacks the full generality of epistemic malevolence as Baehr understands it, it is still recognizably a form of epistemic malevolence. A different response to the concern about the narrowness of the tobacco strategy would be to look for less restricted forms of epistemic malevolence to illustrate the phenomenon. For example, the epistemic malevolence of certain tabloid newspapers and news channels seems quite general. They undermine the epistemic well-being of their readers and viewers in a more general sense by presenting propaganda as news and implicitly promoting the lowering of epistemic standards.

What is the relationship between epistemic malevolence and epistemic insouciance? They are conceptually distinct though often allied in practice. The conceptual distinction is the distinction between not caring about something and actively opposing it. Epistemic malevolence is different from epistemic insouciance precisely because it is *not* a matter of being excessively casual or nonchalant about the challenge of finding answers to complex questions or tending to view such questions as less complex than they really are. Whatever else the tobacco industry can be accused of it surely isn't that. Unlike the epistemically insouciant, the epistemically malevolent don't find the need to find evidence in support of their views an inconvenience. They are in the business of actively undermining what, in private, they recognize as good evidence in favour of the views they seek to undermine. It is precisely because the epistemically malevolent *do* care what the evidence shows, or what the facts are, that they are in the business of subverting the evidence or putting forward alternative facts. The tobacco industry cared very much what the evidence showed about harmful effects of smoking and a good number of them gave up smoking when they saw the evidence. What they didn't want was for their customers to do the same and that is not at all the same as not giving a shit about the evidence.

A very natural way to capture these intuitive distinctions is to conceptualize epistemic malevolence as a stance rather than a posture.

Stances aren't distinguished by the presence or absence of a particular affective quality and much the same goes for epistemic malevolence. Epistemic malevolence is an attitude but not an *affective* attitude like epistemic insouciance. The tobacco strategy shows clearly that one can be epistemically malevolent without being epistemically insouciant. Baehr suggests at one point that malevolence involves a kind of 'hostility or contempt for the good' (2010: 190), and this might make this attitude appear no less 'affective' than epistemic insouciance. However, hostility or contempt for the epistemic good isn't essential for epistemic malevolence. What motivated the tobacco strategy wasn't contempt for knowledge but economic self-interest. The tobacco industry's epistemic malevolence, like epistemic malevolence generally, was a matter of policy rather than a passive posture, the policy of spreading doubts about the dangers of smoking. It was open to the industry to adopt or reject this policy. Epistemic malevolence is voluntary in a way that postures are not. One doesn't decide not to care about whether one's views are adequately supported by the evidence in the way that one decides whether to undermine another person's knowledge or the evidence on which their knowledge is based.

Despite the relatively clear conceptual distinction between epistemic insouciance and epistemic malevolence, it can be hard to know which vice a person's conduct exemplifies. It is reasonably clear that the tobacco strategy was epistemically and morally malevolent, but what about the way that some Leave campaigners argued in favour of Britain's exit from the EU? For example, they claimed that Britain sends £350 million a week to the EU and that this amount would be available for the National Health Service after Britain's exit. Yet the £350 million figure was misleading since it took no account of money paid to Britain by the EU.[30] Indeed, the £350 million a week claim was hastily withdrawn by the official Leave campaign after its victory in the 2016 referendum.[31]

---

[30] Daniel Thornton has pointed out to me that the £350 million claim was inaccurate in three different ways: it didn't take account of the UK rebate, it didn't take account of the funds that the EU provides to programmes in the UK, and it didn't take account of the fiscal impact of the economic damage from Brexit.

[31] The story of the Brexit debacle is told by James Ball in Ball 2017, chapter 1. Ball sees the successful Brexit campaign as the triumph of bullshit but much of what he describes is epistemically malevolent rather than mere bullshit. In keeping with what I have been arguing Ball sees bullshit as involving a 'casual attitude to truth' (2017: 13).

To describe the attitude of those responsible for this strategy as epistemically insouciant may be overgenerous. In its own way, the spreading of misleading information about the economic benefits of leaving the EU was as epistemically malevolent as the tobacco strategy. The active promotion of political and economic ignorance was the *policy* of some senior figures in the Leave campaign, and not just a reflection of an epistemic *posture*. Yet some of these same figures also displayed what I have been calling epistemic insouciance. Exactly where epistemic insouciance ends and epistemic malevolence begins is sometimes hard to say, and the attitude of many politicians in democratic political systems is a mixture of the two. What, if anything, can be done about this is an important question, but not for discussion here.

What does need to be discussed here is the basis on which epistemic insouciance, epistemic malevolence, and other such epistemic attitudes are classified as epistemic *vices*. For Baehr, epistemic malevolence isn't necessarily vicious. Whether it is an epistemic vice or not depends on its motivation, and Baehr wants to allow for the possibility that epistemic malevolence might have an 'epistemically appropriate *ultimate* motivation, such that it is not really an intellectual vice' (2010: 190, n. 2).[32] From an obstructivist perspective, the crux of the matter is whether attitudes like epistemic insouciance and epistemic malevolence get in the way of knowledge and are blameworthy or otherwise reprehensible.[33] If they do get in the way of knowledge, and do so systematically, then we

---

[32] In a book about the coalition government that was in power in the UK for five years from 2010 former cabinet minister David Laws describes a conversation about Michael Gove between prime minister David Cameron and deputy prime minister Nick Clegg. When Clegg complained to Cameron about Gove's behaviour Cameron laughed and said, 'The thing you've got to remember with Michael is that he is basically a bit of a Maoist. He believes that the world makes progress through a process of creative destruction' (Laws 2017: 368). What if Gove's attitude in the Brexit debate is seen as epistemically malevolent to some degree (as well as epistemically insouciant) but as motivated by the belief Cameron attributed to him, together with a desire to destroy the established order in the name of progress? Would this be an example of epistemic malevolence with an epistemically appropriate ultimate motivation? This is a hard question to answer since the example is underdescribed. In particular, it's not clear what kind of progress is at issue and whether Gove's motivation would count as epistemically appropriate if his belief about the supposed benefits of creative destruction is false. The path to hell is paved with good intentions, even allowing that Gove's intentions were good.

[33] They might be blameworthy or otherwise reprehensible on account of their motives, but having bad motives isn't necessary for an epistemic vice to be blameworthy or otherwise reprehensible. See Chapter 1.

need to understand *how* they do that on the account of knowledge that I've been recommending.

Different attitude vices bear on different dimensions of our knowledge. Intellectual arrogance systematically obstructs the gaining and the sharing of knowledge. For example, the arrogant and dismissive attitude of senior members of the Bush administration prevented them from coming to know how many troops would be needed in Iraq. It did that by making it impossible for them to learn from those who actually knew the answer to their question. By the same token, those who knew the answer were prevented from sharing their knowledge. Prejudice is another attitude that obstructs the gaining and sharing of knowledge. The jury's prejudice against black men prevented Tom Robinson from sharing his knowledge with them and thereby also prevented the jury from knowing what actually happened to Mayella Ewell. With epistemic malevolence the primary impact is on the gaining and keeping of knowledge. For those who knew nothing about the link between smoking and cancer the aim of the tobacco strategy was to prevent them from coming to know about it. With regard to people who already knew about the link the aim was to deprive them of their knowledge. As for the epistemic consequences of epistemic insouciance, lack of concern about the truth makes it harder to know the truth, while the casual disparaging of experts prevents them from sharing their knowledge with the rest of us. In addition, the half-truths and outright falsehoods that are the natural by-product of epistemic insouciance make it harder for us to retain our knowledge. Being subjected to a relentless barrage of misleading pronouncements about a given subject can deprive one of one's prior knowledge of that subject by muddying the waters and making one mistrust one's own judgement.

These impacts of attitude vices on our knowledge are made intelligible by the account of knowledge I gave in Chapter 1. On that account, one knows that P only if P is true, one is reasonably confident that P, and one has the right to be confident. One way for an attitude vice to get in the way of knowledge is for it to make one's beliefs less likely to be true. All of the attitude vices I have been describing have that effect. The evidence in favour of a belief is evidence for its *truth*, and beliefs with adequate evidential backing are much more likely to be true than beliefs that lack such backing. One way that attitude vices, like epistemic vices generally, get in the way of knowledge is by making one's beliefs less likely to be evidence-based. The jury's prejudice in *To Kill a Mockingbird* meant that they didn't base their belief in Tom Robinson's guilt on the evidence, and as a result ended up with the false belief that he was guilty. Similarly, it wasn't just bad luck that Rumsfeld's beliefs about the number of US troops that would be needed in Iraq were false. They were false because they weren't based on the evidence and they weren't based on the evidence because his intellectual arrogance led him to ignore that evidence. Someone who is epistemically insouciant as well as intellectually arrogant is even less likely to end up with true beliefs: not caring about the evidence is hardly conducive to forming beliefs that are evidence-based.

Another way for attitude vices to get in the way of knowledge is by undermining one's confidence and making it more difficult for one to hold on to one's true beliefs. This is the essence of the tobacco strategy. The surest way to deprive someone of their knowledge of the link between smoking and cancer is to instil doubts in their mind about whether there really is a link. The more one doubts the existence of a link, the less confident one is that it is genuine. Beyond a certain point this loss of confidence implies loss of belief and, by implication, loss of knowledge. However, the person who is deprived of knowledge by the vice of epistemic malevolence is not the person with the vice. Epistemic malevolence is in this respect different from other epistemic vices, whose primary epistemic impact is on those whose vices they are. Epistemic malevolence is other-directed, and its effectiveness is an indication of the close relationship between knowledge, belief, and confidence. Instilling doubts about the link between smoking and cancer is only effective as a means of depriving a person of knowledge of this link on the assumption that knowledge requires confidence.

This point is worth making because the idea that epistemic confidence is a condition of knowledge is not uncontroversial. It has often been pointed out, correctly, that knowledge doesn't require certainty, and some epistemologists have even questioned the idea that belief is a condition of knowledge.[34] If knowledge doesn't require belief then depriving someone of their belief that smoking causes cancer doesn't necessarily deprive them of their knowledge that smoking causes cancer. If knowledge doesn't require confidence then undermining one's

---

[34] Radford 1966.

confidence that smoking causes cancer doesn't necessarily deprive one of one's knowledge of this fact. However, it is easy to turn this argument on its head: if confidence and belief are not required for knowledge then the tobacco strategy would not be nearly as effective as it is. The datum is that the tobacco strategy *is* an effective knowledge-deprivation strategy, and the best explanation of this datum is that without a suitable degree of confidence in one's beliefs there is no knowledge.

Just how easily an individual can be caused to lose confidence in a particular belief of theirs depends, no doubt, on the nature of the belief and the nature of the individual. A person who is presented with good grounds for doubting whether P might continue to be confident that P, but the question in such cases is whether their confidence is justified. This points to a third way for attitude vices to get in the way of knowledge: by depriving one of one's right to be confident that P rather than by depriving one of one's confidence. Imagine a variation on Harper Lee's story in which Tom is guilty but where the jury's confidence in his guilt is the result of prejudice rather than a sober consideration of the evidence. In that case the jury would have no right to be confident that Tom is guilty and wouldn't know he is guilty, even if he is. It isn't always easy to be sure on what basis someone has a particular belief but to the extent that a person's belief that P is attributed to an attitude vice, or indeed any another epistemic vice, their right to be confident that P or to believe that P is called into question. It can happen that a person's belief is evidence-based but their interpretation of the evidence is itself unduly influenced by one or more of their attitude vices. This is another way for attitude vices to get in the way of knowledge: even if a particular attitude vice isn't the basis on which a person believes P, it might be the basis on which they interpret their evidence as indicating P. If this happens, they may not have the right to be confident that P. In the same way, they may lack the right to be confident that P if prejudice, epistemic insouciance, or some other attitude vice is the basis on which they reject evidence against P or interpret such evidence as misleading.

From the fact that an epistemic attitude systematically gets in the way of knowledge it doesn't follow immediately that the attitude is a *vice*. Genuine vices are also blameworthy or otherwise reprehensible. One is only blameworthy for attitudes for which one is responsible and there is more than one way of understanding the idea of responsibility. Using the terminology introduced in Chapter 1, there is a case for saying that the members of the jury in the trial of Tom Robinson were not 'acquisition responsible' for their prejudice. To hold them acquisition responsible one would have to suppose that they came to be prejudiced by choice rather than, as seems far more plausible, by passively absorbing the racial prejudices of the day. Fricker argues that the jury was nevertheless culpable since it failed to exercise any critical awareness regarding the prejudice that was clearly distorting its perception of Tom Robinson. The jurors had 'ample opportunity to grasp and make good the conflict between the distrust which their corrupted sensibility spontaneously delivers and the trust which a proper attention to the evidence would inspire—a proper attention which others present, white as well as black, are clearly able to give' (2007: 90).[35] What if the jurors are deemed incapable of a critical awareness of their prejudice and can do nothing to correct for their prejudice? Even so, their racist attitudes are still reprehensible and reflect badly on them. Whether or not they can be blamed for their prejudice, they can certainly be criticized for it.

It is easier to see epistemic malevolence as fully blameworthy since it is a stance that one can adopt or reject. The extent to which epistemic insouciance can be blameworthy is less obvious. One might argue, for example, that epistemic insouciance is among what José Medina describes as the 'epistemic vices of the privileged' (2013: 31). Being in positions of power and privilege can easily result in intellectual overconfidence or a cognitive superiority complex, and these epistemic vices might in turn find expression in the excessive casualness or nonchalance which are at the heart of epistemic insouciance.[36] This is a structural analysis of epistemic insouciance, one that traces this vice to a person's membership of a particular social class. However, even if such an analysis is accepted, it is not incompatible with viewing a privileged individual as

---

[35] It might seem that Fricker regards the jurors as culpable because, in my terms, she regards them as 'revision responsible' for their prejudice, that is, capable of modifying their attitude towards Robinson. It's not clear that this is what Fricker has in mind. What she requires isn't that the jurors can *alter* their prejudiced perception of Robinson but that they can *correct* for it. Correcting for a defect isn't the same as eliminating it. Fricker argues that even if the jurors were to be 'partially forgiven' for the way their perceptions of black people had been 'saturated with the powerful racial prejudices of the day', they were still 'starkly culpable in failing to respond appropriately to the heightened testimonial experience afforded by the trial' (2007: 90).

[36] Epistemic insouciance and bullshitting are, of course, not the exclusive preserve of the privileged but might nevertheless be correlated with power and privilege.

blameworthy on account of their epistemic insouciance. Like many attitudes, epistemic or otherwise, epistemic insouciance can be changed. However one comes to be epistemically insouciant, this is not an attitude that a person is generally stuck with and can do nothing to alter. In the terminology of Chapter 1, epistemic insouciance is a posture for which a person can be revision responsible. This, combined with its harmfulness, is the basis on which epistemic insouciance qualifies as an epistemic vice. There is more about the issue of responsibility for one's epistemic vices in Chapter 6.

The last question for this chapter concerns the relationship between attitude and other epistemic vices. When a person is described as intellectually arrogant this can be a comment about their character or their attitude. When they are described as epistemically insouciant this can be interpreted as a comment about their character or about their attitude. However, there is this asymmetry between the two readings: it makes no sense to suppose that a person's character traits include epistemic insouciance without also supposing that they have an epistemically insouciant attitude to the task of finding answers to complex questions. This is a reflection of the fact that one's character traits are a function of one's attitudes in a way that one's attitudes are not a function of one's character traits.[37] It makes perfect sense to suppose that a person might display a particular attitude in response to a particular question even if they lack the corresponding character trait; their attitude in this case might be 'out of character'. What it is for a person's attitude in a given case to be epistemically insouciant can be explained without reference to epistemic insouciance as a character trait, but the character trait can't be explained without reference to the attitude. One way of putting this would be to say that the attitude is more basic than the character trait: one starts with the attitude and works up from there to an understanding of the character trait.

The relationship between attitudes and ways of thinking is less clear but there is a case for saying that epistemic postures are partly a reflection or function of how one thinks. A person with an epistemically insouciant or intellectually arrogant attitude must be disposed to think in characteristic ways. Attitudes aren't just ways of thinking but they

---

[37] For Medina it seems that character traits are *composed* of attitudes, and an epistemic vice is 'a set of corrupted attitudes and dispositions that get in the way of knowledge' (2013: 30).

involve thinking, or being disposed to think, in particular ways. At the same time these ways of thinking can't be properly explained or understood without reference to the attitudes they manifest. If this is so then neither the attitude nor the way of thinking is more basic than the other, though both are more basic than the character traits to which they correspond. It has to be said, though, that while questions about the basicness or explanatory priority of one kind of vice over another might be of considerable philosophical interest, their practical interest is limited. For my purposes the important point isn't that attitude vices are more or less basic than character or thinking vices but that attitude vices exist as a distinctive type of epistemic vice. This point seems obvious enough once it is made, and the neglect of attitudes in philosophical accounts of epistemic vice is difficult to understand.[38] It shouldn't be in the least bit surprising that there are attitudes that are conducive to the gaining, sharing, and keeping of knowledge and attitudes that have the opposite effect. The challenge in thinking about these issues from a philosophical standpoint is not to assume that these attitudes are 'propositional attitudes'. Attitude vices are 'attitudes' in a much more ordinary sense: the sense in which contempt and indifference are attitudes but belief is not. It is the affective dimension of ordinary attitudes that I have emphasized because it is easily missed. More generally, it's worth keeping in mind the importance of posture in one's intellectual or cognitive life, as in one's physical life. The importance of one's physical posture in doing physical work is widely recognized. The importance of one's epistemic posture in doing epistemic work is not. Poor physical posture causes all manner of physical problems, and a poor epistemic posture causes all manner of intellectual problems. So the best advice to the epistemically insouciant and intellectually arrogant is: improve your posture.

[38] One person who isn't guilty of neglecting attitudes in her work on epistemic virtues and vices is Alessandra Tanesini. See, for example, Tanesini 2016.

5

Vice and Knowledge

I've read a fair amount about the Holocaust. I'm not a historian but I've read enough over the years to know that the Holocaust happened. The systematic murder of millions of Jews was undertaken by the Nazis with the aim of exterminating the Jewish population of Europe. If challenged to explain how I know that the Holocaust happened, I can point to various things I have read over the years, and documentaries I have watched. However, although I have read a certain amount about the Holocaust, I haven't read anything by David Irving. I know that Irving has written extensively about the Third Reich and argues that the Holocaust is a myth.[1] Among his claims are that Hitler didn't order the extermination of the Jews in Europe, that there were no gas chambers at Auschwitz, and that not nearly as many Jews were killed by the Nazis as is commonly supposed.[2] I know that Irving produces what he regards as evidence in support of these claims but I've never felt the need or intellectual obligation to engage with this evidence or with Irving's work, despite having firm views about the Holocaust that his work disputes. If challenged to rebut a specific piece of documentary evidence produced by Irving I might find it difficult to do so since I lack the relevant expertise. However, I take myself to be justified in ignoring Irving's arguments and his supposed evidence because I know that the Holocaust happened and can infer from this that any evidence to the contrary must be misleading. Why should I expose myself to evidence that I know to be misleading?

Some might describe my attitude towards Irving as dogmatic and closed-minded but it can be argued that in this particular case dogmatism

---

[1] Irving's views are described in Evans 2002.

[2] These are among the basic tenets of Holocaust denial. See Evans 2002: 118–19. On the issue of whether Irving was a Holocaust denier see chapter 4 of Evans 2002.

and closed-mindedness are justified. There are some ideas to which my mind is not open and these include the idea that there was no Holocaust. The notion that dogmatism is sometimes justified is one of the implications of what has come to be known as Saul Kripke's 'dogmatism paradox'.[3] The dogmatic view, as Kripke describes it, is that 'since we know all sorts of things we should now make a resolution not to be swayed by any future evidence' (2011: 45). If I know that P then I know that any evidence against P is misleading and I should resolve not to be influenced by it. I might resolve not to look at any alleged evidence against P or to ignore any such evidence. If P is the proposition that the Holocaust happened then my resolution to ignore Irving's work is an example of this kind of dogmatism in action.

It is important that P is something I really know. Compare the discussion in Chapter 2 of Eli Zeira's attitudes towards evidence that Egypt and Syria were on the verge of attacking Israel in 1973. Suppose that on 5 October Zeira has reasoned that since Egypt and Syria weren't going to attack, any evidence indicating an impending attack must be misleading and therefore could safely be ignored. This wouldn't have been a case of justified dogmatism in Kripke's sense because Zeira didn't *know* that Egypt and Syria weren't going to attack. He couldn't possibly have known this because they *did* attack the very next day. Kripke's view is that dogmatism can be justified in cases in which a subject A genuinely *knows* that P. He writes:

[S]ometimes the dogmatic strategy is a rational one. I myself have not read much defending astrology, necromancy, and the like ... Even when confronted with specific alleged evidence, I have sometimes ignored it although I did not know how to refute it. I once read part of a piece by a reasonably well-known person defending astrology ... I was not in a position to refute specific claims but assumed that this piece was of no value. One epistemological problem is to delineate cases when the dogmatic attitude is justified.   (2011: 49)

To see why the dogmatic strategy is sometimes rational, suppose I know that P but subsequently encounter evidence against P which I don't know how to refute. One result might be that I give up my belief that P or lose my confidence that P. Alternatively, even if I continue to believe that P, exposure to evidence against P that I am unable to refute might result in

---

[3] Kripke 2011.

my no longer having the *right* to be confident that P. To put it another way, my belief that P is no longer justified. Either way, I no longer know that P. So if I want to avoid a 'loss of knowledge' (Kripke 2011: 49), then the dogmatic strategy looks like it has a lot going for it. By resolutely averting my eyes from evidence against what I know, I protect my knowledge.

The idea that dogmatism can protect knowledge is also a theme in Hume's discussion of miracles. He tells the story of Cardinal de Retz who, on passing through Saragossa, was shown a man who had allegedly regained a missing limb by rubbing holy oil on the stump.[4] Hume makes much of the number and quality of witnesses to the miracle but still commends the Cardinal for being unmoved. The Cardinal 'considered justly, that it was not requisite, in order to reject a fact of this nature, to be able accurately to disprove the testimony, and to trace its falsehood, through all the circumstances of knavery and credulity which produced it' (1975: 124). Hume has been accused of being overly dogmatic for concluding that the supposed miracle was 'more properly a subject of derision than of argument' (1975: 124), but Peter Millican is one commentator who argues that Hume's dogmatism, if that is what it is, is rational:

Hume seems to be suggesting that all of us are prone to lose sound critical judgement if we get drawn too much into the peculiarities of specific tales. That being so, experience can teach us that sometimes it is rational *not* to rely on careful and detailed critical assessment, but instead to prefer the verdict of a general rule without giving the matter too much thought. A modern example might be the persuasive and polished advertising (for investments, prize draws, novel therapies, conspiracy theories, etc.) that regularly bombard us, where reading the advertiser's seductive arguments is typically not only a waste of time, but worse, carries the danger of being persuaded.   (Millican 2011: 181–2)

As with Kripke's defence of dogmatism, the emphasis here is on knowledge preservation: ignoring or dismissing evidence against what one knows is rational to the extent that it helps to retain one's knowledge.

This account of the epistemic benefits of dogmatism might seem tough to reconcile with the story I've been telling about the nature of epistemic vices. I've been arguing that epistemic vices get in the way of knowledge by obstructing its acquisition, transmission, or retention. I've also been assuming that dogmatism is an epistemic vice. The dogmatism that Kripke describes isn't a character trait but an epistemic attitude, a

---

[4] Hume 1975: 123.

posture towards certain kinds of evidence. Now it turns out that this posture doesn't get in the way of knowledge. Indeed, it appears that it can even be *conducive* to knowledge by facilitating its retention. In these cases what dogmatism obstructs is not knowledge but *loss* of knowledge.

In effect, then, we have arrived at the following inconsistent triad:

1. Dogmatism is an epistemic vice.
2. Epistemic vices get in the way of knowledge.
3. Dogmatism doesn't get in the way of knowledge.

Since these claims can't all be true, something has to give. The question is what. However, before getting into that there is a question about the formulation of the inconsistent triad. The central tenet of 'obstructivism' is that epistemic vices *normally* or *systematically* obstruct the gaining, keeping, or sharing of knowledge. To say that epistemic vices systematically get in the way of knowledge is to say that they do so non-accidentally and on balance.[5] The sense in which they normally get in the way of knowledge is that they obstruct the gaining, keeping, or sharing of knowledge in the normal course of events. Neither formulation is committed to the view that epistemic vices are invariably knowledge-obstructive. What they are committed to saying is that cases in which epistemic vices like dogmatism aren't knowledge-obstructive or are even knowledge-conducive are unusual or exceptional.

With this in mind, examples such as those put forward by Hume and Kripke can be accommodated by obstructivism by making the case that they are unusual or exceptional. The following is, after all, not an inconsistent triad: dogmatism is an epistemic vice, epistemic vices systematically get in the way of knowledge, dogmatism doesn't always get in the way of knowledge. To pursue this line of thinking one would need to show that scenarios in which dogmatism is conducive to knowledge by aiding its retention are unusual or exceptional and it's not immediately apparent how to do that. I will come back to this. First, there is an even more basic issue to consider. For aside from dogmatism's role in possibly preventing the *loss* of knowledge, there are further potentially

---

[5] 'On balance and nonaccidentally' is Julia Driver's gloss on 'systematically'. See Driver 2001: xviii. To use her analogy, seatbelts save lives in car accidents and do so systematically. This is consistent with allowing that there may be rare occasions where they lead to a worse outcome. They don't invariably save lives.

embarrassing questions for obstructivism about dogmatism's role in abetting the *acquisition* of knowledge in non-exceptional cases. These questions are brought into focus by reflecting on the nature and intellectual preconditions of scientific inquiry. Consider Kuhn's account of 'normal' science in *The Structure of Scientific Revolutions*. It is natural to think that scientific inquiry is a basic source of knowledge, so it would be a problem for the notion that dogmatism is an epistemic vice if a dogmatic attitude turns out to be an essential feature of normal science. This is Kuhn's view and even Karl Popper, whose views about science are different from Kuhn's in many important respects, observes that 'the dogmatic scientist has an important role to play' (1970: 55).[6]

For Kuhn, normal science is 'research firmly based upon one or more past scientific achievements, achievements that some particular scientific community acknowledges for a time as supplying the foundation for its further practice' (2012: 10). Preconception and resistance to innovation are the rule rather than the exception in normal, mature science and jointly constitute what Kuhn calls its 'dogmatism' (1963: 349). Far from choking off scientific progress, a deep commitment to a particular way of viewing the world and of practising science is 'fundamental to productive research' because it defines for the scientist 'the problems available for pursuit and the nature of acceptable solutions to them' (1963: 349). Normal science is 'paradigm-based' (1963: 349) and presupposes a deep commitment to a paradigm that isn't lightly given up.[7] This is reflected in scientific education, which 'remains a relatively dogmatic initiation into a pre-established problem-solving tradition that the student is neither invited nor equipped to evaluate' (1963: 351).

Even on the basis of this brief summary of Kuhn's defence of dogmatism in science it is easy to see why obstructivism can't easily get off the hook by insisting that dogmatism normally gets in the way of knowledge, even if it doesn't invariably do so. If Kuhn is right, then scientific research is a basic source of knowledge to which dogmatism is fundamental. If *normal* science is dogmatic then dogmatism doesn't *normally* get in the way of knowledge, at least not in the way of scientific knowledge. The position is rather that dogmatism is normally *conducive* to the acquisition of knowledge, to the extent that it is indispensable for science. In that

---

[6] Rowbottom 2011 is a helpful discussion of Popper and Kuhn on dogmatism in science.
[7] On the elusive notion of a 'paradigm' see Kuhn 2012.

case, how can dogmatism be an epistemic vice? By the same token, Kuhn's discussion calls into question the view of most virtue epistemologists that open-mindedness is an epistemic virtue. Open-mindedness is only an epistemic virtue if it is normally conducive to knowledge, but it is hard to make the case that this is so if, as Kuhn argues, the individual scientist is very often not open-minded and this lack of open-mindedness is conducive to scientific research. The individual scientist is not an uncommitted searcher after the truth, and if the results he expects from his research are not forthcoming 'he will struggle with his apparatus and with his equations until, if at all possible, they yield results which conform to the sort of pattern which he has foreseen from the start' (Kuhn 1963: 348). Facts like these 'do not bespeak an enterprise whose practitioners are notably open-minded' (1963: 348).

It seems, then, that the epistemic benefits of dogmatism are considerable: it can protect knowledge we already have and it can abet the acquisition of knowledge by scientific research. What is more, there is nothing unusual or exceptional about scenarios in which dogmatism doesn't get in the way of knowledge or abets its acquisition. So if Kuhn is right then the inconsistent triad remains a problem for obstructivism. This leaves obstructivism with the following options:

A. Concede that dogmatism isn't an epistemic vice but argue that this doesn't affect the status of other standard epistemic vices. Maybe dogmatism is just a special case, one in which what is widely regarded as an epistemic vice turns out not to be so. On this account obstructivism isn't the problem. The problem is with the inclusion of dogmatism in standard lists of epistemic vices.

B. Abandon the core tenet of obstructivism, the idea that what makes epistemic vices epistemically vicious is that they get in the way of knowledge. On a *motivational* conception of epistemic vices what makes them epistemically vicious is that they have, or incorporate, bad motives.[8] As long as dogmatism has epistemically bad motives it is still an epistemic vice, even if its epistemic consequences are good.

C. Rebut the suggestion that dogmatism doesn't normally or systematically get in the way of the acquisition or preservation of knowledge.

---

[8] This is a core tenet of 'responsibilist' accounts of epistemic vice. See Battaly 2014 for further discussion.

One possibility is that the epistemic attitudes described by Kripke and Kuhn aren't genuinely dogmatic and are only epistemically beneficial, to the extent that they are, because they don't amount to dogmatism, properly so called. The other is that these attitudes are genuinely dogmatic but not knowledge-conducive or epistemically justified. On this view, a resolution made in advance to ignore certain types of evidence is more problematic than the discussion so far suggests.

These, then, are the three options to consider: *Concede, Abandon*, or *Rebut. Concede* targets the first element of the inconsistent triad. *Abandon* targets the second element, while *Rebut* targets the third element. I want to make a case for *Rebut*.

Concession looks like the easiest and most straightforward of the three options but it's important not to underestimate its difficulties. For a start, the discussion so far has been one-sided and focused exclusively on the supposed epistemic benefits of dogmatism. But account also needs to be taken of the factors that have made dogmatism look epistemically dubious to many vice epistemologists. When these factors are taken into consideration, the notion that dogmatism isn't an epistemic vice after all is harder to stomach. Another potential problem with conceding that dogmatism isn't an epistemic vice after all is that the reasons for making this concession might also be reasons for rethinking the status of other prominent and closely related epistemic vices, such as closed-mindedness. Philosophical accounts of epistemic vice start with lists of exemplary vices and try to make sense of the fact that the listed items are epistemically vicious. These initial lists of exemplary vices aren't set in stone and it's always possible that some items don't belong, but beyond a certain point one starts to wonder what is at issue if many supposedly exemplary vices turn out to have been misclassified. It's hard to think of two more exemplary vices than dogmatism and closed-mindedness. If dogmatism isn't an epistemic vice then why not say the same thing about closed-mindedness?

For a clearer understanding of the issues here we need a better understanding of what dogmatism is. As Roberts and Wood note, dogmatism in the primary sense pertains to those of a person's beliefs that rise to the status of *doctrines*:

A doctrine is a belief about the general character of the world, or some generally important aspect of the world, which bears the weight of many other beliefs. Thus a mother who refuses, in the face of what should be compelling evidence, to give up her belief that her son is innocent of a certain crime, is perhaps stubborn, obstinate, or blinded by her attachment, but she is not on that account dogmatic. By contrast, someone who holds irrationally to some fundamental doctrine, such as the basic tenets of Marxism or capitalism or Christianity, or some broad historical thesis such as that the Holocaust did not occur, is dogmatic.

(2007: 194–5)

On this account, dogmatism is an irrational attachment to a doctrine. The doctrines to which dogmatists are attached might be tissues of falsehoods, and their attachment is manifested by their disposition to 'respond irrationally to oppositions to the belief, anomalies, objections, evidence to the contrary, counterexamples, and the like' (2007: 195). As it happens, Roberts and Wood's example of a dogmatist in their sense is none other than David Irving, who they claim 'presents a case of dogmatism so extreme as to be almost a caricature of the vice' (2007: 196).[9] Here is someone who, in the interests of defending his view of the Holocaust, engages in tendentious summary, partial quotation from historical documents, the systematic abuse of evidence, and use of methods of historical argument that are manifestly ill-suited to discover the truth.[10]

There is no question of Irving's dogmatism serving to protect his knowledge that the Holocaust never happened because, of course, he knows no such thing. In his account Kripke focuses on the case in which a subject S knows some garden-variety truth P and resolves on this basis to ignore certain types of evidence. In more standard examples of dogmatism P is a doctrine rather than a garden-variety truth and S only *thinks* he knows P. Whether S actually knows P is a further question. For Zeira, the proposition that Egypt and Syria wouldn't attack

[9] According to Roberts and Wood, 'a dogmatist must believe his dogmas' (2007: 197) and at some level Irving believes his story about the Holocaust. However, since he uses arguments that he knows to be bogus he is in a fog about what he believes. Roberts and Wood claim that 'dogmatic persons cannot know very clearly what they believe, because of the contrariety between the beliefs they held dogmatically and their means of defending them' (2007: 198).

[10] In his judgment in Irving's unsuccessful libel case against Deborah Lipstadt, who had accused Irving of being a Holocaust denier, Mr Justice Gray summed up by saying that 'Irving treated the historical evidence in a manner which fell far short of the standard to be expected of a conscientious historian'. He had 'misrepresented and distorted the evidence which was available to him' and was incontrovertibly a Holocaust denier. These quotations from Mr Justice Gray's judgment are from Evans 2002: 235.

Israel was a dogma, a mistaken doctrine that bore the weight of many other beliefs about the military situation. For Irving it was a dogma that the Holocaust never happened, a mistaken doctrine that bore the weight of many other false beliefs about Nazi Germany. If P is false then S doesn't actually know that P, and his resolution to ignore evidence against P doesn't protect his knowledge of P because *ex hypothesi* there is no knowledge to protect. Far from abetting the retention or acquisition of knowledge Irving's dogmatic attachment to the view that the Holocaust never happened distorted his interpretation and presentation of historical documents and made it impossible for him to function as a competent historian capable of knowing the truth about what happened in Nazi Germany. His dogmatic attitude, which resulted in his rejection of compelling evidence that the Holocaust happened, was neither rational nor epistemically justified.

But what if P turns out to be true? Imagine that the Arab attack on Israel in 1973 had been called off at the last minute. In that case Zeira's belief that there would be no war would have been true, but the charge of dogmatism would have stood and his dogmatism would still not have been epistemically beneficial. A manifestation of his dogmatism was his response to indications of an impending war, including the emergency evacuation of Soviet personnel from Egypt and Syria. His dogmatic commitment to the doctrine that there would be no war prevented him from attaching to this evidence the weight that it deserved, and this would have adversely affected his ability to *know* there would be no war even if there actually was no war. For Zeira to have known that there would be no war in these circumstances he would need to have had the *right* to be confident there would be no war, but the role of dogmatism in sustaining his belief would have prevented him from having this right. Another way of making the point would be to say that a belief sustained by dogmatism rather than reasoned consideration of the evidence is not justified. So if, as is commonly supposed, knowledge requires justified belief then Zeira would have been stopped by his dogmatism from *knowing* that there was going to be no war even if his belief that there was going to be no war was a true belief.

Why would Zeira not have had the right to be confident that there would be no war? Why would his belief that there would be no war not have been a justified belief even if it turned out to be correct? For a person to have the right to be confident that P their confidence must be properly grounded. This means that it must be guided by the evidence rather than, say, the subject's own prejudices. If the evidence clearly indicates that P, and S is confident that P on the basis of this evidence, then S has the right to be confident that P and their belief that P is justified. Where P is just a dogma to which S is attached in such a way that they would still be confident that P regardless of the evidence then S isn't guided by the evidence and doesn't have the right to be confident. By the same token, S doesn't know that P in these circumstances even if P, by some chance, turns out to be true.[11]

The negative epistemic effects of closed-mindedness are closely related to those of dogmatism. I argued in Chapter 2 that closed-mindedness is a mode of epistemic being that one would expect to have an impact on a person's epistemic conduct generally. Dogmatism is more limited in scope and pertains to one's doctrinal commitments rather than to one's epistemic conduct generally. It's an attitude rather than a character trait and one's doctrinal commitments may have more to do with the particular content of those commitments than with a general disposition. Nevertheless, it should be noted that the tendencies associated with closed-mindedness, such as the denial of information inconsistent with one's prior views, are also associated with dogmatism. If dogmatism isn't an epistemic vice it is hard to see how closed-mindedness can be an epistemic vice, but it now appears that the right response to the inconsistent triad is not to concede that dogmatism isn't an epistemic vice. Such a concession would be hard to reconcile with the range of real-world cases in which dogmatism seems to be the cause of people holding on to manifestly false beliefs, or to result in some of their true beliefs not being epistemically justified. Given the sheer range and ordinariness of cases in which dogmatism, like closed-mindedness, gets in the way of knowledge, *Concede* doesn't look like a promising response to the inconsistent triad.

The issue of whether dogmatism does or doesn't get in the way of knowledge is only really pressing on the assumption that its getting in the

---

[11] Linda Zagzebski makes a similar point about the role of closed-mindedness in preventing us from having knowledge. As Zagzebski notes, 'closed-mindedness tends to prevent a person from going through the process that would justify his beliefs or would give him a high quality grasp of the truth' (1996: 188–9) in cases where his closed-minded beliefs happen to be true.

way of knowledge is what makes an epistemic vice epistemically vicious. This is the consequentialist idea that epistemic vices are identified and delineated by their epistemic consequences, by their impact on our capacity to know. According to the *Abandon* response to the inconsistent triad, epistemic vices may or may not have bad epistemic consequences but their status as epistemic vices is a reflection of their motives rather than their consequences. On this account, dogmatism can genuinely abet the acquisition and retention of knowledge and still come out as an epistemic vice as long as it has bad motives. The suggestion, then, is that the real casualty of the inconsistent triad is epistemic consequentialism, of which obstructivism is a version. From this perspective, the extent to which epistemic vices do or don't get in the way of knowledge can be left open.

The idea that epistemic vices have bad motives has come up several times in previous chapters and some of the examples discussed in this chapter show exactly what is wrong with this idea. What motivates motivational accounts of epistemic vice is, at least in part, the desire to have people come out as responsible for their epistemic vices. If we are responsible for our bad motives then we can perhaps also be responsible for the epistemic vices that result from them. However, leaving aside the question of whether we can be held responsible for our motives, it is false that bad motives are necessary for epistemic vice. The Kripkean or Humean dogmatist who dismisses reports of miracles or the merits of astrology is motivated by the desire to protect their knowledge and not to be led astray by spurious claims they didn't know how to refute. Zeira refused to believe reports of an impending Arab attack on Israel because he thought that these reports were misleading and he didn't want to be misled. The desire to protect one's knowledge or not to be misled don't sound like bad motives.[12]

If Zeira's motives weren't bad then either his attitude wasn't dogmatic (because true dogmatism requires bad motives) or dogmatism isn't necessarily an epistemic vice (because sometimes dogmatism can have good motives). There is something right about the suggestion that some

---

[12] It might be argued that the problem in these cases is not that the subject has epistemically bad motives but that he is insufficiently well motivated. It's not clear that this is right. Zeira certainly can't be accused of having an inadequate or excessively weak desire for knowledge. See the discussion of the motivational approach in Chapter 1.

of the examples I've been discussing might not be examples of dogmatism properly so called, and I'll have more to say about this suggestion in relation to the *Rebut* response to the inconsistent triad. However, the problem with the motivational approach is that it lacks a plausible account of the bad motives that would make a person's attitude count as genuinely dogmatic. What, exactly, *are* the bad motives that are required for true dogmatism? One issue is whether true dogmatism requires bad *epistemic* motives or bad motives in a broader sense. Irving's dogmatic insistence that the Holocaust is a myth is partly motivated by his desire to exonerate the Nazis, and that is an ethically terrible motive. But if dogmatism is an *epistemic* vice then one would expect it to have *epistemically* bad motives, yet none of the standard examples of epistemically bad motives is applicable in this case. One such motive is 'wanting to believe whatever is easiest' (Battaly 2014: 65), but Irving can hardly be accused of that. Perhaps he has other epistemically defective motives, but the notion that he presents a case of dogmatism so extreme as to be almost a caricature of the vice is based more on his epistemic conduct than his epistemic motives.

The truth is that people's motives are much harder to fathom than their epistemic vices and this should make one suspicious of the notion that commonly attributed epistemic vices have much to do with the specific epistemic motives of those to whom epistemic vices are commonly attributed. Many of our attitudes and much of our epistemic conduct is driven by a tangle of motives, some good and bad, and speculation about their motives is rarely the basis on which a person is deemed dogmatic. The focus in our thinking about dogmatism and other such vices is on the subject's actual epistemic attitudes and conduct rather than on their motives. Of course there can be arguments about whether a person's attitude in a given case—say, Kripke's attitude towards astrology—is genuinely dogmatic, but these are best understood as arguments about the epistemic consequences of that attitude. This is how the *Rebut* response to the inconsistent triad sees things and it is to this response that I now turn.

Rebut disputes the suggestion that dogmatism doesn't normally get in the way of the acquisition or retention of knowledge. The argument for this suggestion came in two stages. In the first stage examples were given of the supposed epistemic benefits of dogmatism. In the second stage, these examples were held to be non-exceptional, and therefore to undermine the idea that epistemic vices normally get in the way of knowledge. The point of *Rebut* is that these are either cases that have been misclassified as cases of dogmatism or ones in which the epistemic benefits of dogmatism have been grossly exaggerated and its epistemic drawbacks underestimated.

It is easy to make the case that what Kuhn describes in his account of normal science isn't really dogmatism but another attitude with which dogmatism is all too easily confused. Normal science, as Kuhn describes it, presupposes a commitment to 'one paradigm-based way of looking at the world' that tells scientists 'the questions that may legitimately be asked about nature' and 'the techniques that can properly be used in the search for answers to them' (1963: 359). Kuhn complains that 'the dependence of research upon a deep commitment to established tools and beliefs' (1963: 369) has received the very minimum of attention, and it is this commitment that he describes as 'quasi-dogmatic' (1963: 349). For Kuhn the scientist is a puzzle solver, like a chess player, whose commitment to the *status quo* 'provides him with the rules of the game being played in his time' (1963: 349). That is why these beliefs and these tools cannot be lightly given up. Scientific research would be impossible if every time a scientist encounters a problem which he fails to solve he abandons his existing tools and beliefs. Instead, the scientist takes it that his failure 'only speaks to his lack of skill' (1963: 362). It cannot call into question the rules supplied by his paradigm 'for without those rules there would have been no puzzle with which to wrestle in the first place' (1963: 363). When scientists resist paradigm change what they are defending is 'neither more nor less than the basis of their professional life' (1963: 363).

To sum up, what Kuhn calls the 'dogmatism of mature science' consists in its having deep commitments to established tools and beliefs, where the depth of this commitment has to do both with its importance for scientific research and the scientist's reluctance to abandon the *status quo*. Why call this dogmatism? A dogmatist is someone who holds irrationally to some fundamental doctrine, but there is no irrationality in the scientist's resistance to change. Indeed, Kuhn goes out of his way to make such resistance look perfectly reasonable and, indeed, indispensable for science. The fact that a commitment is not lightly given up doesn't make it dogmatic because a belief that is lightly given up is by definition not a commitment. Kuhn gives the impression it is in the nature of commitments to be dogmatic but that can't be right. A better label for what Kuhn describes is firmness or tenacity. As Roberts and Wood note, 'we cannot and must not be open to change our deeper views at the first appearance of contrary evidence' and it is entirely proper that the first thing we do when we encounter a putative reason for deeper change is 'to look for ways to refute the objection or accommodate the anomaly to our current understanding of things' (2007: 183). The contrary of firmness isn't open-mindedness but intellectual 'flaccidity' (Roberts and Wood 2007: 185), that is, the absence of firmly held convictions and a willingness to go whichever way the wind happens to be blowing. Far from being admirable, flaccidity is an intellectual weakness that gets in the way of knowledge because it gets in the way of belief. Flaccid thinkers have no deeply held beliefs or convictions. They lack knowledge because they lack confidence in their beliefs.

The reality of the contrast between dogmatism and firmness can be brought home by reflecting on Kuhn's account of how, in science, even deeply held commitments come to be given up and paradigms swept aside. According to Kuhn, the scientist doesn't try to uncover novelties of fact or theory but nevertheless uncovers new and unexpected phenomena for which he isn't prepared by his existing tools and beliefs. Such phenomena are *anomalies*. The recognition of anomaly 'need not draw any profound response' (Kuhn 2012: 81) since there are always discrepancies in science and scientists may be willing to wait for a solution. The point at which science is plunged into crisis by an anomaly is the point at which, for a variety of reasons, the anomaly comes to seem 'more than just another puzzle of normal science' (2012: 82) and is seen by scientists as indicating that 'something is fundamentally wrong with the theory upon which their work is based' (1963: 367). This recognition leads eventually to the rejection of the existing paradigm and the decision to accept another. The ability and willingness to acknowledge fundamental flaws in established tools and beliefs, and abandon those tools and beliefs, is what distinguishes firmness from dogmatism. A scientist with a firm commitment to a particular way of looking at the world will not lightly give up his view but will eventually do so when it becomes apparent, perhaps over a long period of time, that the *status quo* is unsustainable. The behaviour of the true dogmatist is nothing like this. He has neither the ability nor the willingness to recognize fundamental flaws in his commitments and the abandonment of those commitments is unthinkable for him. When a true dogmatist like David Irving finds documentary evidence that can't be reconciled with his view of the Holocaust he *still* doesn't alter his view. Instead, he alters the evidence or dismisses it as not genuine or unreliable.[13] If this is how a true dogmatist behaves then Kuhn's normal scientist is no dogmatist and Kuhn shouldn't be representing himself as making a case for dogmatism. He is doing no such thing. He certainly doesn't show that dogmatism, as distinct from firmness, is conducive to the acquisition of scientific knowledge or the making of scientific discoveries. The scientist's tenacity is knowledge-conducive but the same cannot be said for Irving's dogmatism.

It's one thing to argue that some alleged epistemic benefits of dogmatism are the real epistemic benefits of a different attitude that has been misclassified as dogmatism. Could it not still be true that dogmatism properly so called has real epistemic benefits? For example, Kripke's idea that dogmatism can *protect* our knowledge is still in play. What does *Rebut* have to say about this? To make things vivid here is an example: P is the proposition that the collapse of the World Trade Center twin towers on 9/11 was caused by aircraft impacts and the resulting fires. P is true and I know that it is. I want to protect my knowledge so, in line with Kripkean dogmatism, I resolve in advance not to look at any evidence that points to the falsity of P. I avoid conspiracist websites and books by proponents of the view that the towers were demolished by explosives planted in advance by government agents. The supposed evidence e for this conspiracy theory is at the same time evidence against P but I'm not troubled by it because I have already decided not to look at it. By averting my eyes from e, Kripke suggests, I retain my knowledge of P. Suppose, next, that despite my best efforts to avoid e I am confronted by it. It's now too late for me to avoid e but not too late to ignore it. So even though I don't know how to refute e, I disregard it on the basis that I do, after all, know P. The suggestion is that I preserve my knowledge of P by ignoring e and that this is precisely a case in which, as Kripke puts it, 'the dogmatic attitude is justified'(2011: 49).

One question that can be raised about my attitude towards P and e is whether it is truly dogmatic, but suppose we bracket this issue and focus instead on the following:

---

[13] This tactic of Irving's is brilliantly exposed in Evans 2002, and in the judgment in Irving's unsuccessful libel action against Deborah Lipstadt, who had accused Irving of manipulating and falsifying the historical record. See Lipstadt 1994 and footnote 9 above.

1. Do I protect my knowledge that *p* by *avoiding e*?
2. Do I protect my knowledge that *p* by *ignoring e*?

A resolution to avoid *e* is supposed to protect my knowledge that P by reducing the danger that I will be persuaded by *e* and abandon my belief that P. I am in no danger of being persuaded by the alleged evidence against P if I don't know what it is. There is, however, a simple response to this line of thinking: if you know that P then why are you so afraid of *e*? *Ex hypothesi* I know that *e* is misleading so I shouldn't fear it, even if I think that engaging with it is a waste of my time. However, this assumes that I trust myself not to be taken in by *e* if I encounter it. What if I lack this kind of self-trust or am worried that *e* might be so seductive or persuasive that I am in danger of being taken in by it even if P is true and *e* is spurious? In that case it might make sense for me to avoid *e* in order to protect my knowledge, but there are limits to how far this line of thinking can be taken. A thinker who is concerned about having his mind changed by spurious or misleading evidence is a thinker who lacks epistemic self-confidence, and lack of epistemic confidence is itself a threat to knowledge. To know that P is, in basic cases, to have confidence in one's belief that P and in one's reasons for believing *p*.[14] If I fear facing *e* then it looks like I lack confidence in my belief that P or in my reasons for believing that P. In that case it is open to question whether I actually know that P. But if I don't know that P then there is no knowledge for my resolution to avoid *e* to protect. If I know that aircraft impacts and the resulting fires brought down the twin towers, and have confidence in my reasons for thinking that this is what happened, then I shouldn't need to take steps to avoid evidence that supports a contrary view. I shouldn't need to be dogmatic if I really know.

---

[14] The idea that knowledge requires epistemic self-confidence is not uncontroversial. A standard counter-example is the case of the unconfident examinee who knows that the Battle of Hastings was in 1066 even though he isn't confident that the Battle of Hastings was in 1066. However, this is not the basic case, and I am not in the position of the unconfident examinee in my belief about the fate of the twin towers. In what I am calling the 'basic' case, a person who knows that *p* is confident that *p*. Whether their confidence needs to take the form of certainty is a further question. See Radford 1966 on the unconfident examinee and Rose and Schaffer 2013 for a response. For different views of the relationship between knowledge and certainty, see Unger 1975 and Stanley 2008. The idea that knowledge depends on self-trust is defended in Lehrer 1999. The idea that loss of confidence can lead to loss of knowledge is developed by Miranda Fricker. See her 2007: 48–51.

What if, despite my best efforts, I am forced to confront *e*? Can I still protect my knowledge that P by ignoring *e*? That depends in part on what it would be to 'confront' *e*. Suppose that *e* takes the form of an article arguing that it is physically impossible for aircraft impacts and the resulting fires to have brought down the towers. Perhaps the article is written by engineers who cite various calculations in support of their view. Suppose that the sense in which I am 'confronted' by this alleged evidence is that I read the article. I have no idea how to refute the evidence presented by the article and the sense in which I ignore this evidence is that I take no account of it in my thinking about 9/11. I continue to maintain that P is true. But if I have encountered what purports to be conclusive evidence against P, and I have no idea how to refute that evidence, then it seems that I no longer have the right to be confident that P, regardless of whether I ignore *e* in my thinking. If, as a result of my confrontation with *e*, I no longer have the right to be confident that P, then I no longer know P and the knowledge that my decision to ignore *e* was supposed to protect has disappeared anyway.

This point is related to one that Harman makes in his response to Kripke's dogmatism paradox. He argues that my knowledge that P 'does not warrant me in simply disregarding any further evidence, since getting that further evidence can change what I know. In particular, after I get such further evidence I no longer know that it is misleading' (1973: 149). In my terms, I no longer know that the new evidence is misleading because this evidence deprives me of the right to be confident that P and thereby deprives me of my knowledge that P. If I no longer know that P then I no longer know that the new evidence is misleading. Kripke doesn't deny this and notes that in the cases that he has in mind the subject resolves in advance to avoid specific counter-evidence to P precisely because he 'wishes to avoid a loss of knowledge such as Harman describes' (2011: 49). But the policy of avoiding *e* in order to avoid a loss of knowledge only makes sense if I believe that *e* poses a genuine threat to my knowledge of P. If that is what I really think then am I not under an epistemic obligation, as a responsible inquirer, to pay attention to *e*? By paying no attention to it I appear to make myself vulnerable to the charge of no longer having the right to believe that P, and hence to the charge of no longer knowing P, the very thing that the resolution to avoid *e* was supposed to save me from.

One might worry that this makes it too easy for us to lose our knowledge in a world in which we are constantly bombarded by dubious or crackpot views that are contrary to what we know but that we also don't know how to refute. If I don't know how to refute a specific 9/11 conspiracy theory *and* I can't protect my knowledge that P by avoiding or ignoring the alleged evidence against P then doesn't it follow that I don't really know that aircraft impacts and the resulting fires brought down the twin towers? Conspiracy theorists would no doubt concur but there is a way to avoid such a loss of knowledge. The way to do that is to engage with the alleged evidence against P and figure out, at least in broad outline, where it goes wrong. This might be unrealistic if learning how to refute the evidence against P involves learning physics or engineering, but there are other options. One might be able to refute the supposed evidence against P by consulting experts and working out who is most likely to be right. In the case of more dubious theories it should be correspondingly easier to find reasons to reject them. Kripke is doing himself a disservice when he claims that he doesn't know how to refute the 'evidence' in favour of astrology, necromancy, and the like.[15]

Notice that the envisaged response to the 9/11 conspiracy theory isn't dogmatic. It is not a question of ignoring the evidence against P on the basis of one's presumed knowledge of P, though there is nothing dogmatic about ignoring such evidence on the basis of *other* things one knows. Conspiracy theorists challenge one's right to be confident that the twin towers were brought down by aircraft impacts, and this challenge calls for a serious response, just as the claims of Holocaust deniers call for a serious response. By a serious response I mean a *rebuttal* rather than the mere denial of such claims. If one is unwilling or unable to rebut the claims of 9/11 conspiracy theorists that weakens one's entitlement to suppose that the twin towers were brought down by aircraft impacts. As Adam Morton notes, 'when you believe something for a reason you can defend it against attacks or undermining' (2014: 165). If one can't be bothered to argue against conspiracy theories one can hardly complain if people end up believing them.

If this is right then the attitude towards Holocaust denial I described at the start of this chapter is nothing to be proud of. I started with the

---

[15] It presumably isn't beyond Kripke to work out what is wrong with the idea that it is possible to predict the future by communicating with the dead.

observation that I've never felt any need or obligation to engage with the work of people like Irving because I know that the Holocaust happened and am therefore justified in ignoring arguments to the contrary. But if it is important that people *know* that the Holocaust was no myth then it is important that they know why Irving is wrong. Knowing why he is wrong isn't just a matter of knowing that he has false beliefs about the Holocaust. It is also a matter of knowing why his evidence is unreliable and his arguments are no good. In practice, knowing these things isn't that difficult. For example, one might read Richard J. Evans' devastating critique of Irving's views in his book *Telling Lies about Hitler*. Evans describes his book as being about 'how we can tell the difference between truth and lies in history' (2002: 1) and this is exactly what we *all* need to be able to do in order to protect our knowledge about the Holocaust from being undermined by the work of Holocaust deniers. It is incumbent on us as knowers to base our views on the evidence, and that means taking the trouble to find out what the evidence actually is and what it does (and doesn't) show. Dogmatism is not the answer.

A worry about this approach is that it places excessive demands on knowers and does that because it makes our knowledge out to be more difficult to attain and retain than it really is. It's all very well suggesting that people read Evans on Irving but how many people have the time to do that or the patience to read a lucid but scholarly 272-page book by an academic historian? How many ordinary citizens are competent to refute the claims of 9/11 conspiracy theorists, even with the help of experts whose pronouncements are themselves viewed by conspiracy theorists as part of an establishment cover-up? Digital technology has exacerbated the problem by facilitating the spread of countless theories that are at odds with so-called 'official' accounts of many major historical or polit-ical events. Faced with this digital onslaught, few of us have the time, energy, or intellectual resources to fight back. In a recent discussion of this problem Matthew D'Ancona recommends that 'we must all become editors: sifting, checking, assessing what we read' (2017: 113). That sounds like a worthy ideal but how many of us can actually do this effectively?

The optimistic answer to this question is that most people are perfectly capable of sifting, checking, and assessing what they read or hear. The focus should be on doing it better rather than on watering down the requirements on knowledge to the point that a person can count as knowing that P even if they haven't the faintest idea how to defend P against attacks or undermining. Suppose that P is the true claim that Hitler knew about and approved of the extermination of the Jews. Now imagine a subject S who is confident that P. S is no historian but has always assumed that P is true. One day S discovers quite by chance that a self-styled historian called David Irving disputes P and claims to have documentary evidence against it, including an instruction allegedly given by Hitler to Himmler in 1941 that there was to be no liquidation of the Jews. S can still be confident and have the right to be confident that P but what gives her this right? One thing she might do, if she has never heard of Irving, is to Google him. By doing this she will quickly learn that Irving was found by a court to have 'deliberately misrepresented historical evidence to promote Holocaust denial'.[16] What about the instruction to Himmler? It doesn't take much additional time or effort to establish that Irving's interpretation of this instruction has been discredited, not least by Evans.[17] Having established these things S has every right to be confident that P and dismiss Irving's argument but S has *earned* this right by checking the facts. This sort of fact checking isn't always necessary but it becomes necessary when the facts are in dispute.

Is this asking too much of S? It's certainly at odds with the notion that S can retain her right to be confident that P, and her knowledge that P, without having to lift a finger, without having to make *any* effort to work out why Irving is not to be believed regarding P. If asking 'too much' of S means requiring her to do *something* to protect her knowledge then it's true that too much is being asked of her. This interpretation of what it is reasonable to expect from knowers is too undemanding. Knowers have responsibilities, including the responsibility not to dismiss challenges to their beliefs without good reason. In many cases the amount of time and effort required to discharge this epistemic obligation is not great, and certainly not beyond the reach of anyone with access to the internet and an attention span of more than five minutes. That's as much time as it is necessary to spend online to discover that there is, to say the least,

---

[16] This is from the Wikipedia entry on Irving.

[17] According to Irving, a phone log of a conversation between Himmler and Heydrich on 30 November 1941 provided incontrovertible evidence of Hitler's instruction that there was to be no liquidation of the Jews. However, as Evans clearly demonstrates, Hitler's instruction concerned *one* transport of Jews from Berlin. The phone log 'did not contain any *general* order from *anyone* to stop the killing of Jews' (2002: 87).

something fishy about Irving's claims about what Hitler did or didn't know. This is the upside of digital technology. While the internet enables the propagation of crackpot theories it also supplies the resources required to rebut them. What is needed is for citizens to *avail* of these resources in defence of the truth.

What if large numbers of people are unwilling or unable to avail of widely available online resources to rebut challenges such as Irving's challenge to S's belief that P? In that case, large numbers of people know less than they think they know. It is precisely because it is possible to be deprived of one's knowledge by dubious theories such as Irving's that it is important to learn how to deal with them. If dogmatism isn't the answer then the only hope for a society that cares about knowledge is to equip its citizens with the intellectual and other means to distinguish truth from lies. Education can play a vital role here, especially if it can focus on the development of pupils' critical faculties and epistemic virtues such as rigour and respect for evidence.[18] Only the inculcation and cultivation of the ability to distinguish truth from lies can prevent our knowledge from being undermined by malevolent individuals and organizations that peddle falsehoods for their own political or economic ends.

---

[18] D'Ancona is right to suggest, therefore, that it should be a core task of primary education 'to teach children how to discriminate from the digital torrent' (2017: 114).

6

Vice and Responsibility

In January 1980 Fritz Stiefel was visited in his home near Stuttgart by Gerd Heidemann.[1] Stiefel was a collector of Nazi memorabilia and Heidemann was a journalist for the German magazine *Stern*. Heidemann, whose obsession with Germany's Nazi past had led him to buy Hermann Göring's yacht and befriend former SS generals, had heard rumours that Stiefel had somehow obtained Hitler's personal diary. When Heidemann asked him whether there was any truth in the rumour Stiefel took him to a vault and handed him a slim volume which he said was Hitler's diary from January to June 1935. Heidemann seems never to have doubted that the diary was authentic and the story of the consequences of his encounter with Stiefel has been told many times, most notably by Robert Harris in *Selling Hitler* and Charles Hamilton in *The Hitler Diaries*.[2]

Having convinced himself that the diary was genuine Heidemann bypassed *Stern*'s editors and convinced the magazine's parent company to part with a large sum of money for all twenty-seven volumes. Although efforts were made to authenticate the diary the authentication process was woefully inadequate. As Harris notes, 'if *Stern* had been properly sceptical, the magazine would have commissioned a thorough forensic examination of a complete diary volume. Instead, they concentrated on securing the bare minimum of authentication felt necessary to satisfy the rest of the world' (2009: 178). The newspaper magnate Rupert Murdoch secured serialization rights for the *Sunday Times*, but just as the serialization began in 1983 the diaries were unmasked as forgeries, written on post-war paper, using post-war ink. Forensic tests revealed

---

[1] My account of this meeting and of the entire Hitler diaries affair is based on Harris 2009. The meeting with Stiefel is described in Chapter 7.
[2] Harris 2009 (originally published in 1986) and Hamilton 1991.

that they had been produced within the last two years. The diaries were the work of a forger and conman called Konrad Kujau, who had a particular talent for copying other people's handwriting. As Phillip Knightley observes in his obituary of Kujau, the fraudster could not have known when he started producing his forgeries that 'one day a gullible fool like Heidemann would turn up on his doorstep, having heard about the diaries—and then offer him £2.5m of *Sterns*'s money for them'.[3] Murdoch's comment on the whole affair was 'After all, we are in the entertainment business'.[4]

It's hard to imagine a better example of vice in action than the Hitler diaries affair. It seems that the ordinary vice of greed combined with recognizably epistemic vices such as gullibility and foolishness to produce the debacle. Much has been written about Heidemann's gullibility and at a press conference in 1984 he wailed 'We were all gullible'.[5] To be gullible is to be easily duped, that is, to be susceptible to being duped in circumstances in which a non-gullible person would not be duped. Heidemann was not the only person to have been fooled by Kujau but the ease with which the deception was uncovered by others and the poor quality of the forgery is evidence that he was easily duped, at least on this occasion, if not others.[6] There had been other indications over the years of Heidemann's gullibility, of what Harris calls his 'almost pathetic eagerness to believe what he was told' (2009: 80).[7] Heidemann's response to the fake diaries was not out of character, and in this case wishful thinking also played a significant role. To quote Harris once again, 'by the end he *wanted* to believe in the existence of the diaries so desperately', not least because 'he had put more work into it than Kujau' (2009: 126). Epistemic vices rarely work in isolation.

It is easy to blame Heidemann for his gullibility and foolishness, and many people have done so, but even if he had these traits, did he deserve

---

[3] Knightley 2000.   [4] See Harris 2009: 368.

[5] As reported by Charles Hamilton. See Hamilton 1991: 106.

[6] One issue here is whether gullibility is a low-fidelity or a high-fidelity vice. See Chapter 2 for more on this. Just as a single act of gross dishonesty can make a person with an otherwise unblemished record dishonest, so one might think that a single example of grossly gullible conduct is enough to make a person gullible. If this is right then gullibility, like dishonesty, is a low-fidelity vice and Heidemann's conduct in the Hitler diaries saga is sufficient to establish his gullibility.

[7] See chapter 6 of Harris 2009 for other examples of Heidemann's gullibility. These examples suggest that Heidemann was gullible even if gullibility is high fidelity.

to be blamed for them?[8] In order to answer this question we need an account of blameworthiness, bearing in mind that for obstructivism a character trait, attitude, or way of thinking is an epistemic vice only if it is blameworthy or otherwise reprehensible. Strictly speaking, blame for a vice attaches to the person whose vice it is rather than to the vice itself: a blameworthy vice is one for which the person whose vice it is deserves blame. In the case of epistemic vices the blame that is at issue is, or includes, epistemic blame, that is, blame directed at a person on account of their specifically epistemic failings. As argued in Chapter 1, such failings may or may not also qualify as moral failings that deserve moral blame.

The plan for this chapter is to develop an account of blameworthiness based on the simple notion that in order to deserve blame for a vice a person must be, in the relevant sense, responsible for it. I suggested in Chapter 1 that blame and criticism are not the same thing, and that the conditions on blameworthiness are more stringent on those for justified criticism.[9] This makes it possible to criticize Heidemann's gullibility and foolishness, and regard these traits as reprehensible, without blaming him for them.[10] One of the aims of this chapter will be to explain and defend the distinction between blame and criticism, and make it plausible that epistemic vices can merit criticism without being blameworthy. This isn't to deny that some epistemic vices are blameworthy; the conditions on blameworthiness aren't so stringent that they can't be fulfilled. However, traits that are neither blameworthy nor otherwise reprehensible aren't epistemic vices.

If gullibility and foolishness are epistemic vices they are character vices.[11] Suppose that S is a person and V is one of their putative character vices. S is blameworthy for V only if V is epistemically harmful and S is responsible for V. We don't generally blame people for harmless characteristics or ones for which they aren't responsible. But how is the

---

[8] Pickard 2013 gives a helpful account of blame.

[9] As Julia Driver notes, we often 'make critical comments about a person's intellect without blaming them for it' (2000: 132).

[10] By 'reprehensible' I mean 'deserving of criticism'. Given the distinction between blame and criticism it is possible for something to be reprehensible without being blameworthy. Blame for a vice attaches to the person whose vice it is rather than to the vice itself, but criticism can be directed at the vice as well as the person whose vice it is. It is possible to criticize Heidemann's foolishness as well as Heidemann for his foolishness. Where the vice is one for which the person is not responsible it might be more natural to criticize the vice than the person.

[11] That is, epistemic vices that are character traits.

notion of responsibility to be understood? One view is that responsibility is *answerability*.[12] This view has been used to account for our responsibility for our beliefs. As Pamela Hieronymi puts it, 'it seems plausible that we are responsible for our own beliefs in at least the minimal sense that we can be asked our reasons for believing' (2008: 358). If I believe that it's raining and this belief is genuinely my responsibility then I can be asked why I believe that it is raining. It is my business why I believe it and it is for me to say. But this can't be the sense in which we are responsible for character vices such as foolishness. To view a person as responsible for being foolish is not to suppose that they can be asked their reasons for being foolish. There may be no such reasons. In this case, and quite possibly in the case of other epistemic vices, responsibility is not a matter of answerability but of *accountability*: to view a person as responsible for being foolish or gullible is to regard them as accountable for their vice. To put it another way, the character vices for which a person is responsible are ones for which they can be held to account.

What does it take for S to be accountable for a vice V? One possibility is that S is accountable for V to the extent that S's past actions, omissions, choices, or decisions resulted in her acquiring or developing V.[13] When this is the case S has *acquisition responsibility* for V. To describe S as responsible for V in this sense of 'responsible' is to imply that S brought it about that she has V. On a different interpretation an epistemic vice for which S is accountable is one that S has the ability to control or revise by her own efforts. When this is the case S has *revision responsibility* for V. If S can control V then S is responsible for *having* V, whether or not she is responsible for *acquiring* V. We don't blame people or hold them responsible for traits that they can't help having, just as we don't blame them or hold them responsible for doing things that they literally can't help doing. But if S is revision responsible for V then it's not true that she can't help it that she is, or has, V.

What if S is neither revision responsible nor acquisition responsible for V? Would it follow that V is not an epistemic vice? Not necessarily. Apart from the fact that criticism of S might still be in order, there can also be

---

[12] See Hieronymi 2008: 359.

[13] There are various complications about whether S knew, or should have known, that her past actions, omissions, choices, and decisions would have the effect of cultivating V. For present purposes I'm going to ignore these complications.

individual variations in blameworthiness. Even if having V is not something for which S is responsible it doesn't follow that nobody who has V is responsible for having it or that nobody deserves to be blamed on account of being or having V. For example, the dogmatic Taliban recruit might be neither responsible nor blameworthy for his dogmatism but it does not follow that a person is never responsible for being dogmatic or never deserves blame for being dogmatic. The fact that dogmatism *can* be blameless does not entail that it *is* always blameless or that it is not an epistemic vice.[14]

The essence of revision responsibility is control: to be revision responsible for V is to be able to exercise control over V. What kind of control? This question is important because there are different types of control. One is *voluntary* control, as defined here by Robert Merrihew Adams:

To say that something is (directly) within my voluntary control is to say that I would do it (right away) if and only if I (fully) tried or chose or meant to do so, and hence that if I did it I would do it *because* I tried or chose or meant to do it, and in that sense voluntarily. (1985: 8)

If I have voluntary control then there must be something *over which* I have voluntary control, and one type of thing over which we have voluntary control is our own actions. In the case of bodily actions we might also be said to have voluntary control over (parts of) our own bodies. If I raise my arm because I choose to do so then I have voluntary control over the position of my arm and the action of raising my arm. If I raise my arm voluntarily, without being forced to raise it, then I am in this sense responsible for raising it.

Notoriously, we lack voluntary control over our own beliefs. Belief is not voluntary. To believe that it's raining is to take it to be true that it's raining and this isn't something we can do at will. We do, however, have a different type of control over our own beliefs, namely, *evaluative* control, and this is sufficient for us to count as revision responsible for our beliefs. This is how Pamela Hieronymi explains evaluative control:

Consider a belief that it will take forty-five minutes to get to the airport. If we learn we must leave at rush hour, we then reconsider how long the drive will take

---

[14] The Taliban example is from Battaly 2016. Her view, which she calls 'personalism', says that 'we need not be praiseworthy or blameworthy for being epistemically virtuous or vicious' (2016: 100). That seems right but it's not clear in what sense epistemic vices are *vices* unless they are at least open to criticism.

and the belief changes accordingly. So, in a certain sense, we might also be said to 'control' our own beliefs . . . [W]e control our beliefs by evaluating (and reevaluating) what is true. Call this 'evaluative' control.   (2006: 53)

Evaluative control is not only different from voluntary control but also from what Hieronymi calls *managerial* control.[15] We have this kind of control 'when we manipulate some ordinary object to accord with our thoughts about it' (2006: 53). So, for example, I have managerial control over the layout of the furniture in my study: I can change the layout by shifting things around. It's also possible, though unusual, to exercise managerial control over one's own beliefs. If I want to believe that I am not chronically unfit then I should look for evidence that I'm not chronically unfit. In the absence of evidence it is open to me to resort to other methods of belief management, such as self-hypnosis or positive thinking, whose aim is to manipulate my mind so as to produce in me the desired belief.

It is sometimes suggested that we are only responsible for what is voluntary, but this suggestion is false. Beliefs aren't voluntary but we are still responsible for our own beliefs. There are also emotions such as contempt, anger, and jealousy over which we lack voluntary control but for which we are still responsible.[16] The natural view is that I'm responsible for my beliefs to the extent that I have evaluative or, in some circumstances, managerial control over them. Responsibility for hatred and contempt is more complicated. If my contempt for another person reflects my beliefs about them I'm responsible for my contempt as long as I have evaluative control over these beliefs. If my beliefs are unjustified, and I have no other basis for my attitude, then I can be condemned for my contempt. But what if my contempt is irrational in the sense that it doesn't reflect my underlying beliefs? In that case, there is still the question whether I have managerial control over my attitude. The assumption that we are responsible for our beliefs and other attitudes is the assumption that we have control over them, managerial if not evaluative.

When it comes to our character traits, one view is that we have no control over them and that there is nothing we can do about what we are given. In that case we have no revision responsibility for our character

---

[15] Hieronymi also refers to managerial control as 'manipulative control' (2006: 53).
[16] As noted in Adams 1985.

traits—because they are unrevisable—and so can't be blamed for them because we can't help being the way we are.[17] The more optimistic contrary view is that, as Michele Moody-Adams puts it, 'people can change or revise their characters' (1990: 117). There are two claims here. The first is that character traits aren't fixed and unchanging, and people do change over time. For example, it is possible to go from being open-minded to closed-minded, perhaps as a result of a religious or political conversion. The second claim is that character traits are *malleable*. These claims are distinct. For example, from the fact that the weather is changeable it doesn't follow that it can be controlled or reconfigured, as the notion of malleability implies. People can only change or revise their characters or character traits if their characters or character traits can be actively reconfigured. This is only possible, if it is possible at all, by exercising managerial control over one's character traits. There is no question of evaluative or voluntary control in this case. A closed-minded person can't make himself open-minded by willing it or by evaluating what is true. If there is no possibility of managerial control over one's character then there is no possibility of control period and no revision responsibility. In the absence of both revision and acquisition responsibility there is no blameworthiness.

In arguing this way I'm assuming that one can't properly be blamed for something over which one has no control. This assumption is questioned by George Sher.[18] He argues that it only seems compelling because it is apparently needed to explain two intuitions. The first is that we can't blame people for acts and omissions over which they have no control. The second is that we can't blame people for such physical or mental defects as being clumsy or ugly or stupid. In response Sher argues that the control assumption isn't needed to explain these intuitions. One reason people can't be blamed for acts over which they have no control or for their physical or mental defects is that these acts and these defects do not reflect badly on them. Since 'no one can deserve blame for anything that does not stand in a close enough relation *to* him to reflect badly *on* him' (2006: 57), a car driver whose brakes failed doesn't deserve blame for injuring a pedestrian and a stupid person doesn't deserve

---

[17] I'm assuming that we aren't acquisition responsible for our character traits. Sher explains why not in Sher 2006: 54–5.

[18] See Sher 2006, chapter 4.

blame for being stupid. In contrast, a bad trait like cruelty does reflect badly on those who have it since it is an element of their character.[19] So people can be blamed for traits like cruelty even if they have no control over them. Another consequence of Sher's view is that the notion that we are responsible for our traits is not just false but incoherent. Responsibility, Sher argues, is a causal notion but we aren't causally responsible for our traits.[20]

The traits that Sher is concerned with are moral traits, but similar considerations might be employed to show that responsibility for epistemic traits is incoherent and that we are blameworthy for our epistemic character vices not because we have control over them but because they reflect badly on us. The first thing to notice about Sher's view is that the control he thinks we lack over our character traits, and that is irrelevant to our blameworthiness for bad traits, is control over their *formation*.[21] The formation of one's epistemic character is something that generally happens early in one's life, and control over this process requires a degree of maturity and sophistication that children by and large do not have. In my terms, this means that we lack acquisition responsibility for our epistemic character traits. What we don't necessarily lack, however, is revision responsibility. As Sher concedes, 'there are . . . various techniques that someone who wants to become a better person can use. He can, for example, reflect on his past lapses, force himself to do what does not (yet) come naturally, imitate exemplary others, and avoid those whom he knows to be bad influences' (2006: 55). In my view, the availability of such techniques makes us revision responsible for some of our harmful moral and epistemic traits and blameworthy for them. These traits also reflect badly on those who have them, but that isn't enough for blameworthiness in the absence of control.

I've been arguing that we are blameworthy for our character vices to the extent that we have managerial control over them. This claim will need to be qualified but first there is the question: *do* we have managerial control over our character vices? If Sher is right that there are various techniques that someone who wants to become a morally better person can use then why shouldn't there also be techniques that someone who wants to become an epistemically better person can use? I'll have more to

---

[19] Sher 2006: 58.   [20] Sher 2006: 67.   [21] See Sher 2006: 54–5.

say about this question in Chapter 8 but here are some preliminary observations: on the face of it there *are* practical steps one can take to combat some of one's character vices. For example, one might combat one's arrogance by exposing oneself to superior intellects or one's closed-mindedness by forcing oneself to think long and hard about the merits of opinions with which one disagrees. Such self-improvement strategies are not guaranteed to succeed but nor are they guaranteed to fail. If they succeed they are examples of a person exercising managerial control over their vices. They see their character as something that can be reshaped, at least to some extent. Unlike managerial control over ordinary objects, managerial control over our own character vices is indirect. The layout of the furniture in my office can be changed by moving bits of furniture. Changing one's character or a particular character trait is a matter of doing other things that will hopefully have the desired effect.

For one to exercise effective managerial control over a character vice it isn't enough that the trait is open to manipulation. One also needs to know that one has it and be motivated to change. Self-knowledge can be hard to acquire but I will argue in Chapter 7 that it is possible, in the right circumstances, to know one's epistemic vices. The motivation to tackle them might be lacking but a person whose epistemic vices have got them into serious trouble might be motivated to do something about them. Another possibility is that one is motivated to modify or eliminate a particular trait by one's negative evaluation of it. A person who strongly disapproves of closed-mindedness might be motivated to be less closed-minded once they recognize that they are closed-minded. In this case, change is motivated by one's disapproval, but the control one exercises over one's closed-mindedness is not evaluative in anything like the sense in which control over one's attitudes is evaluative. We don't control our character traits by evaluating what is true, and disapproval of what one recognizes as one of one's own character traits is not sufficient to effect a change in that trait. It is one thing for the disapproval to motivate change but the change itself is the result of self-manipulation.

The assumption that self-improvement depends on self-knowledge points to one way that a person can be responsible and blameworthy for an epistemic vice over which they *lack* managerial control. Suppose that V is a malleable character vice but S doesn't realize that she has V. If S knew she has V she might be able to undo it, but her ignorance ensures that she lacks effective managerial control over V. Is ignorance an excuse? That depends on why S is ignorant of V. Suppose S has at her disposal excellent evidence that she has V, can grasp the significance of that evidence, but refuses to believe that she has V because this would be at odds with her desire to think of herself as epistemically virtuous. In these circumstances S is responsible and blameworthy for her self-ignorance. If she is culpably self-ignorant, and her self-ignorance accounts for her lack of managerial control over V, then she is potentially blameworthy for V despite her lack of managerial control.

Suppose, next, that S knows that she has V but isn't motivated to do anything about it. V is not immune to revision but S has no interest in trying to reconfigure this aspect of her character. One question in this case is whether S can still be said to have effective managerial control over V. If not, and S's lethargy is not due to depression or some other condition for which she is blameless, then this is potentially another example of blameworthiness without managerial control. S is blame-worthy for V because she is blameworthy for the lethargy that deprives her of managerial control over V. If, on the other hand, lack of motiv-ation doesn't amount to lack of managerial control, then managerial control and the revision responsibility it implies are insufficient for blameworthiness. If S isn't motivated to tackle V because she is too depressed then she isn't blameworthy for failing to exercise her man-agerial control over V and isn't blameworthy for V.[22]

These considerations suggest that the relationship between blame-worthiness for a character vice and managerial control over it is far more complicated than one might suppose. It isn't just that the notion of managerial control isn't straightforward. It also needs to be acknow-ledged that one can be blameworthy for a character vice over which one lacks managerial control. It all depends on why one lacks managerial control. However, this should not be allowed to obscure the basic picture: to the extent that we have effective control over our character vices that control is managerial rather than voluntary or evaluative. Managerial control is also the kind of control that is necessary for blameworthiness unless one's lack of managerial control is culpable. Furthermore, man-agerial control over our character vices is usually sufficient for us to count as revision responsible for them. Insofar as we have managerial

---

[22] Assuming that S isn't acquisition responsible for V.

control over our character vices, and these vices are epistemically harmful, we are generally also blameworthy for them. I haven't proved that we actually have managerial control over our character vices but if there are actual cases of people exercising managerial control over their character vices then that suggests such managerial control is possible, both in principle and in practice.

Applying these considerations to the Heidemann case, the question I asked earlier was whether he was blameworthy for his gullibility and foolishness. Relevant issues include the extent to which gullibility and foolishness are epistemically harmful, the extent to which they are malleable, and the extent to which Heidemann had managerial control of his gullibility and foolishness. If he lacked managerial control, what accounts for this? If he turns out not to be blameworthy then is this a case in which criticism might nevertheless be in order? How can it be legitimate to criticize a person's gullibility or foolishness if blame isn't appropriate? More generally, how are we to understand the distinction between blame and criticism? These are the questions to which I now turn.

It isn't controversial that gullibility and foolishness are epistemically harmful. To be foolish, in the particular sense in which Heidemann appears to have been foolish, is to have poor judgement and to be lacking in wisdom and good sense. This is a defect that is almost certain to get in the way of the gaining, keeping, or sharing of knowledge. The same goes for gullibility, which is arguably a form of foolishness. A key issue for Heidemann was whether the diaries were genuine but his gullibility prevented him from finding out. It did so by causing him not to raise the question of authenticity or carry out the type of conscientious inquiry that would have cast light on the issue. He believed Stiefel when he shouldn't have, and he wouldn't have believed him if he hadn't been so gullible. We would know very little without trusting other people but an effective inquirer is one who also knows when *not* to trust. A gullible person is someone who does not know when not to trust and this is what gets them into trouble, epistemically speaking.

The effect of gullibility on the keeping of knowledge is no less obvious. Imagine a person like Heidemann who initially knows and believes that there are no Hitler diaries but comes into contact with Stiefel. When Stiefel shows him the fake diary he believes that it is genuine even though there are plenty of reasons to be suspicious. What has happened in this case is that the subject has lost a piece of knowledge. He has gone from believing truly that there are no Hitler diaries to believing falsely that the diaries exist, and this transition is due to his gullibility. To put it another way, he is confident that the diaries exist as a result of his meeting with Stiefel, but his confidence is unjustified and entirely the result of his gullibility. Indeed, his confidence would have been unjustified even if Stiefel hadn't been lying. Given the circumstances of his meeting with Stiefel and the clear possibility that Stiefel was lying, a possibility that he did nothing to exclude, his belief wouldn't have been justified to the extent that it was the product of his gullibility.

To what extent are gullibility and foolishness malleable? An antidote to gullibility is proper scepticism.[23] Heidemann wouldn't have been conned if he had been properly sceptical and this suggests that one way for someone like him to become less gullible is to cultivate a more sceptical attitude. If scepticism is an attitude that can be cultivated then one can make oneself less gullible by cultivating it. The thought that Heidemann *should* have been more sceptical in response to Stiefel's offer reflects the natural assumption that he *could* have been more sceptical. In the same way, the thought that he should have been less foolish reflects the assumption that he could have been less foolish. The assumption that foolishness isn't incurable is built into the intuitive distinction between foolishness and stupidity. Stupidity has been interpreted as the lack of intelligence and foolishness as the failure of intelligence.[24] One might assume that there isn't much that people with low intelligence can do to make themselves more intelligent but a person whose judgement is poor or who is deficient in good sense can work to correct these flaws. There is, after all, such a thing as learning from one's mistakes and it is at least conceivable that by a combination of self-analysis, practice, and experience one might improve one's judgement. Even if stupidity is untreatable, foolishness is not.

What if this turns out to be too optimistic a view and that gullibility and foolishness aren't malleable? One might think that these traits aren't malleable because character vices generally aren't malleable or because

<hr>

[23] Proper scepticism is an appropriate degree or level of scepticism. As Harris points out, *Stern* and Heidemann weren't 'properly sceptical' (2009: 178).

[24] This is how Robert Musil distinguishes the two. See Mulligan 2014 for an account of Musil's views. Understood as the absence of intelligence, stupidity is 'something one is born with' whereas foolishness is a 'vice or bad habit, which either endures or occurs' (Mulligan 2014: 78).

these traits in particular are hard-wired in such a way that no one who has them can do anything about them. *If* this is right, then this is the point at which the possibility of criticism without blame becomes important. People like Heidemann are criticized for their gullibility and foolishness whether or not they are blamed. The next question, therefore, is whether the distinction between blame and criticism can be sustained. Certainly the distinction deserves closer scrutiny. One might suggest that blame is a form of criticism that implies responsibility whereas criticism per se does not, but this only raises more questions. If it isn't fair to blame someone for what is beyond their control, how can it be fair to criticize them for what is beyond their control? If it is fair to criticize a person's gullibility, then why isn't it also fair to criticize their physical defects like blindness?

One way to make progress with these issues would be to think about the distinction between asking whether a trait is blameworthy and asking whether it reflects badly on those who have it. Sher thinks it's a truism that people can only be blamed for what reflects badly on them, but it isn't a truism that they can be blamed for whatever reflects badly on them.[25] If it is possible for a trait to reflect badly on those who have it even if they can't be blamed for it then this opens up the possibility that the incurably gullible and foolish can be criticized for their gullibility and foolishness because these traits reflect badly on them. In contrast, since physical defects such as blindness don't reflect badly on those who have them there is no question of the blind being open to criticism on account of their blindness despite the fact that not being able to see does get in the way of certain kinds of knowledge. The next challenge, then, is to explain what it is for a trait to reflect badly on a person.

A way to explain the notion that some traits do, while others do not, reflect badly on a person, or cast a negative shadow over them, is to distinguish between deep and superficial traits or between deep and superficial evaluations.[26] As Angela Smith puts it: 'Assessments of people as beautiful or ugly, intelligent or stupid, and athletic or unathletic . . . seem to be "superficial" forms of evaluation. Though others may (cruelly) mock

[25] On the truism that people can only be blamed for what reflects badly on them see Sher 2006: 58.

[26] On the idea that some traits cast a 'negative shadow' over people who have them see Sher 2006: 58.

or despise us for our basic physical or intellectual attributes, it seems that they cannot properly fault or reproach us for them' (2008: 373).

On the most demanding interpretation, a person's deep characteristics define who they are, and it's not unreasonable to deny that the defects listed by Smith are deep in this sense. However, when it comes to the identification of intellectual or epistemic failings—which is what epistemic vices are—what counts is not whether they define the kind of *person* one is but whether they define the kind of *thinker* or *knower* one is. On this reading, stupidity *is* a deep intellectual defect and does cast a negative shadow over those who suffer from it, even if they are not blameworthy for their stupidity. The same goes for gullibility and foolishness. It *does* reflect badly on Heidemann to say that he is gullible and foolish insofar as these are negative traits that define the kind of intellectual or epistemic agent he is. These traits are not separate from him; they are a part of him and of who he is.[27] Furthermore, to say that these traits reflect badly on Heidemann is to say that he can be criticized for them even if not blamed for them. This is what allows these and other such traits to count as epistemic vices regardless of whether they are blameworthy. If it turns out that they are also blameworthy then the classification of them as epistemic vices is even more straightforward, but the issue of blameworthiness can't be settled without also settling the question as to whether these traits are malleable. I'm inclined to think that they are but my point here is that they don't *have* to be malleable in order to count as epistemic vices if we take seriously the idea that epistemic vices are blameworthy or *otherwise reprehensible*, that is to say, reprehensible without necessarily being blameworthy.

To sum up, suppose that V is an epistemically harmful trait like gullibility. We want to know if V is an epistemic vice so we start by asking if it is blameworthy. That depends on whether V is malleable and on whether those who have this trait are revision responsible for having it. If V is malleable and the kind of trait for which people are revision responsible then we can be reasonably confident that V is blameworthy. If V isn't malleable then people lack revision responsibility for having V and aren't blameworthy. But V can still be an epistemic vice if people can be criticized for the trait. They can be criticized for having V if it is a

---

[27] Compare Linda Zagzebski's suggestion that virtues and vices 'come closer to defining who the person is than any other category of qualities' (1996: 135).

trait that reflects badly on those who have it. Whether this is in fact the case depends on the nature of V (on its harmfulness) and on whether it is a deep rather than a superficial trait, that is, one that defines, or helps to define, the kind of thinker or knower one is. In order for V to reflect badly on a person it isn't necessary that they are revision responsible or blameworthy for V. My contention is that gullibility and foolishness are traits that cast a negative shadow over a person like Heidemann regardless of whether he is blameworthy for having them. Whether he *is* blameworthy is a question that doesn't need to be settled here.

The discussion so far has focused on epistemic character vices. The next question is: what kind of control do we have over vices that I have called epistemic postures or attitudes? In Chapter 4 I described attitudes generally as 'affective postures'. Examples are contempt, jealousy, and regret. One *feels* contempt, jealousy, or regret and this is the sense in which these attitudes are 'affective'. Epistemic attitudes are epistemically focused affective postures, that is, affective postures towards knowledge, evidence, or other epistemic objects. Our control over our affective postures is partly evaluative. This is a reflection of the fact that, as Angela Smith writes, such attitudes 'seem to be partially constituted by certain kinds of evaluative judgments or appraisals' (2005: 250). For example:

To feel contempt toward some person, for example, involves the judgment that she has some feature or has behaved in some way that makes her unworthy of one's respect, and to feel regret involves the judgment that something of value has been lost. There seems to be a conceptual connection between having these attitudes and making, or being disposed to make, certain kinds of judgments. (2005: 250)

If I *judge* that a person has behaved in a way that makes her unworthy of respect then, normally, I also *believe* that her behaviour makes her unworthy of respect.[28] The link between attitudes and judgements therefore also implicitly links affective postures with beliefs. Since beliefs are subject to evaluative control it is hard to see how the postures they underpin could fail to be subject, at least to some extent, to evaluative control. Suppose I feel contempt for a particular politician because I believe he has been stirring up racial hatred. Beliefs are controlled by

---

[28] For an account along these lines of the relationship between judging and believing see Cassam 2010.

evaluating what is true. So if I discover that the politician I have in mind hasn't been stirring up racial hatred then I will abandon my belief that he has been stirring up racial hatred. By the same token, I should no longer feel contempt for him unless I have other reasons for regarding him with contempt.

Because humans are less than perfectly rational, there are limits to our evaluative control over our attitudes and emotions generally. A familiar illustration of this phenomenon is fear of spiders. If I judge that spiders are nothing to be afraid of then I should no longer fear them, but the judgement that something is not fearful doesn't necessarily extinguish one's fear. Judging, knowing, and believing that most spiders are neither fearful nor threatening is no guarantee that one will not continue to fear them. More fancifully, judging that a politician for whom one feels contempt has done nothing to merit one's contempt is no guarantee that one will not continue to feel contempt for them. One's posture might prove recalcitrant in the sense that it is unresponsive to one's considered judgement. However, such a failure of evaluative control leaves open the possibility that the recalcitrant attitude is nevertheless susceptible to managerial control. One might develop strategies for managing one's attitude, and people who go to hypnotists or therapists in order to overcome their fears or other emotions are trying to exercise managerial self-control. There is no guarantee of success but also no guarantee of failure.

Epistemic attitude vices are no different. Suppose that a person's intellectual arrogance is underpinned by a firm belief in their own intellectual superiority. If their alleged superiority is put to the test and proved to be non-existent then they ought to revise their belief and change their attitude. They should stop regarding other people with disdain. If the evidence leads them to revise their belief in their intellectual superiority then they have displayed evaluative control of their belief. If the change of belief leads to an appropriate change in attitude then they have, in addition, displayed evaluative control over their attitude. As with other attitudes, a person's arrogant attitude might prove recalcitrant. They might continue to believe in their intellectual superiority or they might fail to change their attitude despite revising their belief. In either case they are guilty of irrationality. 'Irrational' is a term of epistemic appraisal, and to describe a person as irrational on account of their failure to change their attitude is to imply that they are responsible for their attitude and their failure to change it. The responsibility at issue here is revision responsibility and the assumption that we are revision responsible for our attitude vices, together with the epistemic harmfulness of such vices, justifies the judgement that they are blameworthy.

I've argued that not all character vices are blameworthy. In some cases criticism rather than blame is the appropriate response. In that case, are there also attitude vices that are not blameworthy? Consider prejudice, an attitude that is epistemically as well as morally vicious. One way that prejudice is epistemically harmful is that it obstructs the sharing of knowledge. Miranda Fricker gives a nice example of this phenomenon from *The Talented Mr Ripley*.[29] In Patricia Highsmith's story, Herbert Greenleaf's son Dickie has disappeared. Marge Sherwood, Dickie's fiancée, knows something about the disappearance, but Greenleaf senior's gender prejudice prevents her from sharing that knowledge with him. He is dismissive of Marge's testimony because she is a woman and so fails to exhibit what Fricker calls the virtue of testimonial justice. Although Greenleaf was at fault Fricker argues that he wasn't *culpably* at fault given the prevalence and 'normality' of gender prejudice in the society in which his attitudes were formed.[30]

Fricker's focus is not on whether Greenleaf was revision responsible for his prejudice but whether he should have known better. However, these two issues are related. If prejudice isn't malleable then the question of revision responsibility doesn't arise. On the other hand, even if prejudice is seen as malleable in principle, it is arguable that Greenleaf's historically contingent circumstances would have made it practically impossible for him to undo his gender prejudice.[31] For a start he wouldn't have recognized his prejudice as a prejudice or as something that he needed to undo even if such a thing is possible. He would have lacked a critical awareness of his vice, and this lack of critical awareness would have deprived him of effective control of his attitude. This supports the notion that Greenleaf's prejudice wasn't blameworthy.

---

[29] Fricker 2007: 9. Fricker's discussion is based on Anthony Minghella's screenplay of *The Talented Mr. Ripley*.

[30] See Fricker 2007: 100.

[31] As Fricker described them these circumstances include the 'absence of a critical awareness of gender prejudice in the society in which his ethical and epistemic second nature were formed' (2007: 100).

It doesn't support the notion that his gender prejudice wasn't reprehensible or that he couldn't justly be criticized for it. Even if his attitude wasn't blameworthy it still cast a negative shadow over him. His attitude was epistemically damaging and not separate from him. It is not just the attitude itself that can be criticized. *Greenleaf* can be criticized for his attitude because it was truly *his* attitude. In such cases, our criticism is a response to the content of Greenleaf's attitude *and* to Greenleaf himself as the subject of the attitude. So here is another case that brings out the importance of the distinction between blame and criticism. Without this distinction it is hard to do justice to our reaction towards historically contingent attitude vices. If they are vices, then criticism must be in order in these cases.[32]

A third kind of epistemic vice is ways of thinking that get in the way of knowledge. Examples include closed-minded thinking and wishful thinking. Thinking is a mental action over which thinkers normally have voluntary control. Deciding to think about Brexit can be all it takes for one to think about Brexit. However, just because one has voluntary control over *whether* to think about Brexit it doesn't follow that one has voluntary control over *how* one thinks about it. A person can have voluntary control over their walking, in the sense that they can decide whether to walk rather than sit or run, but little or no voluntary control over how they walk, over their gait or walking style. If ways of thinking are like ways of walking then not only is there no question of voluntary control over how we think, there is also arguably very little scope for evaluative or managerial control. On a pessimistic view, how one thinks is not constituted by certain kinds of evaluative judgements, and there may be very little one can do to change how one thinks.

It isn't clear, though, that the analogy between ways of thinking and ways of walking is a good one. One reason for being sceptical about the analogy is that it underestimates the extent of our managerial control

---

[32] As Fricker puts it, 'we need to qualify our exculpation of Greenleaf, for surely he is not altogether off the hook. If history puts blame out of court, is there some other form of moral resentment that remains in play?' (2007: 103). For Fricker, the form of moral resentment that remains in play is 'a certain *resentment of disappointment*' that is grounded in the sense that Greenleaf 'could have done better' (2007: 103). I agree with Fricker that Greenleaf is not altogether off the hook. In my terms he is liable to criticism rather than blame, on account of his attitude. Criticism of Greenleaf needn't be based on the idea that he could have done better. If he could have done better then he was revision responsible and blameworthy for his prejudice.

over our thinking. Consider this example: in the run-up to the Brexit vote I believed that the result would be a vote for Britain to remain in the European Union. There was plenty of contrary evidence but I was swayed by evidence of a defeat for Brexit. I was wrong. A few months later, I failed to attach sufficient weight to evidence of Donald Trump's growing popularity in the last days of the 2016 US presidential election campaign and assumed that Hillary Clinton would be victorious. I was wrong. In retrospect, I see that my beliefs about the outcomes of the two votes were at least in part the result of wishful thinking: I thought that Brexit would lose and Clinton would win because these were the outcomes I wanted. Next time I will be more careful. I will be on my guard against supposing that the actual outcome in such cases will be the outcome I hope for. I will make a special effort to question my assumptions and be more sceptical about opinion polls and other data that suggest that things are going just the way I want them to go. I will do my best not to make the same mistake again.

It might turn out that my best isn't good enough and that, despite my determination not to fall into the same trap again, that is exactly what I do. But things needn't turn out that way. There is no guarantee that I will be successful but no guarantee that I won't be. Suppose that the next time I manage to change my thinking and avoid making the same mistake. If that is how things turn out then I will have exercised managerial control over my way of thinking. Instead of comparing ways of thinking with ways of walking one might instead compare them to ways of driving. A person whose reckless driving causes them to crash repeatedly is expected to change how they drive. If they are prone to reckless driving they are expected to exercise greater self-control after their crashes and to change their driving. There are all sorts of techniques for doing that, including going back to driving school. The reckless driver who makes no effort to change and goes on driving recklessly despite being involved in multiple crashes is held responsible for their conduct. Their failure is a failure to exercise control over their way of driving, and they cannot escape responsibility by declaring that they have no control over how they drive. What goes for vicious driving goes for vicious thinking: we are responsible for how we think because, and to the extent that, we can modify how we think by taking the appropriate steps. The idea that a person who understands that they are prone to wishful thinking can do nothing about it is no more compelling than the view that reckless drivers can do nothing about their reckless driving. On this account, we are revision responsible for our thinking vices and blame-worthy for them.

This line of thinking might appear hopelessly naïve in the light of research in cognitive psychology that suggests that our thinking is shaped by more or less universal, sub-personal cognitive biases that are built into the way our minds work. Wishful thinking is, on this view, either a cognitive bias in its own right or a way of thinking that is closely related to well-established cognitive biases such as confirmation bias. Cognitive biases are inescapable and so, it seems, is wishful thinking. For example, Elisha Babad points to the prevalence of wishful thinking among voters. When voters are asked to predict the result of a forth-coming election, 'their predictions vary in an optimistic direction as a function of their preferences' (1997: 105). To put it crudely, people predict the result they want. While remedies designed to reduce wishful thinking do have some effect, practically speaking 'the power and inten-sity of wishful thinking is far stronger than psychological interventions and remedies that have been invented to counter it' (1997: 122). Such remedies include promising voters financial rewards for accurate predic-tions and providing them with accurate polling information. If the overall high intensity of wishful thinking is unchanged by such remedies, what reason is there to believe that wishful thinking is something over which thinkers have managerial control or for which they are blameworthy?

The results reported by Babad and many others are a useful corrective to the view that wishful thinking and other thinking vices are easy to control or counteract. It is worth noting, however, that the psychological interventions described by Babad are about remedying other people's wishful thinking. They do not study the prospects for controlling one's own wishful thinking by reflecting on one's past errors. In the case of the overoptimistic Clinton supporter and Brexit opponent the aim is to learn from one's mistakes. The reflective politics student who sees a pattern in his tendency to predict the outcome he wants needn't and shouldn't be seen as a prisoner of his thinking vice. Having been caught out by Trump and Brexit he is just as likely to overcompensate in the opposite direction as to repeat his mistake. The next time he is desperate for a particular result he might find himself betting against the result he wants on the basis that 'I was wrong about Trump and Brexit so maybe I should assume that the outcome this time will be the opposite of what I want'.

Going from excessive optimism to excessive pessimism is all too common and doesn't suggest that wishful thinking is unavoidable. For all the talk of cognitive biases the natural and understandable reaction to cases in which a person is repeatedly caught out by their own wishful thinking is 'You should have known better'.

The view of responsibility I have been defending in this chapter is a control-based view according to which, as I've emphasized, the key to being responsible for one's epistemic character traits, attitudes, or thinking styles is to be able to control or modify them through one's own efforts. To be in control of something is to be able to modify it. To be in control of a vehicle is to be able to modify its direction and speed. To be in control of one's thinking or attitudes or character traits is to be able to modify them. This approach to responsibility has been strongly criticized in a series of papers by Angela Smith so it would be appropriate to conclude this chapter by looking at Smith's criticisms and the merits of the *rational relations* approach she recommends.

Smith's target is what she labels the 'volitional theory of responsibility'. This theory assumes that 'choice, decision, or susceptibility to voluntary control is a necessary condition of responsibility (for attitudes as well as actions)' (2005: 238). For example, one version of the volitional theory says that responsibility for an attitude requires that it is connected in some way to choices made in the past that led to the development of the attitude in question. This corresponds to what I've been calling 'acquisition responsibility'. A different volitional theory says that a person is responsible for her attitudes only if she has the ability to modify them through the choices she makes in the future. This is a form of what I've been calling 'revision responsibility'. In reply Smith argues that:

[W]e attach (moral) significance to a wide variety of attitudes and mental states, many of which do not arise from conscious choice or decision, and many of which do not fall under our immediate voluntary control. While it may be true that we could, over time, exert an influence on many of these patterns of awareness and response by voluntarily pursuing various projects of self-improvement, I do not think that this fact plays a role in explaining either our willingness to take these attitudes as a legitimate basis for (moral) appraisal or the nature of the appraisals we in fact make. When we praise or criticize someone for an attitude it seems we are responding to something about the content of that attitude and not to facts about its origin in a person's prior voluntary choices, or to facts about its susceptibility to influence through a person's future voluntary choices. (2005: 250–1)

These observations are the basis of the rational relations approach to responsibility. This says that rational judgement rather than choice or voluntary control is the fundamental condition of responsibility: 'to say that an agent is morally responsible for something, on this view, is to say that that thing reflects her rational judgement in a way that makes it appropriate, in principle, to ask her to defend or justify it' (2008: 369).

Although Smith talks here about *moral* responsibility, her view can also be interpreted more broadly as offering an account of what it takes for a person to be responsible in a wider sense for her attitudes, including the attitudes that I have classified as epistemic vices: if V is an attitude vice then S is only responsible for V if V reflects her rational judgement. For example, suppose that V is the vice of epistemic insouciance, defined as an attitude towards evidence or inquiry, and that this attitude depends on an evaluative judgement about the value or importance of evidence and inquiry. On the rational relations view, the sense in which a person is responsible for her epistemic insouciance is not that it falls under her immediate voluntary control. The point is rather that it is appropriate in principle to ask her to justify or defend the underpinning judgement.

Smith is clearly right that responsibility for our attitudes doesn't require immediate voluntary control over them. It is also true that when we criticize people for their attitudes we are responding to something about the content of the attitude. But none of this precludes the notion that being responsible for such attitudes is also partly a matter of being able to control them. We clearly don't need to suppose that people have immediate voluntary control over their attitudes in order to count as responsible for them. Equally, we don't need to suppose that such attitudes originate in people's prior choices. But if we were truly convinced that there is literally nothing that a person with vicious attitudes can do to modify them, that they literally have *no* control over them and not just no voluntary control, then this really does raise questions about the extent of their responsibility.

This is even clearer when it comes to responsibility for character and thinking vices. These are vices to which the rational relations view doesn't apply since they needn't reflect a person's evaluative judgements. Equally, when we criticize someone for wishful thinking we aren't responding to something about the content of their attitude because wishful thinking is not an attitude. What we are responding to is its harmful effects and the possibility of doing something about it by changing how we think. The control we have over our epistemic vices is nothing like our voluntary control over our actions, but no sane volitional theory would suppose otherwise. Where voluntary control is absent evaluative control may still be present. Where there is no evaluative control there may still be managerial control. Where there is no voluntary control, no evaluative control, and no managerial control there is in most cases also no responsibility.

It's worth adding that even on the rational relations view, it remains the case that responsibility is tied to the possibility of modification and, in this sense, to the possibility of control, though not voluntary control. For Smith, in order for a creature to be responsible for an attitude, 'it must be the kind of state that is open, in principle, to revision or modification through that creature's own process of rational reflection' (2005: 256). So the issue is not *whether* the states for which we are responsible must be open to modification but *how* they are open to modification. The rational relations view draws attention to the key role of rational reflection in modifying one's own attitudes, and this is an important insight which the control view I've been defending in this chapter tries to respect. On the underlying issue of whether modifiability is a condition of responsibility the control and rational relations views are in complete agreement.

7

Stealthy Vices

A few days before Donald Trump's inauguration as the 45th president of the United States *New York* magazine reported that ever since Trump's election David Dunning's phone had been ringing off the hook.[1] Dunning was one of the authors of a famous paper published in 1999 in the *Journal of Personality and Social Psychology*.[2] The paper's central idea is that in many social and intellectual domains incompetent individuals lack the skills needed to know that they are incompetent. As a result, they have inflated views of their performance and abilities. For example, participants in a test of logical reasoning generally overestimated their reasoning skills but those in the bottom quartile exhibited the greatest miscalibration. This came to be known as the Dunning-Kruger effect, a less polite version of which is quoted by *New York* magazine: some people are too dumb even to know it. The phone calls to Dunning were a reflection of the increasing popularity of the view that Trump personified this effect. The headline of the *New York* article was 'Donald Trump, the Dunning-Kruger President'. In a similar vein a 2017 *New York Times* op-ed labelled Trump the 'all-time record holder of the Dunning-Kruger effect'.[3] Dunning himself seemed to concur with this analysis. In an article published before Trump's election he speculated that the Dunning-Kruger effect 'may well be the key to the Trump voter—and perhaps to the man himself' (Dunning 2016).

Being too incompetent to understand one's own incompetence is, or results in, a form of self-ignorance. If Trump is the personification of the Dunning-Kruger effect then what he lacks is a vital piece of self-knowledge, knowledge of his own incompetence. Trump's self-ignorance, if that is what it is, is often put down to a chronic lack of self-awareness. One memorable profile of Trump notes that the walls of the Trump

---

[1] Pressler 2017.   [2] Kruger and Dunning 1999.   [3] Brooks 2017.

Organization headquarters are lined with framed magazine covers, 'each a shot of Trump or someone who looked a lot like him', and that these images 'seemed the sum of his appetite for self-reflection' (Singer 2016: 32).[4] However, the notion of Trump as the Dunning-Kruger president suggests that his lack of self-knowledge isn't just the result of a lack of interest in self-reflection.[5] The implication is rather that even if Trump were to reflect on his competence he would in all likelihood remain self-ignorant because of the Dunning-Kruger effect. The most effective way to increase an incompetent person's ability to determine his level of competence is to improve his level of competence, but that isn't always possible.

The Dunning-Kruger effect is limited in its application. Golf, for example, is not a domain in which the incompetent are likely to be unaware of their lack of skill, and this might be a reflection of the fact that competence in this domain is mainly determined by certain physical skills that are not the very skills needed to evaluate one's competence as a golfer.[6] The domains in which the Dunning-Kruger effect applies are those in which the skills needed for competence are 'the very same skills needed to evaluate competence in that domain—one's own or anyone else's' (Kruger and Dunning 1999: 1121). In these domains a lack of competence obstructs its own detection, and this is the essence of the Dunning-Kruger effect. Another way to describe the effect is in terms of the negative impact of incompetence on metacognition, 'the ability to know how well one is performing' (1999: 1121). In these terms, the thesis is that incompetence obstructs metacognition.

The notion of a flaw or incapacity that obstructs its own detection raises the following question: do epistemic vices block their own detection? Epistemic vices that obstruct their detection are inherently hard to detect. Such vices are *stealthy vices*.[7] There are good reasons to think that

---

[4] See also Wolff 2018.

[5] Trump is reported as having said in an interview, 'I don't like to analyse myself because I might not like what I see'. See https://yougov.co.uk/news/2016/10/28/donald-trumps-self-awareness-self-analysis-contemp. If he really said this then he isn't (or wasn't) completely lacking in self-awareness.

[6] Clearly people can be deluded about their golfing prowess and think they are better at golf than they are, but in this case it isn't their lack of golfing prowess that explains their ignorance of their lack of golfing prowess.

[7] In case it isn't obvious, stealthy vices as I understand them are inherently hard to detect by people whose vices they are. They needn't be hard to detect by others. Trump's vices

some epistemic vices are stealthy.[8] Incompetence per se isn't an epistemic vice and there are forms of incompetence—at golf, for example—that are of no epistemic significance. However, if there is such a thing as what Alvin Goldman calls 'epistemic incompetence' (2011: 21), then this is presumably not just an epistemic vice but a stealthy vice, one that is subject to the Dunning-Kruger effect. To be epistemically incompetent is to be an incompetent inquirer or knower, perhaps in virtue of one's possession of other epistemic vices such as laziness, closed-mindedness, and epistemic insouciance. If one needs to be epistemically competent in order to determine one's level of epistemic competence then the epistemically incompetent are in a particularly bad position to know that they are epistemically incompetent. Another stealthy vice is closed-mindedness. The closed-minded are unlikely to recognize their own closed-mindedness since doing so requires a degree of open-mindedness that one is unlikely to have if one is closed-minded. In contrast, intellectual carelessness is a less obviously stealthy vice. Being intellectually careless needn't prevent one from recognizing one's own carelessness since no great care is required for one to recognize one's lack of care.

Why does it matter whether any epistemic vices are stealthy? It matters if it matters whether one knows, or is in a position to know, one's own epistemic and other vices. There is a link here to the discussion in Chapter 6. Suppose that a person S has a character vice V. Is S blameworthy for V? Suppose that S's blameworthiness for V depends on whether S has revision responsibility for V. Whether S has revision responsibility for V depends on whether S has control over it.[9] However, in order to have control over a vice like closed-mindedness one needs to know that one has it. How is S supposed to be able to exercise control over an epistemic vice that she doesn't even know she has? So if V is stealthy enough for one not to know that it is one of one's epistemic vices then it looks like this is going to have an impact on one's blameworthiness for it.

As noted in Chapter 6, there is a way for someone to be blameworthy for a character vice over which she lacks control. S might be blameworthy

might not be apparent to him but are all too obvious to the rest of us, excluding his fans. For further discussion of the notion of a 'stealthy vice' see Cassam 2015a.

[8] I leave open the question whether all epistemic vices are stealthy, at least to some degree. Even if that is so, some epistemic vices are stealthier than others.

[9] I take it that the control that is at issue in this case is managerial control.

for V if she lacks control over it because she doesn't know she has V and her self-ignorance is itself culpable. I gave the example of the person who has good evidence that she has V but doesn't believe she has V because such a belief would be at odds with her desire to think of herself as epistemically virtuous. What if V is the vice of closed-mindedness and S refuses to accept compelling evidence of her closed-mindedness simply because her mind is closed to the possibility that she is closed-minded? In that case, is her ignorance culpable? More generally, what effect does the stealthiness of our epistemic vices have on their blameworthiness? Are epistemic vices that block their own detection more or less culpable than those which do not?

As well as its potential impact on questions of responsibility and blameworthiness the stealthiness of some of our epistemic vices also has a potential impact on the possibility of self-improvement. Self-improvement, understood as the project of undoing or combatting one's epistemic character vices, requires managerial control over them.[10] If self-ignorance can undermine one's managerial control over one's vices then the stealthiness of some of our epistemic vices is a barrier to self-improvement as well as self-knowledge. If, as is often supposed, self-knowledge is the first step towards self-improvement then the stealthiness of our epistemic vices is a barrier to self-improvement at least in part *because* it is a barrier to self-knowledge. This raises an important practical question: is there any way of breaking through the veils of self-ignorance woven by our stealthy vices? Stealthy vices are inherently hard to detect but being hard to detect doesn't make them undetectable. How, then, is knowledge of one's own stealthy vices possible?

Here, then, are three questions, or clusters of questions, about stealthy vices to which it would be good to have answers:

1. What makes an epistemic vice stealthy? What are the obstacles to knowledge of one's own epistemic vices, and which are the stealthier or stealthiest vices?
2. How, if at all, is it possible to overcome the obstacles to knowledge of our stealthy vices?
3. Can we be held responsible for our stealthy vices? Does the stealthiness of an epistemic vice diminish our responsibility for it?

---

[10] Self-improvement can, of course, also pertain to attitude and thinking vices.

The rest of this chapter will attempt to provide answers to these questions. Chapter 8 will be about the prospects of self-improvement.

What makes an epistemic vice stealthy? Some obstacles to vice detection are prosaic: one might fail to discover one's own vices simply because, like Trump, one can't be bothered (or is afraid) to think about them. It is also possible that one lacks the conceptual resources necessary to know one's own epistemic vices. To know that one is, say, dogmatic, one needs to know what dogmatism is, but this is knowledge the dogmatist might lack. A person can be highly dogmatic without knowing what dogmatism is. The greater one's conceptual repertoire and intellectual sophistication, the better able one is to know one's own vices. Another possibility is that one has all the necessary concepts but one's self-conception makes it hard for one to accept that one has a particular epistemic vice. Perhaps I know perfectly well what dogmatism is but I firmly believe I am undogmatic. My dogmatic belief about myself makes it hard for me to accept that I am dogmatic even if my dogmatism is apparent to other people. Anything that makes it hard for a person to *accept* that they have vice V also makes it hard for them to *know* that they have V. Perhaps V is perceived by them or by their community as a particularly bad epistemic vice and this can be an obstacle to recognizing that they have V. Or there is the opposite case in which they recognize that they have V but don't perceive V as a vice at all. A racist who lives in a community of racists might see nothing wrong with being racially prejudiced. Members of such a community may know that they are prejudiced but they still lack insight into their vice: not realizing that one's epistemic vices are vices is a form of self-ignorance.

These obstacles to knowledge of one's own epistemic vices do not support the notion that some vices are *inherently* harder to detect than others. Because two people with the same vice V have different self-conceptions it might be harder for one of them to know that they have V, but this doesn't make V inherently harder to detect than any other vice. However, some epistemic vices *are* stealthier. The first thing to notice is that epistemic vices aren't self-intimating: a person who has an epistemic vice V needn't know she has V. Coming to know one's epistemic vices usually requires effort, even if it is only the effort of reflecting on one's own epistemic vices. Reflection on one's epistemic vices is what Fricker calls 'active critical reflection' (2007: 91), but—and this is the key point—active critical reflection requires the exercise of a range of epistemic *virtues.* Suppose that V* is one such virtue and that V is a contrary epistemic vice. The sense in which V is contrary to V* is that a person who has V either *can't* have V* or is *unlikely* to have V*. This would then be a way for V to obstruct active critical reflection and thereby to obstruct its own detection: V is an obstacle to its own detection to the extent that it nullifies or opposes the very epistemic virtues on which active critical reflection depends. Maybe not all epistemic vices obstruct their own detection by active critical reflection but those that do are inherently hard to detect. They are stealthy vices.

Even if inherently stealthy vices evade detection by active critical reflection there may be other sources of knowledge of one's epistemic vices. For example, is it not possible to know one's own epistemic vices by being told about them? If such 'testimonial' knowledge of one's vices is possible then it is a further question whether epistemic vices that obstruct their detection by active critical reflection also obstruct their discovery by testimony. One issue here is whether testimonial self-knowledge depends on active reflection or whether it is a wholly independent source of self-knowledge. If self-knowledge by testimony depends on active critical reflection then obstacles to the latter are also obstacles to the former. I'll come back to this. The immediate priority is to arrive at a better understanding of active critical reflection, the epistemic virtues on which it depends, and the epistemic vices that get in the way of it.

The sense in which active critical reflection on one's own epistemic vices is active is that it is something that one *does*, and does intentionally. It doesn't just happen. Any number of things can trigger it. For example, people who have been taken in by a conman might ask themselves whether they are especially gullible. One can imagine Heidemann reflecting in this spirit on his gullibility after the Hitler diaries fiasco. Being the victim of a plausible and sophisticated scam doesn't necessarily make one gullible and needn't prompt much soul searching, but Heidemann's case was different. If he went in for some active critical reflection after the diaries were unmasked as forgeries it wouldn't be hard to work out why: such reflection was the appropriate response. Another case in which active critical reflection is appropriate is one in which a person has it pointed out to her that all her friends and acquaintances are white. Such a person might be led to reflect on whether she has a prejudice against non-whites. There is of course no guarantee that this will happen, just as there was no guarantee that Heidemann would be led to think about his epistemic vices as a result of being conned by Kujau. Active critical reflection on one's epistemic vices is a form of self-criticism. There are individuals—perhaps Trump is one of them—who are incapable of self-criticism, but thankfully such individuals are few and far between. Even if a person concludes that he has no epistemic vices, active critical reflection requires at least openness to the *possibility* that one isn't vice-free. The supposition that one has no epistemic vices is itself an epistemic vice, the vice of epistemic hubris.

This account of active critical reflection makes it easy to identify the epistemic virtues on which it depends. A willingness to engage in self-criticism requires epistemic humility and openness. Epistemic vices are epistemic deficits, and being open to the possibility that one has such deficits is a form of epistemic humility, that is, 'attentiveness to one's own cognitive limitations and deficits' (Medina 2013: 43). Such attentiveness is clearly needed for critical reflection on one's epistemic vices. Even to ask the question whether one is, say, gullible is already to display a degree of attentiveness to one's limitations. An even greater degree of attentiveness to one's limitations is required in order to investigate one's epistemic vices by subjecting oneself to serious intellectual self-scrutiny. Beyond a certain point self-criticism can undermine one's self-confidence and induce intellectual paralysis; it is possible to be too humble. In moderation, however, epistemic humility not only facilitates active critical reflection on one's epistemic vices, it also affords more general intellectual benefits.[11]

The openness required for active critical reflection is related to open-mindedness, but the emphasis is somewhat different. An open-minded person has been described as one who 'characteristically moves beyond or temporarily sets aside his own doxastic commitments in order to give a fair and impartial hearing to the intellectual opposition. He is willing to follow the argument where it leads and to take evidence and reasons at face value' (Baehr 2011: 142). In contrast, the openness needed for active critical reflection isn't a matter of being willing to set aside one's doxastic commitments, other than a commitment to the notion that one has no

---

[11] As Medina notes, 'insofar as humility involves epistemic attitudes and habits conducive to the identification of cognitive lacunas, it can facilitate learning processes and one's overall cognitive improvement' (2013: 43).

epistemic vices worth investigating. There is no 'intellectual opposition' to which a fair and impartial hearing needs to be given, and it isn't in this sense that critical reflection depends upon openness. The openness that *is* vital is a willingness to listen to evidence of one's epistemic vices and follow the evidence wherever it leads. The person who is aware of being repeatedly taken in by conmen has *prima facie* evidence of his gullibility and must be open to concluding that he is gullible. *Prima facie* evidence of one's gullibility may not be conclusive. Perhaps the evidence can be explained away but it must be given a fair hearing. The openness required for active critical reflection on one's epistemic vices is the openness required for rational inquiry and is a core component of the virtue of open-mindedness. It is the willingness to update one's beliefs, in this case one's beliefs about one's epistemic vices, in the light of the evidence.

The epistemic vices that are contrary to epistemic humility are arrogance, vanity, and hubris. It is possible to be arrogant and humble about different things, and it is even possible to be arrogant and humble about the same thing, as when one is in two minds about it. However, a person who is *intellectually* arrogant is unlikely to be seriously attentive to his cognitive deficits and limitations since he may well think that he doesn't have any serious deficits or limitations. By the same token he is unlikely to have much interest in the project of *reflecting* on his limitations and deficits, even though regarding oneself as intellectually superior to other people isn't strictly speaking incompatible with recognizing that one is not vice-free. A person with an intellectual superiority complex can acknowledge that he is far from perfect, but his cognitive imperfections are likely to strike him as less important and less worthy of serious critical reflection than would be the case if he didn't have the sense of himself as special.

The vices that are contrary to openness are closed-mindedness and dogmatism. The matters concerning which one is closed-minded might be different from those concerning which one has an open mind. However, one's mind can't be both open and closed in relation to one and the same topic. A closed-minded person is unlikely to be open-minded in relation to evidence of their closed-mindedness if their starting point is that they are not closed-minded. This is a reflection of the fact that closed-mindedness is a matter of being reluctant to consider novel information and change one's mind once a given conception has been adopted. If one regards oneself as epistemically virtuous, and one's commitment to this self-conception can't be shaken by compelling evidence to the contrary, then one is to that extent also dogmatic. One has an irrational commitment to a particular view of oneself and this is incompatible with the openness that is needed for active critical reflection on one's epistemic vices.

If active critical reflection depends on humility and openness, and the contrary vices are arrogance and closed-mindedness, then it follows that people who have these vices are in a particularly bad position to know by active critical reflection that they are arrogant and closed-minded. This is the vice epistemological equivalent of the Dunning-Kruger effect. An amusing illustration of how arrogance can be a barrier to its own discovery is a remark attributed to former White House chief of staff John Sununu. He is quoted as once saying, 'People say I'm arrogant, but I know better'.[12] Sununu was chief of staff to President George H. W. Bush from 1989 to 1991. He had a high opinion of himself and a correspondingly low opinion of others. The *Washington Post* ran a piece entitled 'Sununu's Arrogance', which described him as an 'arrogant fellow' who seemed to think that 'everyone else is a bit slow'.[13] Tiberius and Walker note that Sununu betrayed his arrogance as he denied it, and point to the way that arrogance can function as a barrier to the arrogant person's acquiring information from others.[14] What is equally striking is how one's arrogance can block awareness of itself. Sununu's arrogance made him inattentive to his own epistemic vices and apparently disinclined to engage in intellectual self-criticism. Since arrogance was one of the epistemic vices to which his arrogance made him inattentive, it stymied its own discovery by means of active critical reflection.

Closed-mindedness is, if anything, even stealthier than arrogance. There are some people who admit to being arrogant and even regard their arrogance as a virtue, but few of us are happy to admit to being closed-minded. As mentioned in Chapter 2, there are thinkers who make the case for closed-mindedness as the best protection against being led astray by what they see as harmful or misguided notions.[15] Such thinkers are in a small minority. Most of us see open-mindedness as an intellectual virtue and like to think of ourselves as open-minded.

[12] In Tiberius and Walker 1998.   [13] Cohen 1991.
[14] Tiberius and Walker 1998: 382.   [15] Sayyid Qutb is one such thinker.

For many closed-minded individuals it is their closed-mindedness that ensures ignorance of their closed-mindedness by obstructing active critical reflection and causing them to dismiss or ignore evidence of their closed-mindedness. There is nothing like being closed-minded to prevent one from realizing that one is closed-minded and there are few epistemic vices that are as antithetical to critical reflection.

What would be an example of an epistemic vice that isn't stealthy, or is at least less stealthy than closed-mindedness and arrogance? Consider the vice of intellectual carelessness, that is, the disposition to take insufficient care in one's reasoning or inquiries. A person can have evidence of his carelessness in this sense, reflect on this evidence, and conclude that he is intellectually careless. Being intellectually careless needn't prevent him from acknowledging and reflecting on evidence of his intellectual carelessness or concluding that he is indeed intellectually careless. In the same way, he might conclude from the fact that he has been taken in by conmen that he must be gullible. He might be reluctant to draw these unflattering conclusions out of a general desire to think well of himself, but being careless is not *in itself* a significant obstacle to recognizing that one is careless in the way that being closed-minded is *in itself* a significant obstacle to recognizing that one is closed-minded. Carelessness and gullibility do get in the way of knowledge—otherwise they wouldn't qualify as epistemic vices—however, they aren't specifically obstacles to their *own* detection. Another relatively non-stealthy vice is prejudice in the psychological sense.[16] This has been defined as 'an attitude that encompasses dislike, disrespect, and even hatred' (Banaji and Greenwald 2016: 47). The fact that one is prejudiced needn't stop one recognizing that one is prejudiced.[17] If people with strong prejudices fail to recognize that fact, or are reluctant to engage in active critical reflection on their prejudices, it needn't be their prejudices that are the obstacle to their own recognition. The obstacle to self-knowledge in this case is that prejudice is associated with other epistemic vices, such as

---

[16] According to a report in the *Independent*, around a quarter of British people polled in 2015 were prepared to describe themselves as 'slightly racially prejudiced'. In philosophy and psychology much has been written about implicit biases or prejudices but in the population at large prejudice is all too explicit. See http://www.independent.co.uk/news/uk/politics/half-of-ukip-voters-say-they-are-prejudiced-against-people-of-other-races-10062731.html.

[17] Unless the prejudice is against the idea that one is prejudiced.

closed-mindedness, that hamper active critical reflection, including reflection on one's own prejudices.

On this account the difference between comparatively stealthy and non-stealthy vices isn't primarily a difference in consciousness. What places carelessness at the less stealthy end of the spectrum and closed-mindedness at the stealthier end isn't that carelessness is conscious in a way that closed-mindedness is not. This is one respect in which stealthy vices are different from the implicit biases described by psychologists.[18] These have been described as 'hidden' in the same sense that uncon-scious mental processes are hidden.[19] An example of such a bias is a strong automatic preference for one racial group over another. Implicit biases are akin to stealthy vices in being hard to detect but what makes them hard to detect—the fact that they are unconscious—is not what makes stealthy vices hard to detect. Closed-mindedness is hard to detect not because it is unconscious but because it obstructs critical reflection. It is the cognitive role of closed-mindedness as a barrier to critical reflec-tion that accounts for its stealthiness.

Part of the problem with interpreting the stealthy/non-stealthy dis-tinction as the same as the unconscious/conscious distinction is that there are epistemic vices to which the latter distinction has no applica-tion. For example, intellectual carelessness is neither conscious nor unconscious. When a state is conscious there is something that it's like to be in that state. There is nothing that it's like to be careless but this doesn't make carelessness unconscious. Understood as a character trait, carelessness is the wrong kind of thing to be conscious or unconscious. The same goes for other character vices. For example, it makes no more sense to ask whether a person's closed-mindedness is conscious than to ask whether their courage is conscious. Attitude vices are more of a mixed bag. While it might be legitimate to ask whether an attitude such as prejudice is conscious, it's not clear what it would be for a person's epistemic insouciance to be conscious, unless this is just a way of describing it as intentional. While the stealthiness of some attitude vices might be explained by reference to their being unconscious, this isn't true of all attitude vices, let alone all epistemic vices.

[18] For a philosophical perspective see the essays in Brownstein and Saul 2016. They define implicit biases as 'largely outside of conscious awareness and control' (2016: 7).
[19] See Banaji and Greenwald 2016.

The next question concerns the prospects of overcoming the obstacles to knowledge of one's own vices. How, if at all, can we come to know our own stealthy vices? As I have noted, active critical reflection isn't the only source of self-knowledge, so the fact that a given vice obstructs such reflection doesn't entail that it is undetectable by the person whose vice it is. Another source of self-knowledge is testimony. For example, whether or not one is disposed to engage in active critical reflection, it is possible to discover that one has a vice V by being told that one has that vice. One doesn't always believe what one is told but suppose that one is told that one has V by someone very close, such as a spouse, or by a friend for whom one has great respect. This is a way for one to come to know that one has V without the effort of active critical reflection on whether one has V.

In reality, the testimonial route to self-knowledge is far less straightforward than this suggests. Wilson and Dunn note that:

> Rather than taking an objective look at how other people view them and noticing the fact that this view might differ from their own, people often assume that other people see them the way they see themselves. Deciphering others' views may also be difficult because people often try to hide their negative assessments, out of politeness or a desire not to hurt someone's feelings. Finally, as with any theory, there is a confirmation bias with self-views, whereby people are more likely to notice and recall instances in which other people seem to share their views than instances in which they do not.   (2004: 508)

If I am closed-minded, the mere fact that someone I trust tells me I am closed-minded may not result in my realizing that I am closed-minded even if my informant is in a position to know. If their words are open to interpretation then I may seize on a more favourable interpretation of what they say. Even if they tell me outright 'You are closed-minded', I might assume that they don't really mean it or focus instead on the more favourable opinions of others. If I am closed-minded then that very fact might make me unwilling to listen even when a close and trusted friend tells me I am closed-minded. Like John Sununu I might think, 'She thinks I'm closed-minded but I know better'. Closed-mindedness can prevent one from gaining self-knowledge by testimony as effectively as it can stymie the acquisition of self-knowledge by active critical reflection.

There are two ways of understanding this. On one interpretation, self-knowledge by testimony involves active critical reflection in such a way that obstacles to the latter are also obstacles to the former. On another interpretation, active reflection and testimony are independent sources of self-knowledge and the fact that closed-mindedness gets in the way of self-knowledge by testimony has an independent explanation. Why should anyone think that self-knowledge by testimony involves active critical reflection? A natural thought is that when one is told something by another person one has to work out whether to believe them. Relevant questions include 'Are they trustworthy?', 'Are they likely to know what they are talking about in this case?', 'Does what they are telling me fly in the face of other things that I already know?', and so on. Only if these and other questions have satisfactory answers do I take their word for it. The thought is not that I explicitly go through a reasoning process when deciding whether to believe another person when they tell me something but that reasoning and inference are implicitly involved.[20] These forms of reasoning are themselves forms of critical reflection, including critical reflection on the credentials of one's informant, and it is because of this that obstacles to active critical reflection are also obstacles to testimonial knowledge. The closed-minded person who concludes that he knows better than his informant whether he is closed-minded has effectively engaged in such reflection. It is the impact of his closed-mindedness on his reflection on how much his informant is likely to know that leads him to conclude that he isn't closed-minded.

This picture of testimonial knowledge can be criticized for overintel-lectualizing the phenomenon and making it sound much more active than it really is. On a different picture, knowledge by testimony is non-inferential and in this sense direct. It is not the result of any reasoning process, and assumptions about the trustworthiness of informants don't figure as premises in explicit or even implicit inferences. However, this doesn't make testimonial knowledge undiscriminating. Fricker notes that a hearer gains knowledge by testimony in virtue of exercising what she calls 'doxastic responsibility'. A hearer can be doxastically responsible, but without making any inferences, by exercising 'a rational sensitivity such that [she] may critically filter what she is told without any active reflection or inference of any kind' (2007: 69). The proposal is that 'where the hearer gives a suitably critical reception to the interlocutor's

---

[20] On this account, 'all knowledge by testimony is indirect or inferential. We know that *p* when reliably told that *p* because we make some inference about the reliability and sincerity of the witness' (Coady 1992: 122–3).

word without making any inference, she does so in virtue of the perceptual deliverances of a well-trained *testimonial sensibility*' (2007: 71). So, for example, one might hear one's interlocutor as more or less credible, and believe or disbelieve them depending on one's perception of them.

On this account, testimonial knowledge isn't the product of active reflection but can nevertheless be obstructed by some of the same epistemic vices that obstruct active reflection. In *To Kill a Mockingbird* the jury's prejudiced perception of Tom Robinson as unreliable causes them to disbelieve his testimony.[21] Similarly, vices like dogmatism, gullibility, and closed-mindedness can distort one's testimonial sensibility in ways that damage or distort its capacity to filter the testimony of others. When a closed-minded person is told by someone who knows him well that he is closed-minded, his closed-mindedness might make it difficult if not impossible for him to perceive his interlocutor as a reliable informant on the topic. In this way, closed-mindedness can prevent its unmasking by testimony just as it can prevent its unmasking by active critical reflection. Yet there is no suggestion here that testimony requires active reflection by the hearer.

All of this begs an obvious question: if stealthy vices are so effective at blocking their detection, whether by active reflection or other means, how can one know one's own stealthy vices? Before tackling this question head on, it's worth pausing briefly to look at Kruger and Dunning's account of how it is possible to improve the metacognitive skills of incompetent individuals. It's one thing to say that incompetent individuals lack the metacognitive skills that enable them to tell how poorly they are performing and another to claim that they lack metacognitive skills *because* of their incompetence. The test of causality is whether manipulating competence improves metacognitive skills and the accuracy of self-appraisals. One of Kruger and Dunning's studies established that this is indeed the case. The training of incompetent individuals improved both their levels of competence and their metacognitive skills.

Yet there is something paradoxical about the suggestion that incompetent individuals can be enabled to recognize their incompetence by improving their competence.[22] Once they are no longer incompetent

---

[21] See the account of Harper Lee's novel in Fricker 2007: 23–9.
[22] 'If instead it takes competence to recognize competence, then manipulating competence ought to enable the incompetent to recognize that they have performed poorly.

they are no longer in a position to know they are incompetent. They can't know what is not true. The most that the exercise of their improved metacognitive skills can tell them is that they *were* incompetent. If they are now competent enough to know their level of competence then they will now know that they are in fact competent—at least competent enough to know that they are competent. The question this doesn't address is: how can the incompetent know that they are incompetent while they are still incompetent, prior to any attempt to make them more competent? How is *this* self-knowledge possible in domains where the Kruger-Dunning effect has made its presence felt?

There is a parallel dialectic in the case of stealthy vices. Suppose that what stops an intellectually arrogant person from recognizing his intellectual arrogance is his intellectual arrogance. If it is feasible to send such a person on humility training, and this training works, then they will come back not intellectually arrogant and more inclined to engage in active critical reflection and self-criticism. But when they engage in critical reflection and self-criticism will they discover that they are intellectually arrogant? Presumably not, since *ex hypothesi* they no longer have this vice. They might come to see that they were arrogant prior to their humility training but this doesn't explain how a person can come to know, via active critical reflection, testimony, or some other means, that he is intellectually arrogant while he still is. What is missing is an account of what one might call *present tense* or *here-and-now* vice knowledge as distinct from *past tense* vice knowledge. What is needed for knowledge of one's current stealthy vices is something that is forceful enough to break through the veils of self-ignorance they weave and reveal one's current vices in a compelling way.

What might this 'something' be? Among all the possible answers to this question the one I want to focus on for the rest of this chapter is a kind of *experience*. Instead of thinking of knowledge of one's hitherto stealthy vices as resulting from active critical reflection one might think of it as resulting from traumatic experiences. A traumatic experience is typically 'a sudden, unexpected, and potentially painful event' that 'ruptures part of our way of being or deeply held understanding of the world'

Of course there is a paradox to this assertion. It suggests that the way to make incompetent individuals recognize their own incompetence is to make them competent' (Kruger and Dunning 1999: 1128).

(Rushmer and Davies 2004: ii14). Since traumatic experiences are unplanned and uncontrolled the resulting self-knowledge is accidental, unlike the self-knowledge (if any) that results from active critical reflection. One can undertake to look into one's epistemic vices by engaging in active critical reflection but not by arranging to have a traumatic experience. Traumatic experiences can be *breakthrough* experiences: in the right circumstances they can be sufficiently forceful and revelatory to break through veils of self-ignorance and bring one's stealthy vices to light. By delivering a shock to the system they can overturn or radically alter one's understanding of one's intellectual character. What is more, the way that traumatic experiences can be revelatory looks rather different from the way that active critical reflection can be revelatory, though it remains to be seen precisely to what extent these two potential sources of self-knowledge are genuinely independent.

Here are some examples of the epistemological payoff of some traumatic experiences. A gullible person who loses a fortune as a direct result of his gullibility might come to see for the first time how gullible he is. His experience of losing a fortune, like Gerd Heidemann's experience of losing his reputation and his career, is so shocking and tough to come to terms with that he sees himself in a new light. As a result of his experience he learns something about himself. Next, imagine the shock that Zeira must have felt the day that, contrary to his closed-minded insistence that such a thing would never happen, Egypt and Syria attacked Israel in 1973. It isn't at all hard to imagine a person being traumatized by such a catastrophic demonstration of his own error and, as a result, coming to see something about himself he would otherwise never have seen: his own closed-mindedness. To be clear, the claim is not that traumatic experiences always result in self-knowledge.[23] Some people never learn from their mistakes. Traumatic experiences can be eye openers but there is no guarantee that they will be. A third example of an eye-opening traumatic experience is suggested by the literature on physician overconfidence: imagine an overconfident physician whose

[23] It is an empirical question to what extent traumatic experiences result in self-insight. There is some empirical evidence that they do. See the account in Tedeschi and Calhoun 2004 of 'posttraumatic growth', that is, 'positive psychological change experienced as a result of the struggle with highly challenging life circumstances' (2004: 1). Jayawickreme and Blackie 2014 is a useful survey of the literature on this topic. Thanks to an anonymous referee for drawing my attention to this area of psychological research.

overconfidence and arrogance cause him to make a fatal mistake.[24] Perhaps he fails to request the recommended diagnostic tests in a given case because he is confident—far too confident—that he already knows the answer. When it emerges that he didn't know the answer and should have asked for additional tests he may acknowledge his own overconfidence and arrogance and recognize that these epistemic vices were what led to disaster. Some of these examples (the second and third) are not just examples of epistemic vices being revealed to their subject by a traumatic experience. They are examples of *stealthy* epistemic vices coming to light as a result of a traumatic experience.

Talk of *seeing* oneself in a new light in these cases is appropriate because what the traumatic experience produces is a certain kind of insight. Having things go badly wrong as a result of one's epistemic failings can open one's eyes to those failings and thereby alter one's self-conception. In making sense of this phenomenon it is helpful to think in terms of three notions: *transformative experience, quantum change,* and *cataleptic impression.* Starting with the first of these notions, in her work on transformative experiences L. A. Paul distinguishes two kinds of transformative experience. Some are personally transformative while others are epistemically transformative.[25] When Mary, who has only ever lived in a monochrome room, sees colours for the first time, she learns what it is like to see colour. Her experience teaches her something that she could not have come to know without having that experience and this is what makes it epistemically transformative. Personally transformative experiences are ones that change who you are. Examples include having a traumatic accident, experiencing a horrific physical attack, undergoing a religious conversion, and having a child.[26] A personally transformative experience 'can be life-changing in that it changes what it is like for you to be you' (Paul 2014: 16). 'Transformative experiences' without qualification are both personally and epistemically transformative. An obvious question now is: are the traumatic experiences I've described 'transformative' in anything like Paul's sense?

When traumatic experiences cause people to recognize their own epistemic vices there is a point to calling these experiences epistemically

---

[24] There is an extensive literature on overconfidence as a cause of diagnostic error in medicine. See, for example, Berner and Graber 2008 and Cassam 2017.

[25] Paul 2014: 17.   [26] Paul 2014: 16.

transformative, though not exactly in Paul's sense. What the doctor whose arrogance results in the avoidable and unexpected death of a patient learns is not, or not just, what a certain *experience* is like but what *he himself* is like.[27] Perhaps it is an exaggeration to say that what he learns from his experience couldn't have been learned without the experience. However, it might be right to say that the traumatic experience opens his eyes to certain truths about himself that he would otherwise have had, and did have, difficulty seeing. The experience is also personally transformative, but it changes the doctor by changing how he perceives himself and thereby changing what he knows or believes about himself.

When a traumatic or other experience opens one's eyes to one's hitherto concealed or invisible vices it is tempting to think in terms of an epiphany or sudden insight. Epiphanies or sudden insights are forms of what William Miller and Janet C'de Baca (2001) refer to as quantum changes, that is, vivid, surprising, benevolent, and enduring personal transformations that can occur with or without any salient external event.[28] Scrooge undergoes a quantum change in *A Christmas Carol* and there are many real-life examples of quantum change. Sudden insights are a type of quantum change that are 'different from ordinary reasoning processes, from "coming to the conclusion that" or deciding' (2001: 19). They involve a 'breakthrough realization' or 'change in the personal sense of self' (2001: 39). Epiphanies are another type of quantum change. They are mystical transformations that are experienced as 'quite out of the ordinary, qualitatively different from insightful turning points' (2001: 20). There is more a sense with this type of change of being acted on by a powerful external force, but what the two types of quantum change have in common is the experience of receiving new knowledge. This knowledge is often 'knowledge about oneself' and is accompanied by 'an immediate certainty of its veracity' (2001: 43).

The sudden change in one's self-conception that results from a traumatic experience is more plausibly thought of an insightful rather than a mystical quantum change. However, quantum changes as Miller and de Baca define them have some features that distinguish them from traumatic experiences such as causing the death of a patient. Quantum

---

[27] John Campbell 2015 is critical of Paul for her focus on subjective experience.
[28] Thanks to Susanna Rinard for putting me onto Miller and de Baca's work.

changes are 'not comprehensible as ordinary responses to life event' (2001: 5), but the alteration in the doctor's self-conception following the avoidable and unexpected death of a patient is an ordinary response to a life event. Nor is it necessarily the case that, like genuine quantum changes, the change in the doctor's self-conception is a 'one way door through which there is no going back' (2001: 5). As the memory of the mistake fades the doctor may revert to type and behave as he always behaved before things went wrong. But if the change is deep and long-lasting, and takes the form of a sudden flash of insight, it is like a quantum change. Sometimes self-knowledge is the product of reflection, but traumatic experiences can produce self-knowledge in a way that leaves no room for doubt as to their veracity.

Suppose that the insights that result from traumatic experiences are described as *transformational insights*. These can be insights into the self or other matters but the present concern is with self-directed transformational insights. The trauma-induced realization that one is, or has been, arrogant or closed-minded is a self-directed transformational insight, and what this insight can produce is knowledge of one's stealthy vices. What makes the realization *transformational* is that it radically alters one's self-conception. What makes it an *insight* is that it is a kind of seeing. It's one thing to reason that one has been arrogant or closed-minded and another thing to see these truths about oneself with a flash of insight. The latter produces knowledge that is direct and non-inferential. Transformational insights are instantaneous in a way that reasoning is not. Like insightful quantum changes, they 'center on a grand "aha", an awareness that breaks on the shores of consciousness with tremendous force' (Miller and de Baca 2001: 45). They are, in this sense, breakthrough experiences.

Understood in this way, transformational insights have certain features of so-called 'cataleptic impressions'. As characterized by Martha Nussbaum, these are impressions which, 'by their own experienced quality, certify their own veracity' (1990: 265). By assenting to a cataleptic impression we get ourselves into 'a condition of certainty and confidence from which nothing can dislodge us' (1990: 265). Nussbaum's example of a cateleptic impression is the anguish that, in Proust's novel, reveals to Marcel that he loves Albertine. Because Marcel can neither control nor predict his anguish on hearing that Albertine has left he can conclude that it is an authentic form of emotional knowing. Marcel discovers his true feelings for Albertine by feeling rather than by using his intellect, and this is an obvious point of contact with the traumatic experiences I have been discussing. The anguish caused by traumatic experiences might be regarded as cataleptic and as a kind of emotional knowing.[29] It is not knowledge *of* one's emotions but knowledge *by means of* one's emotions of one's stealthy epistemic vices. Trauma-induced anguish is able to break through the veils of self-ignorance that would otherwise keep one's stealthy vices hidden.

How does this kind of self-knowledge differ from self-knowledge by active critical reflection? Critical reflection involves the use of the intellect in a way that breakthrough experiences do not. Since self-knowledge by critical reflection is *intellectual* self-knowledge it can't fail to be affected to a greater or lesser extent by the very intellectual vices it is trying to uncover, and this is the basis of the Dunning-Kruger effect. This is also a Proustian point. For Proust there is always the danger that what critical reflection produces is not self-knowledge but 'self-deceptive rationalization' (Nussbaum 1990: 264). The more spontaneously emotional one's self-knowledge, the lower the risk of self-deception. As long as transformational insights are not the product of one's intellect there is little danger of their being distorted by one's stealthy vices. The self-knowledge they give us is here-and-now self-knowledge, since traumatic experiences can open one's eyes to one's current epistemic vices and not just vices one has already had to overcome in order to uncover them retrospectively. Being incompetent or closed-minded is not an obstacle to finding out that one is incompetent or closed-minded *if* the finding out is not an act of self-interpretation.

The problem with all this is that it exaggerates the extent to which self-knowledge by transformational insight can really circumvent our dependence on critical reflection for self-knowledge.[30] The worry is that not even breakthrough experiences can avoid some degree of dependence on the intellect and therefore some degree of vulnerability to one's epistemic vices if they are to tell us anything about ourselves. For example, in the case of the doctor whose overconfidence leads to the

---

[29] 'Emotional knowing' is from Nussbaum 1990: 269.

[30] Knowledge of one's own epistemic vices is a form of what, in previous work, I have called 'substantial self-knowledge' (Cassam 2014, chapter 3). For a defence of the view that substantial self-knowledge is inferential see Cassam 2014, chapter 11.

death of a patient it isn't the doctor's traumatic experience that is revelatory. It would be possible for him to be traumatized but not see that the death has anything to do with his epistemic vices. What counts is how the doctor *reflects* on his experience, what he makes of it, but won't this create an opening for his epistemic vices to kick in again and obstruct their discovery? Isn't reflecting on one's experience just the kind of active critical reflection which the insight model was trying to avoid? Impressions require interpretation, and interpreting one's impressions or traumatic experiences is the work of the intellect.[31] So it seems there is no getting away from the potential impact of stealthy vices; they *can* get in the way of self-knowledge by traumatic experience, by causing us to misinterpret these experiences or misunderstand their significance.

This leaves it open, however, whether self-knowledge by transformational insight is *as* vulnerable to the impact of epistemic vices as self-knowledge by active critical reflection. There are two extremes between which there is a plausible middle way. At one extreme is the idea that traumatic experiences or other transformational insights are capable of providing us with knowledge of our own epistemic vices without any dependence on the intellect or any risk of distortion or deception by those vices. At the opposite extreme is the notion that self-knowledge by transformational insight is as vulnerable to the impact of epistemic vices as self-knowledge by critical reflection because transformational insights are always a matter of interpretation. The middle way is to accept that while it is possible for our epistemic vices to distort our supposed transformational insights into our own failings they are less likely to obstruct self-knowledge by transformational insight than self-knowledge by active critical reflection. The directness and instantaneous nature of transformational insights means that there is less scope—but not no scope—for distortion and misinterpretation. Sometimes the message of a traumatic experience about one's own failings is so loud and clear, so lacking in ambiguity, that one can hardly fail to hear it. Of course some people are so well defended and so impervious to bad news about themselves—Trump might be an example of this—that literally nothing can break through, but this is not the norm.

---

[31] See Nussbaum 1990: 270. According to Nussbaum, Proust concedes in a limited way that Marcel was too hasty in dismissing intellect and its scrutiny from the enterprise of self-knowing.

Insofar as traumatic experiences are a potential source of self-knowledge, do they leave the epistemic vices they reveal intact? Suppose that a notably closed-minded person has a traumatic experience which causes him to realize for the first time how closed-minded he is. One might argue that simply in virtue of this realization he is now less closed-minded than he was before. If this is right then the traumatic experience that brings his closed-mindedness to light also changes his intellectual character. This is different from Dunning-Kruger's account of self-knowledge. It isn't that one already has to have overcome one's closed-mindedness, at least to some extent, to have any chance of discovering it. It is rather that the discovery of the vice itself constitutes a change in outlook. But there are limits to how far this line can go. For one thing, while the realization that one is closed-minded might be regarded as a form of open-mindedness, there are many other subjects in relation to which the person in question might remain closed-minded. In any case, it isn't true in general that recognizing that one has a particular vice is a way of no longer having it. One can recognize that one is cruel and still be cruel. In the same way, one can recognize that one is arrogant and still be arrogant. In these cases, self-knowledge is no guarantee of self-improvement.

The remaining question for this chapter can be dealt with more briefly. The question is whether the stealthiness of an epistemic vice diminishes our responsibility for it. I made the point in Chapter 6 that self-ignorance can diminish a person's responsibility and culpability for their epistemic vices if their ignorance isn't itself culpable. For one's self-ignorance to be culpable one must be responsible for it and this creates a special problem in the case of stealthy vices. If it is the nature of a vice V to obstruct its detection, and one's failure to realize that one has V is due to the stealthiness of V, in what sense can one be responsible for one's self-ignorance? To put the same question more simply, how can self-ignorance in the case of stealthy vices be culpable? To make this question more concrete consider Trump again. Is he responsible for his epistemic incompetence? Not if he literally has no idea that he is epistemically incompetent and his ignorance is non-culpable. But is his ignorance non-culpable if it is his epistemic incompetence that is preventing him from realizing he is epistemically incompetent? Only if the epistemic incompetence that is preventing him from knowing he is epistemically incompetent is non-culpable, but the epistemic incompetence that prevents him from knowing he is epistemically incompetent is the epistemic incompetence whose culpability was at issue in the first place. So it seems that we have made no progress and the question whether Trump's epistemic incompetence is culpable remains unanswered.

In practice, there is little temptation to regard Trump's epistemic incompetence as excusable, and this is a reflection of the fact that a person's ignorance of his vices is seen as culpable if his ignorance is caused by his vices. For example, it can happen that a person's cruelty is so pernicious that it prevents him from realizing that he is cruel. Instead he sees his conduct as normal. Few would be tempted to regard the cruel person's ignorance of his own cruelty as non-culpable on the grounds that it is the result of his cruelty. If the only thing preventing one from knowing one's vices is those very vices then one's ignorance is culpable. It is on this basis that Trump's ignorance of his epistemic incompetence can still be deemed culpable. It is no excuse that he is so incompetent that he can't get the measure of his incompetence. That only makes it worse.

8

Self-Improvement

In June 1994 Anthony Greenwald, a University of Washington psychology professor, wrote the first computer program for what came to be known as the Implicit Association Test (IAT).[1] As described by Greenwald and his colleague Mahzarin Banaji in their bestseller *Blindspot* the basic idea was simple but ingenious. In one version of the test—the flower-insect IAT—subjects are presented with four sets of words, flower names (orchid, daffodil), insect names (flea, wasp), pleasant-meaning words (gentle, heaven), and unpleasant-meaning words (damage, poison). What the test confirmed is that, for most of us, it's easiest to connect insect names with unpleasant words and flower names with pleasant words. Linking insect names with pleasant words or flower names with unpleasant words is harder and slower. The reason, Greenwald assumed, is that insect names and unpleasant words share a negative valence whereas flower names and pleasant words share a positive valence. A shared valence is a mental association. Flower names and pleasant words are mentally associated in the sense that they share the more abstract quality of positive valence.[2] The associations that link things to valences are *attitudes* in the psychological sense so the IAT can be interpreted as capturing subjects' attitudes towards flowers and insects by comparing the speed of completing different sorting tasks.[3]

The association between flower names and pleasant-meaning words is not much of a surprise, but things became much more interesting when Greenwald and his colleagues came up with the idea of a Race

---

[1] See the account in Banaji and Greenwald 2016: 40. An online version of the test is available here: https://implicit.harvard.edu/implicit/takeatest.html.

[2] Banaji and Greenwald 2016: 40.

[3] As Banaji and Greenwald put it, the IAT captures attitudes towards flowers and insects 'by comparing the speeds of completing two different sorting tasks' (2016: 41).

IAT. To his own disappointment Greenwald discovered that he was faster at sorting names of famous white people with pleasant words than at sorting names of famous black people with pleasant words. This was so even though he had no conscious or explicit preference for whites over blacks. Yet it was as hard for him to link names of black people and pleasant words as it had been for him to link insect names and pleasant words. He couldn't avoid concluding that he had a 'strong automatic racial preference for White relative to Black' (2016: 45). Such preferences are implicit biases or, as they are sometimes called, implicit attitudes.[4] The possibility that the Race IAT brings to light, and that was illustrated by Greenwald himself, is that people's implicit attitudes can be in conflict with their explicit attitudes.

Banaji and Greenwald describe implicit biases as 'mindbugs', that is, 'ingrained habits of thought that lead to errors in how we perceive, remember, reason, and make decisions' (2016: 4).[5] Habits of thought that do that must be epistemically harmful and much has been written about the epistemic costs of implicit bias, including what Tamar Gendler describes as its tendency to 'interfere with knowledge' (2011: 49). A vivid example of the epistemic and other harms caused by implicit racial bias is provided by Keith Payne in his work on what he calls 'weapon bias'.[6] He developed a laboratory task in which participants made visual discriminations between guns and harmless objects. A human face flashed just before each object appeared. In one version of the test, participants who were shown a harmless object (a hand tool) 'falsely claimed to see a gun more often when the face was black than when it was white. Under the pressure of a split-second decision, the readiness to see a weapon became an actual false claim of seeing a weapon' (2006: 287–8). It was race that

---

[4] The existence of implicit bias and the validity of the IAT have recently been called into question, partly in response to the so-called 'replication crisis' in social psychology. I'm not going to get into this here. If implicit biases don't exist then they can be crossed off the list of human epistemic vices that need to be tackled. For what it's worth, I'm sceptical about blanket scepticism about implicit bias. However, the seriousness of recent challenges to this notion does need to be acknowledged. See Payne et al. 2018.

[5] Banaji and Greenwald are reluctant to describe the implicit biases measured by the IAT as 'prejudices' in the ordinary sense since 'the Race IAT has little in common with measures of prejudice that involve open expressions of hostility, dislike, and disrespect' (2016: 52). Having said that, the Race IAT does predict racially discriminatory behaviour, and Banaji and Greenwald are prepared to say that the Race IAT measures 'implicit prejudice'. See 2016: 46.

[6] Payne 2006.

shaped people's mistakes, and Payne found that African American participants were as prone to weapon bias as white participants. Payne's work is a compelling illustration of how implicit bias can lead to errors in perception. By causing errors in perception weapon bias gets in the way of perceptual knowledge, and the practical consequences hardly need spelling out. In the US innocent African American men are shot with alarming frequency by police officers who think they see a gun when no gun is present. If weapon bias is an epistemic vice then here is proof that some epistemic vices are quite literally a matter of life and death.

Are implicit biases like the weapon bias epistemic vices, given my characterization of epistemic vices as blameworthy or otherwise reprehensible character traits, attitudes, or ways of thinking that are epistemically harmful? Implicit biases are attitudes and many of them are epistemically harmful. They are blameworthy only if we are revision responsible for them, and we are revision responsible for them only if we have control over them. The control that matters is the ability to weaken or even get rid of them. Self-improvement is the key; the idea that we are revision responsible for our implicit biases and other epistemic vices is tied to the idea that self-improvement in respect of them is possible. Indeed, if implicit biases can result in the shooting of innocents then we should be interested in the prospects of self-improvement quite apart from a concern with whether implicit biases are epistemic vices.

Optimism is the view that self-improvement is possible, and that there is often (though not always) something we can do about our epistemic vices, including many of our implicit biases. Optimists argue that epistemic vices are malleable and that vice reduction is an active, goal-directed process by means of which we can take control of our epistemic vices and reshape or regulate them.[7] However, self-improvement is only possible if we are aware of our epistemic vices, are motivated to tackle them, and have the means to do so. The means by which implicit attitudes can be modified might be very different from the means by which other types of epistemic vice can be modified, so the challenge for optimists is to

---

[7] The reshaping of our epistemic vices means deploying the more general ability to reshape our mental lives. As Dorothea Debus notes, 'healthy, mature human beings are able to play an active part in how their own mental lives develop, and thus, healthy, mature human beings are able to shape their own mental lives' (2015/16: 4). When subjects regulate aspects of their mental lives, including their epistemic virtues and vices, they are 'actively involved with their own mental lives in a goal-directed way' (Debus 2015/16: 7).

identify a realistic and effective method of self-improvement for each type of epistemic vice. The main point, however, is that we aren't stuck with our epistemic vices, and this leaves it open that at least some of them are blameworthy.

Pessimism is much more sceptical about the prospects of self-improvement or, at any rate, of lasting self-improvement. Pessimists doubt whether our epistemic vices are malleable and whether, even if they are, we are ever in a position to take control of them and reshape or regulate them as optimists suppose. To be a pessimist is to question the extent to which our epistemic vices are blameworthy, though not necessarily to question the extent to which they are otherwise reprehensible. For pessimists, the focus of inquiry shouldn't be on overcoming our epistemic vices but on *outsmarting* them, that is, finding ways to work around them so as to reduce their ill effects.[8] For example, a very simple way to outsmart the gender or other biases of those responsible for grading examination papers is to insist that all papers are anonymized.

In these terms, Banaji and Greenwald are at the more pessimistic end of the spectrum as far as implicit bias is concerned. They regard mindbugs as 'dauntingly persistent' (2016: 152) and recommend a focus on outsmarting rather than eradication of mindbugs. Although there is evidence that hidden-bias mindbugs can be weakened by relatively minimal interventions, Banaji and Greenwald doubt that such interventions produce durable changes. In their view, the observed changes are likely to be *elastic*: 'like stretched rubber bands, the associations modified in these experiments likely soon return to their earlier configuration' (2016: 152). In contrast, Payne is more optimistic about the possibility of bias reduction at least in relation to weapon bias. He notes that firearms training can effectively reduce weapon bias but emphasizes that people can't will this bias away.[9] Getting rid of implicit bias requires the identification and effective implementation of specific bias-reduction *strategies*.[10]

Obstructivism isn't committed to optimism or pessimism about self-improvement and is compatible with both. Nevertheless, I want to

---

[8] On outsmarting see Banaji and Greenwald 2016, chapter 8. To outsmart a mindbug is to find a way to bypass it.

[9] Payne 2006: 290.

[10] Payne notes that 'although people cannot simply will the weapon bias away, certain specific strategies may be able to eliminate the automatic component of the bias' (Payne 2006: 290).

make the case for a qualified optimism. My claim isn't that lasting self-improvement is always possible but that it sometimes is. Some epistemic vices are resistant to self-improvement strategies but such strategies are sometimes available and effective. We may have to settle for outsmarting rather than eliminating some vices but pessimism about the prospects of vice reduction isn't always warranted. With many if not most epistemic vices there is the possibility of lasting change for the better. When it comes to attitude and thinking vices the notion that self-improvement is possible is easier to accept than in relation to character vices.[11] In non-epistemological contexts we tend to accept that attitude change is not only possible but also something that a person can sometimes bring about. When teachers warn delinquent pupils that they need to change their attitude towards studying if they want to pass their exams it does not seem that the pupils are being asked to do something that can't be done. In that case, why shouldn't it be possible for us to change our explicit and implicit epistemic attitudes? As for the possibility of changing one's thinking, it's worth noting that entire therapies such as cognitive behaviour therapy (CBT) are predicated on such a thing being possible.[12] In that case, why should it not be possible to change epistemically vicious ways of thinking? In contrast, one might think that there is something paradoxical about the idea that it is possible to change one's epistemic character for the better. In order for a closed-minded person to set about making himself more open-minded would he not already have to be open-minded to some degree? Isn't the implication that character vices such as closed-mindedness are not just *stealthy* but also *resistant*, that is, inherently hard to tackle?

All of this suggests a plan of action for this chapter. With respect to each of the three types of epistemic vice I have identified, there are three questions to consider:

1. To what extent is self-improvement possible?
2. To the extent that self-improvement is possible, what are the means by which it is possible?
3. What are the obstacles to self-improvement and how, if at all, can these obstacles be overcome?

---

[11] Intuitively, character vices are the most deeply entrenched.
[12] Edelman 2006 is a useful introduction to CBT.

The answer to the first of these questions depends on the malleability of different kinds of vice, that is, on the extent to which they can be actively eliminated or reconfigured. The second question is a practical one about self-improvement strategies or techniques. It isn't enough for a theory of epistemic vice to identify our vices, comment on their ill effects, and leave it at that. It should also try to explain what, if anything, we can *do* about our vices once their existence has been acknowledged. This means identifying potential obstacles to change and ways of overcoming these obstacles. Where there is no prospect of self-improvement a proper understanding of the extent to which resistant vices can be outsmarted becomes all the more important. However, I will leave discussion of outsmarting strategies until the end of the chapter. For if self-improvement is possible then outsmarting is unnecessary.

Part of what makes the first question hard to answer in relation to implicit attitudes is that psychologists who write on this issue are not in agreement. There are, however, some grounds for optimism. Implicit attitudes are sometimes represented as inflexible on the basis that they are automatic. In a review of the evidence, Irene Blair challenges the common assumption that such automatic processes can't be controlled. She makes what she describes as a 'strong case for the malleability of automatic stereotypes and prejudice in response to the perceiver's motives and strategies, and to variations in the situation' (2002: 257). Motivated individuals can modify the operation of negative stereotypes by employing specific strategies, including the suppression of stereotypes and promotion of counter-stereotypes.[13] She points to evidence that the formation of a specific implementation intention, such as the intention to ignore a person's race or gender, can help to suppress stereotypes.[14] There is also evidence that exposure to counter-stereotypic group members—for example, admired black Americans and disliked white Americans—can alter automatic race prejudice at least to some extent. It has even been suggested a person might rein in her implicit racial biases 'by putting up pictures of admired black celebrities around her office' (Holroyd and Kelly 2016: 121).

These modes of control over one's implicit biases are managerial rather than voluntary or evaluative. Putting up pictures of black celebrities

---

[13] Blair 2002: 248–50.   [14] See the references in Blair 2002: 248.

is a way of manipulating one's implicit attitudes, and there is nothing in the nature of implicit bias that makes them unmodifiable by self-manipulation. The effectiveness of improvement strategies designed to counter one's implicit biases improves with practice and 'any effective strategy takes time and motivation to implement' (Blair 2002: 249). It can also happen that suppression backfires and actually magnifies automatic stereotypes. In addition, as Banaji and Greenwald insist, positive changes may be short-lived. Still, there is no empirical justification for the view that it is impossible to improve one's implicit attitudes, or there is nothing that a person can do to change. Self-improvement in this area is possible and there are specific means by which it is possible, given the requisite level of awareness, motivation, and skill.

This points to some of the potential obstacles to self-improvement. Ignorance of one's implicit biases is one obvious obstacle to doing something about them, although, as obstacles go, it isn't an especially difficult one to overcome. There is, for example, always the option of sitting down at one's computer and taking the IAT. One will not take the test if one is not motivated to take it, and this is one way that lack of motivation can be an obstacle to self-improvement. Even after taking the test one might disbelieve the result. And even if one is motivated to take the test and believes the result one might lack the motivation to implement strategies to counter one's implicit bias. One might be too lazy or complacent to do so or indifferent to the fact that one is biased. These obstacles to self-improvement vary in respect of how easily they can be overcome and also in how well or badly they reflect on us. Ignorance of implicit bias can be an excuse for not doing anything to take remedial action but indifference is no excuse. Failure to tackle one's implicit biases is something for which one can be blamed or criticized, depending on how much one knows, or ought to know, about implicit bias.

What are the prospects of self-improvement in relation to affective postures and epistemic stances? Unlike implicit biases, stances are voluntarily adopted epistemic policies. Improving one's epistemic policies might seem a relatively straightforward matter. If a stance is something one can simply adopt or reject then it is something over which one has voluntary control.[15] In that case it might seem that all it takes to change is

---

[15] On the idea that stances are voluntary see Chapter 4 and Lipton 2004.

to decide to change. If the change is a change for the better then this is a case in which self-improvement is in one's own hands. For example, the shift from full-scale epistemic malevolence to epistemic benevolence is a change in epistemic policy that one can bring about by choosing to be benevolent rather than malevolent from now on. In reality, though, matters are more complicated. As noted in Chapter 4, stances are usually a reflection of what one believes, and this limits our voluntary control over them since we don't have voluntary control over our beliefs. If tobacco industry executives believed that the policy of spreading doubt about the dangers of smoking was the most effective way of achieving their overall objective of maximizing profits then abandoning this policy wasn't an option for them. It would only become an option if they became convinced that their stance was bad for business, or started to care more about the health of smokers than about their profits. Fortunately, such changes in priorities are possible. One can imagine a tobacco industry executive prioritizing health over profit in response to the discovery that a member of his own family has cancer as a result of smoking. Without some such trigger, there may be no self-induced change in epistemic policy. The lesson is that improvements in epistemic policy are usually mediated by other changes—changes in one's beliefs or priorities.

Since epistemic postures are involuntary there is no temptation to suppose that our control over them is voluntary. The involuntariness of postures like contempt is a reflection of the involuntariness of the judgements on which they are based and the feelings or emotions they embed. In the normal course of events one can't change one's judgements or emotions by fiat. In that case, how is self-improvement in respect of our epistemic postures so much as possible? What kind of control do we have over our postures and what can we do to change them? In many cases this question won't arise because we fail to recognize our own epistemic postures—as distinct from those of other people—as epistemically vicious. Take epistemic insouciance as an example. Imagine a politician who implements a policy that flies in the face of all the evidence and expert advice. As it turns out the experts were right and the policy leads to the economic disaster they predicted. One possibility is that the politician is none the wiser. He doesn't recognize his attitude for what it is and isn't motivated to change. He learns nothing about himself from the disaster and changes neither his epistemic attitude nor his conduct. But now consider a less likely but nevertheless possible outcome: the disaster proves to be a breakthrough experience for the politician. He now sees clearly that he shouldn't have been dismissive of expert advice and recognizes the need for a change in his attitude. What can he do to improve?

The first thing to say is that the recognition that he has a problem and needs to change his attitude is itself a change in attitude. The truly insouciant not only don't care about the facts or the evidence, they also don't care that they don't care. The point at which one starts to care about one's epistemic attitude is the point at which the process of altering one's attitude has begun. Further improvements can be brought about by changes in behaviour. It is tempting to think that one behaves differently because one's attitude has changed but there is also the possibility of changing one's attitude by changing one's behaviour. For example, the epistemically insouciant politician who was in the habit of making extravagant claims on the basis of flimsy evidence might refrain from doing so. He might refrain from deriding experts and undertake to treat both them and their claims with greater respect. By *showing* greater respect it is possible to become more respectful and less contemptuous. When that happens, a change in one's posture has resulted from a change in one's conduct.

Another mark of epistemic insouciance is the tendency to regard complex issues as much simpler than they really are. This attitude is often the result of relying on narrow or ill-informed sources for one's understanding of the issues. It's no surprise that people who don't read very much and rely on the television or social media to keep themselves informed often have little time for complexity or nuance. Fortunately, not reading widely is a problem with a simple solution: reading widely. As an aside, it is worth noting that among recent American presidents two—Clinton and Obama—were voracious readers whereas George W. Bush and Trump read very little.[16] Clinton and Obama were often criticized for being too cautious but it is possible to see their caution as a reflection of their appreciation of complexity. In contrast, more reading about Iraqi culture and history might have saved President Bush from the follies described in Chapter 1. When it comes to curing epistemic insouciance, immersing oneself in the work of experts can not only

---

[16] For an amusing description of the contrast between the reading habits of Clinton and Bush see Clarke 2004: 243.

improve the quality of one's knowledge but also open one's eyes more generally to the care and effort required to make sense of complex phenomena. A little reading can go a long way, though it is clearly not the case that being well read makes a person immune to epistemic insouciance. In the case of epistemically insouciant thinkers who can't be accused of not reading enough a different remedy will be required, perhaps one that targets their complacency or sense of superiority if these are the causes of their insouciance.

These examples of practical strategies for improving one's epistemic attitudes are for illustrative purposes only. Whether these strategies would actually work in practice is a further question, but the point here is that there seems no reason in principle why it shouldn't be possible by such means to change one's own attitudes. It isn't in the nature of epistemic or other attitudes to be unmodifiable. They can shift, sometimes through one's own efforts, and if attitudes generally are malleable then there are presumably means by which one can tackle one's epistemically vicious attitudes. The practical challenge is to identify realistic strategies for improving one's attitudes, and there is very little hope of meeting this challenge if one subscribes to the pessimistic view that one's attitudes are unchangeable. Pessimism about the prospects of self-improvement encourages a kind of fatalism about one's own attitudes, but most of us have had life experiences that have led us to modify our attitude about something or someone. Attitudes can be worked on, and epistemic attitudes are no different from other attitudes in this respect.

To what extent is self-improvement possible in respects of epistemically vicious ways of thinking? If one doesn't think well how can one improve one's thinking? The pessimistic view is that there is very little one can do fundamentally to change one's thinking. We are stuck with our individual thinking styles, and the thinking vices they exemplify. What, in that case, does the pessimist make of the existence of apparently effective therapies that are predicated on the possibility of changing one's thinking? Aside from raising questions about their effectiveness the other thing a pessimist might say is that the specific thinking flaws that are supposedly addressed by cognitive therapies aren't *epistemic* vices, and that the sense in which it is possible to change one's thinking is of little relevance to epistemology. To see that this is not so it might be helpful to look at an example of 'changing your thinking' from the cognitive therapy literature.

'Awfulizing' or 'catastrophic thinking' has been defined as the tendency to exaggerate the negative consequences of our life situations:

> We may awfulise about many different issues from minor hassles to more serious problems. Largely inconsequential events such as being kept waiting, having to spend time with someone we don't like, looking silly in front of others or forgetting an appointment can feel like a catastrophe when we perceive it that way. Even serious problems become more distressing than they need be when we dwell on their negative consequences.   (Edelman 2006: 24)[17]

Given that catastrophic thinking is a cause of psychological distress and depression, it's no surprise to find plenty of practical advice in the cognitive therapy and self-help literature on how to combat it.[18] The first step is to recognize one's catastrophic thinking by self-monitoring. However, mere awareness of awfulizing won't change anything. The next stage, therefore, is to dispute one's thinking with a view to decatastrophizing. This means asking oneself a series of simple questions designed to put things into perspective. Examples include: does this really matter? On an awfulness scale of 0 to 100 how bad is this? Will this matter in five years' time? Another form of disputing is behavioural, where the validity of our thinking is put to the test by changing one's behaviour and observing the consequences. There is evidence that practice with these and other such techniques can change how one thinks and reduce one's tendency to catastrophize.[19]

What does this brief excursion into the world of self-help have to do with the project of self-improvement in relation to epistemic vices? The answer is quite a bit. For a start, it's not obvious that catastrophic thinking shouldn't itself be classified as an epistemic vice, a way of thinking that systematically gets in the way of knowledge of one's actual situation or prospects. From a psychological point of view the point of decatastrophizing is to improve one's mental well-being. From an epistemological standpoint the point is to improve one's ability to gain and retain certain types of knowledge. These objectives are related to the extent that how one feels is determined in part by what one knows.

---

[17] Edelman notes that the term 'awfulising' (or 'awfulizing') was coined by Albert Ellis, one of the originators of CBT. Ellis' own preferred label for his approach was 'Rational Emotive Behavior Therapy'. For an overview see the essays in Ellis 2010.

[18] For example, Edelman 2006.

[19] The techniques summarized in this paragraph are described in chapter 3 of Edelman 2006.

Effective strategies for countering catastrophic thinking are also effective strategies for countering a particular form of vicious thinking, and the obvious question to ask is whether similar strategies might be effective in countering the more familiar varieties of vicious thinking described in previous chapters, including closed-minded thinking, wishful thinking, and conspiratorial thinking. To ask the same question in a different way, could there be a kind of cognitive therapy that targets ways of thinking that are epistemologically harmful?

It's hard to see why not. In Chapter 6, I gave the case of a person (me, as it happens) whose desire for a particular outcome to the 2016 Brexit vote and US presidential election led him to predict the results he wanted. Reconstructing my thought processes in retrospect it was perfectly clear that I had been guilty of wishful thinking. As a result I became much more inclined to monitor and dispute my thinking about subsequent political events. Having been burned once I took extra care not to allow myself to be misled again. Taking extra care meant asking myself a series of questions about my thinking about other matters. When, in the 2017 British general election, I came across a last-minute opinion poll that predicted the outcome I wanted, I was much more sceptical than I would have been without my heightened sensitivity to wishful thinking. I was inclined to dismiss the poll (even though it turned out to be correct). In the same way, a person who is motivated to kick his habit of conspiratorial thinking can learn to ask himself challenging questions about his conspiracy theories: is this really the best explanation of the event in question? How many people would need to have been involved in the conspiracy? What are the odds of there being no leaks in a conspiracy involving so many different actors? Clearly one isn't going to ask these questions if one isn't motivated to ask them, but the present question is not: what leads a person to *want* to change his thinking? The present question is: *given* that one is motivated to improve one's thinking, what can one do in practical terms to change it? The answer is not 'nothing'. When it comes to epistemically vicious thinking styles there is actually quite a lot one can do to combat them.

Obviously it's important not to be naïve about the prospects of self-improvement. It may well be the case that wishful thinking can't be eliminated but the issue is not whether it or other forms of vicious thinking can be eradicated. The issue is whether and to what extent they can be controlled and reduced. In Chapter 6 I noted that some kinds of vicious thinking are, or are grounded in, seemingly universal and hard-wired cognitive biases, but that doesn't make self-improvement impossible. Even hard-wired cognitive biases can be countered to some extent and there are many fields of inquiry in which the need to improve our thinking and combat our cognitive biases is indisputable. One field, which is relevant to the discussion in Chapters 1 and 2, is intelligence analysis. In a handbook for intelligence analysts Richards Heuer laments the fact that too little attention is devoted to 'improving how analysts think' (1999: 2), but this complaint is only legitimate if it is possible to improve how analysts think. Heuer thinks that it is, and his book is effectively a self-improvement manual for intelligence analysts. Analytic thinking 'can be taught, it can be learned, and it can improve with practice' (1999: 2). Being an effective analyst means knowing about cognitive bias and Heuer goes to a lot of trouble to instruct his readers in the intelligence community about this subject. In his view, there are tools and techniques that can be used to alleviate the weaknesses and biases inherent in human thinking, and the book is an overview of some of these tools and techniques. None of this proves that self-improvement in respect of thinking vices is possible, but if our thinking can't be improved that would make it one of the few things that humans do that they can't do better with practice and training. There is little justification for such pessimism.

It is in relation to character vices that pessimism comes into its own. It's one thing to accept that it is possible for us to improve our thinking and another to accept that there is any serious prospect of tackling our character vices. The issue has already come up a number of times in previous chapters. The view I've been defending is the reverse of Aristotle's view of moral character. For Aristotle moral character is voluntarily acquired through habitual action, but once character is formed it is fixed and far from malleable. I've been arguing that this is not a plausible account of *intellectual* character. It is rare for a person's intellectual character to be voluntarily acquired. Perhaps those who sign up for the Taliban knowing its reputation for intolerance and dogmatism can be said to have made themselves intolerant and dogmatic when they become intolerant and dogmatic. For the most part, though, our intellectual characters are the result of different influences over which we have little control. Upbringing, education, and culture all play a part. As people mature and their characters form they may *become* more closed-minded or dogmatic but, for the most part, they don't knowingly and actively *make themselves* closed-minded or dogmatic.

However one's intellectual character is acquired or comes to be, it isn't unalterable. It is worth noting, to begin with, that people do sometimes change. Just as they may become more or less outgoing or more or less conservative over the years, they may also become more or less closed-minded or more or less dogmatic. This hardly suggests that such traits are fixed and unalterable. However, it doesn't establish their malleability in the specific sense that I have in mind: it doesn't support the notion that character traits can be actively controlled and modified by the people whose traits they are. The evidence that character is malleable in this more demanding sense is that people do sometimes reform themselves. This example from Jonathan Jacobs makes the point:

Imagine someone with the habit of retailing gossip. This person is always keen to hear gossip and to transmit it, perhaps with embellishment and distortion. For one or another reason (perhaps finding himself on the other side of this sort of thing) he begins to feel that this is a bad practice and begins to doubt whether he should enjoy it quite as much as he does. This initiates a process of trying to break the habit, and the course this takes might be as follows. First, through an effort of self-control, he undertakes not to seek out gossip and pass on the sorts of things that before, he would have eagerly conveyed ... If the effort of self-control succeeds he may find that with the passage of time the appetite for this activity and its pleasures diminishes and it is no longer a matter of restraining himself. Instead the taste for it is gone.   (2001: 18)

Although the focus here is on modifying one's *habits*, the shift from being a gossip to not being a gossip is broadly speaking a change in character. Given the association between character and habit this is no surprise. Being a gossip is not an epistemic vice but if the type of self-transformation described by Jacobs is something that sometimes actually happens, then is it not possible that epistemic character vices are similarly malleable?

Generalizing from Jacobs' example, the idea would be that it is possible for a person to tackle his character vices as long as he knows that he has them, is motivated to tackle them, and is willing and able to make the necessary effort of self-control. On this view, the means by which self-improvement is possible is self-control, and self-control is basically a matter of effort. However, this underestimates the depth of many character traits and is no more plausible than the suggestion that weapon bias can be willed away. In the case of entrenched traits that define who one is as a thinker or knower the effort of self-control is unlikely to be sufficient. What is missing is any account of the practical steps by means of which people can change or revise their characters. If, as I have claimed, intellectual character traits are stable dispositions to act, think, and feel, then changing one's character means changing the relevant dispositions. The more deeply entrenched one's dispositions, the harder they are to modify, and epistemic vices such as arrogance and closed-mindedness tend to be deeply entrenched.

To see what an effective self-improvement strategy might look like consider the vice of intellectual arrogance. Although there is more to being intellectually arrogant than being a poor listener, being intellectually arrogant usually involves being a poor listener. It certainly did in the case of Donald Rumsfeld, whose failure to listen to advice and firm conviction that he knew better than those advising him ultimately led to his downfall. If that is right then what can such a person do to become a better listener, assuming they are motivated to change their ways? One practical suggestion is that paraphrasing exercises can make one a better listener. In paraphrasing exercises, the poor listener is invited to listen to another person talk for a period of time, possibly no more than five or ten minutes, and to paraphrase what they have heard as accurately as possible and without passing judgement on what they have heard. The speaker is then invited to comment on the accuracy, or otherwise, of the paraphrase. Poor listeners are bad at this exercise but improve with practice: they become better listeners.[20]

One worry about this self-improvement strategy is that it misses the point. The sense in which the intellectually arrogant are poor listeners isn't that they don't understand what is said to them or fail to take it in. The problem is that they too frequently lack respect for views that are different from their own and are too quick to dismiss them. For example, one imagines that Rumsfeld understood perfectly well what the military was saying to him about preparations for the Iraq War. He just didn't take it seriously. Not taking contrary views seriously can be the result of failing to engage with the arguments in their favour, and one way to increase the likelihood of a serious engagement with other people's

---

[20] My understanding of paraphrasing exercises is based on Rosenberg 2015: 96–101.

arguments is to practise paraphrasing those arguments before dismissing them or assessing their merits. Paraphrasing an argument for a conclusion, as distinct from merely endorsing or rejecting the conclusion, is a way of forcing oneself to engage and training oneself to be a more empathetic listener. Such self-improvement exercises aren't guaranteed to succeed but they also aren't guaranteed to fail. Success in this context means getting to the point where one's listening dispositions change so that one is able to absorb and engage with arguments for uncongenial conclusions without any special effort. The good listener is someone for whom listening well comes naturally.

Another worry about this self-improvement strategy for intellectual arrogance is that it only addresses one element of this vice. What accounts for an intellectually arrogant person's failings as a listener is their cognitive superiority complex. This complex is one that an effective self-improvement strategy must find a way to tackle, and paraphrasing exercises aren't going to do the job. However, as noted in Chapter 6, there are ways to recalibrate one's sense of one's intellectual standing. The most obvious of these is taking steps to expose oneself to the achievements of superior intellects. Just as one rapidly discovers one's limitations as a tennis player by playing against stronger opponents, so one rapidly discovers one's own intellectual limitations by engaging with higher-ranked intellects.[21]

If these prescriptions have a slight air of unreality about them one reason might be that a person's character vices aren't always a personal matter. Sometimes they have a social or structural explanation, and so can't be undone without addressing their social or structural causes. Consider José Medina's suggestion that intellectual arrogance is one of the epistemic vices of the privileged and the powerful. This points to a social structural explanation of some people's intellectual arrogance: they are that way because of the position they occupy in the social structure, in which case there is little prospect of reform unless there is a change in their position in the social structure. If being privileged makes one intellectually arrogant then loss of privilege may make one less arrogant, especially if the change in one's position is sudden and unexpected. These things do happen, of course, but there is no guarantee that loss

---

[21] You think you're so smart? Try reading Kant or Darwin.

of one's privileges will make one more humble. Bitterness rather than humility is an equally likely outcome.

The proposal that character vices can be undone by self-improvement strategies such as the ones I've described might prompt the thought that these strategies are unlikely to be employed by individuals who are most in need of them. Far from exposing themselves to better intellects intellectually arrogant individuals might consciously or unconsciously avoid people or works that threaten their sense of intellectual superiority. Their sense of superiority might in any case be so entrenched that not even exposure to manifestly superior intellects will have any effect. The implication is that in the case of some of our character vices the vices themselves are obstacles to self-improvement. Vices that obstruct their own reduction or elimination are resistant vices. Just as stealthy vices are inherently hard to detect because they are antithetical to the epistemic virtues needed to detect them, so resistant vices are inherently hard to undo because they are antithetical to the epistemic virtues needed to undo them. For example, one is unlikely to take paraphrasing exercises seriously unless one already has a degree of intellectual humility. If one has the requisite degree of humility then one isn't intellectually arrogant. If one is intellectually arrogant then one probably won't be humble enough to do the exercises. In the same way, the epistemically lazy may well be too lazy to do anything about their laziness, and the complacent too complacent to worry about being complacent. In all of these cases, the problem is that the project of undoing one's character vices is *virtue-dependent*, and those who have the necessary epistemic virtues don't have the epistemic vices.

While there is something right about the notion that many epistemic vices are resistant vices, it's important not to exaggerate the significance of this point. For a start, epistemic vices are not all or nothing and it is conceivable that those who are mildly arrogant or closed-minded might have enough humility or open-mindedness to recognize their epistemic vices and implement vice-reduction strategies. It also helps in these cases to be clear about the role of motivation. In one scenario, S recognizes that he has V but isn't motivated to do anything about it. If V itself is what deprives S of the motivation to do anything about V then V is a resistant vice. Now think of a different scenario is which the consequences of V for S are so disastrous that even S sees that he has a problem and is motivated to tackle V. Imagine Zeira after Yom Kippur 1973 recognizing that he can't go on as an effective military intelligence officer unless he does something about what he now acknowledges as his closed-mindedness. The point at which he recognizes the need for remedial action is the point at which he has already taken the first step on the road to greater open-mindedness. Taking this first step makes it easier for him to take further remedial action and achieve greater open-mindedness. There are indications here of a kind of virtuous circle, with greater open-mindedness at each stage facilitating further remedial action against closed-mindedness. The initial breakthrough is provided by the experience of failure, where the nature and magnitude of the failure leave no room for doubt as to its origins in the subject's intellectual character. The same goes for other epistemic vices. One is already less arrogant at the point at which a breakthrough experience reveals one's arrogance as a problem and motivates one to tackle it. This initial improvement then makes it possible for one to act in ways that further reduce one's arrogance.

Sadly, epistemic vices aren't all like this. The point at which one sees one's arrogance or closed-mindedness as a problem might be the point at which these vices are already in retreat, but the point at which one sees one's own gullibility as a problem isn't the point at which one's gullibility is already in retreat. Being motivated to be less gullible does not itself make one less gullible in the way that being motivated to be less closed-minded makes one less closed-minded. Is gullibility a resistant vice then? That depends on whether measures to combat one's gullibility are countered by that very gullibility. A person who has fallen for an obvious scam could develop a checklist of questions to ask the next time they get an offer that sounds too good to be true.[22] Asking sceptical questions is a way to become less gullible as well as a way to protect oneself against one's gullibility. To be gullible is to be disinclined to ask such questions and this supports the idea that gullibility is a resistant vice. On the other hand, a person who has suffered dire consequences as a result of their gullibility might force themselves to ask questions they aren't inclined to ask. Disinclinations can be overcome, and being gullible makes it harder but not impossible to take steps to counter one's gullibility. So here is another case in which self-improvement in respect of a character vice is possible. For most character vices, there are strategies for countering them.

---

[22] On the importance of checklists more generally see Gawande 2011.

Nevertheless, it needs to be recognized that self-improvement strategies don't always work, and that the self-knowledge, skill, and motivation required for the implementation of these strategies are often absent. In these circumstances, is outsmarting an option? Banaji and Greenwald observe that in 1970 less than 10 per cent of instrumentalists in America's major symphony orchestras were women, and women made up less than 20 per cent of new hires.[23] In subsequent years some orchestras adopted a system of blind auditions and the proportion of women hired by major symphony orchestras doubled. Here was a cheap and simple fix for a gender mindbug.[24] In general, where there is a danger of a decision being unduly influenced by biases, the risk of this happening can be reduced by strategies to diminish their impact.

What are the prospects of outsmarting one's character vices? Imagine a self-protective gambling addict who can't kick the habit but wants to limit the financial damage caused by his addiction. One way for him to outsmart his vice would be to limit his access to his money. Alternatively, he might avoid parts of town where there are betting shops and arrange fixed limits on his online betting transactions. Some epistemic character vices can be handled in the same way. A voter who was taken in by claims made by the winning side in the Brexit debate might resolve not to be so gullible in future and remember to ask Louis Heren's question in such cases: why is this lying bastard lying to me?[25] If the voter has been the victim of financial fraud then he might, in addition, arrange his financial affairs in such a way that it is no longer possible for him to make large payments without the approval of a trusted friend or relation. Asking sceptical questions of lying politicians is a way of *being* less gullible. Rearranging one's financial affairs is not so much a way of being less gullible as of outsmarting one's gullibility. When he tries to outsmart his epistemic vice the gullible person is thinking of himself in a way that is similar to the way that the self-protective gambler thinks

[23] 2016: 146.
[24] This is a case in which, as Banaji and Greenwald note, outsmarting a mindbug 'did not need to be complicated or costly' (2016: 147).
[25] Heren was a journalist who spent his entire career working for the London *Times*. In his memoirs he recalls some advice given to him by his mentor, the industrial correspondent of the old *Daily Worker*: 'When I asked him for some advice before interviewing a senior official, he said, "Always ask yourself why these lying bastards are lying to me"' (Heren 1988: 59).

of himself. They both know that they have a problem and they both want to deal with it.

This way of putting this brings out the extent to which the project of outsmarting an epistemic vice is as dependent on self-knowledge as the project of vice reduction. Just as one is unlikely to embark on the project of eliminating a vice one doesn't know or at least suspect one has, so one is unlikely to embark on the project of outsmarting a vice one doesn't know or suspect one has. In addition, the success of both projects depends on one's level of desire or motivation and the availability of suitable methods. Outsmarting an implicit bias requires 'awareness, a desire to improve, and a method for improving' (Banaji and Greenwald 2016: 147). If the very same combination of knowledge, desire, and method is needed in order to outsmart epistemic vices generally then it would appear that the obstacles to the outsmarting project are no different from the obstacles to projects of self-improvement. In both cases self-ignorance is one major obstacle and lack of desire is another. One has to want to improve if one is to improve and one has to want to outsmart one's vices if one is to outsmart them.

This assumes, however, that outsmarting one's epistemic vices is something that one always does for oneself, but that isn't so. When orchestras instituted blind auditions they were outsmarting the potential or actual implicit biases of hiring committees whose members may have had little to do with the decision to institute blind auditions. In much the same way, one can easily imagine Israeli military intelligence taking steps after the Yom Kippur surprise to make sure that no one individual's closed-mindedness or other epistemic vices could ever again have a decisive influence on its military policy and planning. Institutions that become aware of the actual or potential harms caused by implicit bias or other epistemic vices can try to minimize such harms by implementing outsmarting strategies at the level of the institution. By doing so they take the decision whether to outsmart out of the hands of individuals. But it would be naïve to put too much faith in the managers or directors of large institutions. They, as well as the institutions they manage, have their own vices and can't always be relied on to do the right thing.[26]

---

[26] Institutional vices are an important subject in their own right. See Thompson 2005.

The onus is therefore on us as individuals to minimize the harms done by our epistemic vices. It's worth emphasizing, however, that talk of outsmarting one's vices is, in one sense, an admission of failure. The addictive gambler who prevents himself from betting more than a certain amount is taking appropriate steps to mitigate the financial consequences of his addiction but is not tackling the addiction itself. In the same way, blind auditions don't get rid of implicit biases, they merely prevent them from doing too much damage. Pessimists focus on such measures because they see little prospect of self-improvement, but the message of this chapter is more hopeful: of course there are significant obstacles that stand in the way of self-improvement but these obstacles aren't insuperable. It is only because it is possible to exercise some control over one's epistemic vices that one counts as responsible for them. The challenge is to talk about self-improvement in a way that is neither naïvely optimistic nor morbidly pessimistic. The truth, as always, is in the middle: self-improvement in respect of our epistemic vices, like self-improvement more generally, is difficult but, for most of us, not impossible.

I began this book by quoting Susan Stebbing's remark on the urgent need for citizens of a democracy to think well. I end with more Stebbing:

I am convinced of the urgent need for a democratic people to think clearly, without the distortions due to unconscious bias and unrecognized ignorance. Our failures in thinking are in part due to faults which we could to some extent overcome were we to see clearly how these faults arise. (1939, preface)

In reality there is little prospect of our ever being able entirely to avoid unconscious bias or unrecognized ignorance, but Stebbing is right to insist that some of our failures in thinking can be overcome and that there is an urgent need to overcome them to the extent that this is possible. Some biases can be overcome, and when it comes to epistemic vices more generally we don't have to accept the *status quo* like despondent card players who have been dealt a bad hand. The story I've been telling is one in which epistemic vices of various kinds have been at least partly responsible for a series of political and other disasters. The only hope of avoiding such disasters in the future is to improve our thinking, our attitudes, and our habits of thought and inquiry. The alternative is too ghastly to contemplate.

References

Aaronovitch, D. (2009), *Voodoo Histories: How Conspiracy Theory Has Shaped Modern History* (London: Jonathan Cape).

Adams, R. (1985), 'Involuntary Sins', *Philosophical Review*, 94: 3–31.

Alfano, M. (2013), *Character as Moral Fiction* (Cambridge: Cambridge University Press).

Alston, W. (1980), 'Level-Confusions in Epistemology', *Midwest Studies in Philosophy*, 5: 135–50.

Althusser, L. and Balibar, E. (1979), *Reading Capital* (London: Verso Editions).

Amis, M. (2008), *The Second Plane* (London: Vintage).

Ayer, A. J. (1956), *The Problem of Knowledge* (Harmondsworth: Penguin).

Babad, E. (1997), 'Wishful Thinking among Voters: Motivational and Cognitive Influences', *International Journal of Public Opinion Research*, 9: 105–25.

Baehr, J. (2010), 'Epistemic Malevolence', in H. Battaly (ed.), *Virtue and Vice, Moral and Epistemic* (Chichester: Wiley-Blackwell): 189–213.

Baehr, J. (2011), *The Inquiring Mind: On Intellectual Virtues and Virtue Epistemology* (Oxford: Oxford University Press).

Ball, J. (2017), *Post-Truth: How Bullshit Conquered the World* (London: Biteback Publishing).

Banaji, M. and Greenwald, A. (2016), *Blindspot: Hidden Biases of Good People* (New York: Bantam Books).

Bar-Joseph, U. (2005), *The Watchman Fell Asleep: The Surprise of Yom Kippur and Its Sources* (Albany, NY: State University of New York Press).

Bar-Joseph, U. and Kruglanski, A. (2003), 'Intelligence Failure and Need for Cognitive Closure: On the Psychology of the Yom Kippur Surprise', *Political Psychology*, 24: 75–99.

Baron, J. (1985), *Rationality and Intelligence* (Cambridge: Cambridge University Press).

Battaly, H. (2014), 'Varieties of Epistemic Vice', in J. Matheson and R. Vitz (eds), *The Ethics of Belief: Individual and Social* (Oxford: Oxford University Press): 51–76.

Battaly, H. (2015), *Virtue* (Cambridge: Polity Press).

Battaly, H. (2016), 'Epistemic Virtue and Vice: Reliabilism, Responsibilism, and Personalism', in C. Mi, M. Slote, and E. Sosa (eds), *Moral and Intellectual Virtues in Western and Chinese Philosophy* (New York: Routledge): 99–120.

Beardsley, E. L. (1969), 'A Plea for Deserts', *American Philosophical Quarterly*, 6: 33–42.

Bergesen, A. J. (2008), *The Sayyid Qutb Reader: Selected Writings on Politics, Religion, and Society* (New York: Routledge).

Berman, P. (2004), *Terror and Liberalism* (New York: W. W. Norton & Company).

Berner, E. and Graber, M. (2008), 'Overconfidence as a Cause of Diagnostic Error in Medicine', *American Journal of Medicine*, 121: S2–S23.

Bernstein, C. and Woodward, B. (1974), *All the President's Men* (New York: Simon & Schuster).

Blair, I. (2002), 'The Malleability of Automatic Stereotypes and Prejudice', *Personality and Social Psychology Review*, 6: 242–61.

BonJour, L. (2001), 'Externalist Theories of Empirical Knowledge', in H. Kornblith (ed.), *Epistemology: Internalism and Externalism* (Oxford: Blackwell): 10–35.

Broadie, S. (1991), *Ethics with Aristotle* (Oxford: Oxford University Press).

Brooks, D. (2017), 'When the World Is Led by a Child', *New York Times*, 15 May.

Brotherton, R. (2015), *Suspicious Minds: Why We Believe Conspiracy Theories* (London: Bloomsbury Sigma).

Brotherton, R., French, C., and Pickering, A. (2013), 'Measuring Belief in Conspiracy Theories: The Generic Conspiracist Belief Scale', *Frontiers in Psychology*, 4: 1–14.

Brownstein, M. and Saul, J. (2016), *Implicit Bias and Philosophy, volume 1: Metaphysics and Epistemology* (Oxford: Oxford University Press).

Bruder, M., Haffke, P., Neave, N., Nouripanah, N., and Imhoff, R. (2013), 'Measuring Individual Differences in Generic Beliefs in Conspiracy Theories across Cultures: Conspiracy Mentality Questionnaire', *Frontiers in Psychology*, 4: 1–15.

Burrell, I. (1999), 'Lord Denning, the Century's Greatest Judge, Dies at 100', *Independent*, 6 March.

Campbell, J. (2015), 'L. A. Paul's *Transformative Experience*', *Philosophy and Phenomenological Research*, 91: 787–93.

Cassam, Q. (2009), 'Can the Concept of Knowledge Be Analysed?', in D. Pritchard and P. Greenough (eds), *Williamson on Knowledge* (Oxford: Oxford University Press): 12–30.

Cassam, Q. (2010), 'Judging, Believing and Thinking', *Philosophical Issues*, 20: 80–95.

Cassam, Q. (2014), *Self-Knowledge for Humans* (Oxford: Oxford University Press).

Cassam, Q. (2015a), 'Stealthy Vices', *Social Epistemology Review and Reply Collective*, 4: 19–25.

Cassam, Q. (2015b), 'Bad Thinkers', *Aeon* (https://aeon.co/essays/the-intellectual-character-of-conspiracy-theorists).

Cassam, Q. (2016), 'Vice Epistemology', *Monist*, 88: 159–80.

Cassam, Q. (2017), 'Overconfidence, Diagnostic Error and Self-Knowledge', *Palgrave Communications*, 3: 1–8.

Clarke, R. A. (2004), *Against All Enemies: Inside America's War on Terror* (London: Free Press).

Coady, C. A. J. (1992), *Testimony: A Philosophical Study* (Oxford: Clarendon Press).

Coates, D. J. and Tognazzini, N. A. (2013), 'The Contours of Blame', in D. J. Coates and N. A Tognazzini (eds), *Blame: Its Nature and Norms* (Oxford: Oxford University Press): 3–26.

Cockburn, A. (2007), *Rumsfeld: An American Disaster* (London: Verso).

Cohen, R. (1991), 'Sununu's Arrogance', *Washington Post*, 21 June.

Croskerry, P., Singhal, G., and Mamede, S. (2013), 'Cognitive Debiasing 2: Impediments to and Strategies for Change', *BMJ Quality and Safety in Healthcare*, 22: ii65–ii72.

D'Ancona, M. (2017), *Post Truth: The New War on Truth and How to Fight Back* (London: Ebury Press).

Dahl, E. J. (2013), *Intelligence and Surprise Attack: Failure and Success from Pearl Harbor to 9/11 and Beyond* (Washington, DC: Georgetown University Press).

Darley, J. and Batson, D. (1973), '"From Jerusalem to Jericho": A Study of Situational and Dispositional Variables in Helping Behavior', *Journal of Personality and Social Psychology*, 27: 100–8.

Debus, D. (2015–16), 'Shaping Our Mental Lives: On the Possibility of Mental Self-Regulation', *Proceedings of the Aristotelian Society*, 116: 341–65.

Dennett, D. (2010), *Content and Consciousness* (Abingdon: Routledge Classics).

Doris, J. (2002), *Lack of Character: Personality and Moral Behaviour* (Cambridge: Cambridge University Press).

Dougherty, T. (2012), 'Reducing Responsibility: An Evidentialist Account of Epistemic Blame', *European Journal of Philosophy*, 20: 534–47.

Driver, J. (2000), 'Moral and Epistemic Virtue', in G. Axtell (ed.), *Knowledge, Belief, and Character: Readings in Virtue Epistemology* (Lanham, MD: Rowman & Littlefield): 123–34.

Driver, J. (2001), *Uneasy Virtue* (Cambridge: Cambridge University Press).

Dunning, D. (2016), 'The Psychological Quirk that Explains Why You Love Donald Trump', *Politico Magazine*, 25 May.

Dyer, C. (1999), 'Lord Denning, Controversial "People's Judge", Dies Aged 100', *Guardian*, 6 March.

Edelman, S. (2006), *Change Your Thinking with CBT* (London: Vermilion).

Ellis, A. (2010), *Evolution of a Revolution: Selections from the Writings of Albert Ellis, Ph.D.*, edited by J. McMahon and A. Vernon (Fort Lee, NJ: Barricade Books).

Elton, M. (2000), 'The Personal/Sub-Personal Distinction: An Introduction', *Philosophical Explorations*, 3: 2–5.

Evans, R. (2002), *Telling Lies about Hitler* (London: Verso).

Fetzer, J. (2007), *The 9/11 Conspiracy: The Scamming of America* (Peru, IL: Catfeet Press).

Foster, J. (1985), *A. J. Ayer* (London: Routledge & Kegan Paul).

Frankfurt, H. G. (2005), *On Bullshit* (Princeton, NJ: Princeton University Press).

Frankish, K. (2009), 'Systems and Levels: Dual System Theories and the Personal-Subpersonal Distinction', in J. Evans and K. Frankish (eds), *In Two Minds: Dual Processes and Beyond* (Oxford: Oxford University Press): 89–107.

Freedland, J. (2016), 'Post-Truth Politicians such as Donald Trump and Boris Johnson Are No Joke', *Guardian*, 13 May.

Freeman, D. and Bentall, R. (2017), 'The Concomitants of Conspiracy Concerns', *Social Psychiatry and Psychiatric Epidemiology*, 52: 595–604.

Freeman, I. (1993), *Lord Denning: A Life* (London: Hutchinson).

Fricker, M. (2007), *Epistemic Injustice: Power and the Ethics of Knowing* (Oxford: Oxford University Press).

Gawande, A. (2011), *The Checklist Manifesto: How to Get Things Right* (London: Profile Books).

Gendler, T. S. (2011), 'On the Epistemic Costs of Implicit Bias', *Journal of Philosophy*, 156: 33–63.

Goldman, A. (2011), 'A Guide to Social Epistemology', in A. Goldman and D. Whitcomb (eds), *Social Epistemology: Essential Readings* (Oxford: Oxford University Press): 11–37.

Groopman, J. (2008), *How Doctors Think* (Boston, MA: Mariner Books).

Hamilton, C. (1991), *The Hitler Diaries: Fakes that Fooled the World* (Lexington, KY: University of Kentucky Press).

Hare, W. (1983), 'Open-Mindedness, Liberalism and Truth', *Educational Philosophy and Theory*, 15: 31–42.

Harman, G. (1973), *Thought* (Princeton, NJ: Princeton University Press).

Harman, G. (1999), 'Moral Philosophy Meets Social Psychology: Virtue Ethics and the Fundamental Attribution Error', *Proceedings of the Aristotelian Society*, 99: 315–31.

Harman, G. (2000), 'The Nonexistence of Character Traits', *Proceedings of the Aristotelian Society*, 100: 223–326.

Harman, G. (2003), 'No Character or Personality', *Business Ethics Quarterly*, 13: 87–94.

Harris, R. (2009), *Selling Hitler* (London: Arrow Books).

Haslanger, S. (2015), 'Social Structure, Narrative and Explanation', *Canadian Journal of Philosophy*, 45: 1–15.

Haslanger, S. (2016), 'What Is a (Social) Structural Explanation?', *Philosophical Studies*, 173: 113–30.

Heren, L. (1988), *Memories of Times Past* (London: Hamish Hamilton).

Heuer, R. (1999), *Psychology of Intelligence Analysis* (Langley, VI: Central Intelligence Agency).

Hieronymi, P. (2006), 'Controlling Attitudes', *Pacific Philosophical Quarterly*, 87: 45–74.

Hieronymi, P. (2008), 'Responsibility for Believing', *Synthese*, 161: 357–73.

Hofstadter, R. (2008), *The Paranoid Style in American Politics* (New York: Vintage Books).

Holroyd, J. and Kelly, D. (2016), 'Implicit Bias, Character, and Control', in A. Masala and J. Webber (eds), *From Personality to Virtue* (Oxford: Oxford University Press): 106–33.

Hookway, C. (1994), 'Cognitive Virtues and Epistemic Evaluations', *International Journal of Philosophical Studies*, 2: 211–27.

Hume, D. (1975), 'An Enquiry Concerning Human Understanding', in L. A. Selby-Bigge (ed.), *Enquiries Concerning Human Understanding and Concerning the Principles of Morals*, third edition (Oxford: Oxford University Press).

Imhoff, R. and Bruder, M. (2014), 'Speaking (Un-)Truth to Power: Conspiracy Mentality as a Generalised Political Attitude', *European Journal of Personality*, 28: 25–43.

Jackson, F. and Pettit, P. (1992), 'Structural Explanation in Social Theory', in D. Charles and K. Lennon (eds), *Reduction, Explanation, and Realism* (Oxford: Clarendon Press): 97–131.

Jackson, R. (2015), 'The Epistemological Crisis of Counterterrorism', *Critical Studies on Terrorism*, 8: 33–54.

Jacobs, J. (2001), *Choosing Character: Responsibility for Virtue and Vice* (Ithaca, NY: Cornell University Press).

Janis, I. (1982), *Groupthink*, second edition (Boston, MA: Wadsworth).

Jayawickreme, E. and Blackie, L. (2014), 'Posttraumatic Growth as Positive Personality Change: Evidence, Controversies and Future Directions', *European Journal of Personality*, 28: 312–31.

Johnson, D. (2004), *Overconfidence and War: The Havoc and Glory of Positive Illusions* (Cambridge, MA: Harvard University Press).

Kahneman, D. (2011), *Thinking, Fast and Slow* (London: Allen Lane).

Kean, T. H. and Hamilton, L. (2012), *The 9/11 Commission Report: Final Report of the National Commission on Terrorist Attacks upon the United States* (Seattle, WA: Pacific Publishing Studio).

Keeley, B. (1999), 'Of Conspiracy Theories', *Journal of Philosophy*, 96: 109–26.

Kidd, I. (2016), 'Charging Others with Epistemic Vice', *Monist*, 99: 181–97.

Knightley, P. (2000), 'Konrad Kujau', *Guardian*, 16 September.

Kripke, S. (2011), 'On Two Paradoxes of Knowledge', in S. Kripke (ed.), *Philosophical Troubles: Collected Papers*, volume 1 (Oxford: Oxford University Press): 27–52.

Kruger, J. and Dunning, D. (1999), 'Unskilled and Unaware of It: How Difficulties in Recognizing One's Own Incompetence Lead to Inflated Self-Assessments', *Journal of Personality and Social Psychology*, 77: 1121–34.

Kruglanski, A. W. (2004), *The Psychology of Closed-Mindedness* (New York: Psychology Press).

Kuhn, T. (1963), 'The Function of Dogma in Scientific Research', in A. Crombie (ed.), *Scientific Change* (London: Heinemann): 347–69.

Kuhn, T. (2012), *The Structure of Scientific Revolutions*, 50th anniversary edition (Chicago, IL: University of Chicago Press).

Kvanvig, J. (1992), *The Intellectual Virtues and the Life of the Mind* (Lanham, MD: Rowman & Littlefield).

Laws, D. (2017), *Coalition: The Inside Story of the Conservative-Liberal Coalition Government* (London: Biteback Publishing).

Lehrer, K. (1999), *Self-Trust: A Study of Reason, Knowledge, and Autonomy* (Oxford: Oxford University Press).

Lipstadt, D. (1994), *Denying the Holocaust: The Growing Assault on Truth and Memory* (Harmondsworth: Penguin).

Lipton, P. (2004), 'Discussion: Epistemic Options', *Philosophical Studies*, 121: 147–58.

Madison, B. (2017), 'On the Nature of Intellectual Vice', *Social Epistemology Review and Reply Collective*, 6: 1–6.

Maio, G. and Haddock, G. (2015), *The Psychology of Attitudes and Attitude Change*, second edition (London: Sage).

Mason, M. (2003), 'Contempt as a Moral Attitude', *Ethics* 113: 234–72.

Medina, J. (2013), *The Epistemology of Resistance: Gender and Racial Oppression, Epistemic Injustice, and Resistant Imaginations* (Oxford: Oxford University Press).

Merritt, M., Doris, J., and Harman, G. (2010), 'Character', in J. Doris and Moral Psychology Research Group (eds), *The Moral Psychology Handbook* (Oxford: Oxford University Press): 355–401.

Mill, J. S. (2006), 'On Liberty', in *On Liberty and The Subjection of Women* (London: Penguin).

Miller, W. R. and de Baca, J. C. (2001), *Quantum Change: When Epiphanies and Sudden Insights Transform Ordinary Lives* (New York: Guildford Press).

Millican, P. (2011), 'Twenty Questions about Hume's "Of Miracles"', *Royal Institute of Philosophy Supplement*, 68: 151–92.

Montmarquet, J. (1987), 'Epistemic Virtue', *Mind*, 96: 482–97.

Montmarquet, J. (1993), *Epistemic Virtue and Doxastic Responsibility* (Lanham, MD: Rowman & Littlefield).

Moody-Adams, M. (1990), 'On the Old Saw that Character Is Destiny', in O. Flanagan and A. Rorty (eds), *Identity, Character and Morality: Essays in Moral Psychology* (Cambridge, MA: MIT Press): 111–31.

Morton, A. (2014), 'Shared Knowledge from Individual Vice: The Role of Unworthy Epistemic Emotions', *Philosophical Inquiries*, 2: 163–72.

Mulligan, K. (2014), 'Foolishness, Stupidity, and Cognitive Values', *Monist*, 97: 65–85.

Mullin, C. (1990), *Error of Judgement: The Truth about the Birmingham Bombings*, revised and updated edition (Dublin: Poolbeg Press).

Mullin, C. (1991), 'Evidence to the Royal Commission on Criminal Justice', http://www.chrismullinexmp.com/speeches/evidence-to-the-royal-commission-on-criminal-justice.

Nettle, D. (2007), *Personality: What Makes You the Way You Are* (Oxford: Oxford University Press).

Nichols, T. (2017), *The Death of Expertise: The Campaign against Established Knowledge and Why It Matters* (Oxford: Oxford University Press).

Nussbaum, M. (1990), *Love's Knowledge: Essays on Philosophy and Literature* (Oxford: Oxford University Press).

Oreskes, N. and Conway, E. (2010), *Merchants of Doubt: How a Handful of Scientists Obscured the Truth on Issues from Tobacco Smoke to Global Warming* (London: Bloomsbury).

Owens, D. (2000), *Reason without Freedom: The Problem of Epistemic Normativity* (Abingdon: Routledge).

Parris, M. (2016), 'Tories Have Got to End Their Affair with Boris', *Times*, 26 March.

Paul, L. A. (2014), *Transformative Experience* (Oxford: Oxford University Press).

Payne, K. (2006), 'Weapon Bias: Split-Second Decisions and Unintended Stereotyping', *Current Directions in Psychological Science*, 15: 287–91.

Payne, K., Niemi, L., and Doris, J. (2018), 'How to Think about "Implicit Bias"', *Scientific American*, 27 March.

Pickard, H. (2013), 'Responsibility without Blame: Philosophical Reflections on Clinical Practice', in K. W. M. Fulford, M. Davies, R. Gipps, G. Graham et al. (eds), *The Oxford Handbook of Philosophy and Psychiatry* (Oxford: Oxford University Press): 1134–52.

Pigden, C. R. (2017), 'Are Conspiracy Theorists Epistemically Vicious?', in K. Lippert-Rasmussen, K. Brownlee, and D. Coady (eds), *A Companion to Applied Philosophy* (Chichester: Wiley-Blackwell).

Popper, K. (1970), 'Normal Science and Its Dangers', in I. Lakatos and A. Musgrave (eds), *Criticism and the Growth of Knowledge* (Cambridge: Cambridge University Press).

Pressler, J. (2017), 'Donald Trump, the Dunning-Kruger President', *New York Magazine*, 9 January.

Proctor, R. (2008), 'Agnotology: A Missing Term to Describe the Cultural Production of Ignorance (and Its Study)', in R. N. Proctor and L. Schiebinger (eds), *Agnotology: The Making and Unmaking of Ignorance* (Stanford, CA: Stanford University Press): 1–33.

Proctor, R. and Schiebinger, L. (eds) (2008), *Agnotology: The Making and Unmaking of Ignorance* (Stanford, CA: Stanford University Press).

Radford, C. (1966), 'Knowledge—by Examples', *Analysis*, 27: 1–11.

Reason, J. (2000), 'Human Error: Models and Management', *BMJ*, 320: 768–70.

Ricks, T. E. (2007), *Fiasco: The American Military Adventure in Iraq* (London: Penguin Books).

Roberts, R. C. and Wood, W. J. (2007), *Intellectual Virtues: An Essay in Regulative Epistemology* (Oxford: Oxford University Press).

Rose, D. and Schaffer, J. (2013), 'Knowledge Entails Dispositional Belief', *Philosophical Studies*, 166: S19–S50.

Rosenberg, M. (2015), *Nonviolent Communication*, third edition (Encinitas, CA: PuddleDancer Press).

Ross, L. and Nisbett, R. (2011), *The Person and the Situation: Perspectives of Social Psychology* (London: Pinter & Martin).

Rowbottom, D. (2011), 'Kuhn vs. Popper on Criticism and Dogmatism in Science: A Resolution at the Group Level', *Studies in History and Philosophy of Science*, 42: 117–24.

Rushmer, R. and Davies, H. T. O. (2004), 'Unlearning in Healthcare', *BMJ Quality and Safety in Healthcare*, 13(Suppl II): ii10–ii15.

Ryan, A. (1974), *J. S. Mill* (London: Routledge & Kegan Paul).

Sher, G. (2006), *In Praise of Blame* (Oxford: Oxford University Press).

Shipman, T. (2017), *All Out War: The Full Story of Brexit* (London: William Collins).

Shklar, J. (1984), *Ordinary Vices* (Cambridge, MA: Harvard University Press).

Singer, M. (2016), *Trump and Me* (London: Penguin Random House).

Smith, A. (2005), 'Responsibility for Attitudes: Activity and Passivity in Mental Life', *Ethics*, 115: 236–71.

Smith, A. (2008), 'Control, Responsibility, and Moral Assessment', *Philosophical Studies*, 138: 367–92.

Stanley, J. (2008), 'Knowledge and Certainty', *Philosophical Issues*, 18: 35–57.

Stanovich, K. E. and West, R. F. (1997), 'Reasoning Independently of Prior Belief and Individual Differences in Actively Open-Minded Thinking', *Journal of Educational Psychology*, 89: 342–57.

Stebbing, L. S. (1939), *Thinking to Some Purpose* (Harmondsworth: Penguin Books).

Sternberg, R. J. (1997), *Thinking Styles* (Cambridge: Cambridge University Press).

Swami, V., Coles, R., Stieger, S. et al. (2011), 'Conspiracist Ideation in Britain and Austria: Evidence of a Monological Belief System and Associations between Individual Psychological Differences and Real-World and Fictitious Conspiracy Theories', *British Journal of Psychology*, 102: 443–63.

Swank, C. (2000), 'Epistemic Vice', in G. Axtell (ed.), *Knowledge, Belief, and Character: Readings in Virtue Epistemology* (Lanham, MD: Rowman & Littlefield): 195–204.

Tanesini, A. (2016), '"Calm Down Dear": Intellectual Arrogance, Silencing and Ignorance', *Proceedings of the Aristotelian Society*, supplementary volume, 90: 71–92.

Taylor, G. (2006), *Deadly Vices* (Oxford: Clarendon Press).

Tedeschi, R. and Calhoun, L. (2004), 'Posttraumatic Growth: Conceptual Foundations and Empirical Evidence', *Psychological Inquiry*, 15: 1–18.

Teller, P. (2004), 'Discussion: What Is a Stance?', *Philosophical Studies*, 121: 159–70.

Thompson, D. F. (2005), *Restoring Responsibility: Ethics in Government, Business, and Healthcare* (Cambridge: Cambridge University Press).

Thompson, E. P. (1995), *The Poverty of Theory* (London: Merlin Press).

Tiberius, V. and Walker, J. (1998), 'Arrogance', *American Philosophical Quarterly*, 35: 379–90.

Tilly, C. (2002), *Stories, Identities, and Political Change* (Lanham, MD: Rowman & Littlefield).

Unger, P. (1975), *Ignorance: A Case for Scepticism* (Oxford: Clarendon Press).

van Fraassen, B. (2004), 'Replies to Discussion on *The Empirical Stance*', *Philosophical Studies*, 121: 171–92.

Vyse, S. (1997), *Believing in Magic: The Psychology of Superstition* (Oxford: Oxford University Press).

Walker, C. and Starmer, K. (eds) (1999), *Miscarriages of Justice: A Review of Justice in Error* (Oxford: Blackstone Press).

Wastell, C., Weeks, N., Wearing, A., Duncan, P., and Ebrahimi, W. (2013), 'The Impact of Closed-Mindedness on the Assessment of Threat: An Empirical Study', *Open Psychology Journal*, 6: 10–19.

Williams, B. (1985), *Ethics and the Limits of Philosophy* (London: Fontana Press).

Williams, B. (1993), 'Moral Incapacity', *Proceedings of the Aristotelian Society*, 93: 59–70.

Williamson, T. (2000), *Knowledge and Its Limits* (Oxford: Oxford University Press).

Williamson, T. (2009a), 'Reply to Quassim Cassam', in P. Greenough and D. Pritchard (eds), *Williamson on Knowledge* (Oxford: Oxford University Press): 285–92.

Williamson, T. (2009b), 'Reply to Elizabeth Fricker', in P. Greenough and D. Pritchard (eds), *Williamson on Knowledge* (Oxford: Oxford University Press): 293–301.

Wilson, T. and Brekke, N. (1994), 'Mental Contamination and Mental Correction: Unwanted Influences on Judgments and Evaluations', *Psychological Bulletin*, 116: 117–42.

Wilson, T. and Dunn, E. (2004), 'Self-Knowledge: Its Limits, Value, and Potential for Improvement', *Annual Review of Psychology*, 55: 493–518.

Wohlstetter, R. (1962), *Pearl Harbor: Warning and Decision* (Stanford, CA: Stanford University Press).

Wolff, M. (2018), *Fire and Fury: Inside the Trump White House* (London: Little, Brown).

Wood, J. (1999), 'Extracts from the Transcript of the Trial of the *Birmingham Six*, Lancaster, June 1975', in C. Walker and K. Starmer (eds), *Miscarriages of Justice: A Review of Justice in Error* (Oxford: Blackstone Press): 226–8.

Wood, M., Douglas, K., and Sutton, R. (2012), 'Dead and Alive: Belief in Contradictory Conspiracy Theories', *Social Psychology and Personality Science*, 3: 767–73.

Wright, L. (2011), *The Looming Tower: Al-Qaeda's Road to 9/11* (London: Penguin Books).

Zagzebski, L. (1996), *Virtues of the Mind: An Inquiry into the Nature of Virtue and the Ethical Foundations of Knowledge* (Cambridge: Cambridge University Press).

Zonis, M. and Joseph, C. (1994), 'Conspiracy Thinking in the Middle East', *Political Psychology*, 15: 443–59.

Index

Aaronovitch, David 71n.33
active critical reflection 148–59, 163–4
Adams, Robert Merrihew 125
Adelman, Kenneth 1n.2
agnotology 89
Alfano, Mark 32, 44–6
Alston, William 51n.43
Althusser, Louis 24n.41
AMAN (Directorate of Military
    Intelligence) 28–30, 35, 45–6,
    49–50
Aristotle 5–6, 18–19, 179–80
Armstrong, Neil 33
arrogance, intellectual 2–3, 6–8, 12–14,
    94–5, 128–9, 151, 158, 181–4
attitude 6–7, 13, 81, 83–4, 98–9, 167–8,
    172, 176; *see also* epistemic attitude
attitude vice 79–80, 86–8, 98–9, 137
awfulizing *see* thinking, catastrophic
Ayer, A. J. 10n.22

Babad, Elisha 140–1
Baehr, Jason 5, 88, 90–4, 150–1
Ball, James 80–1, 92n.31
Banaji, Mahzarin 153–4, 167–9, 172–3,
    185–6
Bandman, Lieutenant-Colonel
    Yona 28–30, 41–3, 45–6
Banks, Arron 78
Bar-Joseph, Uri 28–30, 33–4, 38–9, 45–7
Baron, Jonathan 61–2
Batiste, John 3
Battaly, Heather 19–21, 85, 110–11
Beardsley, Elizabeth 17n.29
Berman, Paul 40n.15
Bernstein, Carl 70–1
Birmingham Six 54–7, 63–4, 71, 73
Blair, Irene 172–3
blame 17, 122–3, 132–3, 137–8
blameworthiness 17–19, 122–5, 134–5,
    146–7
Brekke, Nancy 24–5
Bridge, Mr Justice 53–4, 63–5, 71–6
Broadie, Sarah 18n.36

Brooks, David 144n.3
Brotherton, Rob 69n.26
bullshit 80–1
Bush, President George H. W. 152
Bush, President George W. 1–2, 175–6

Cameron, David 79n.3, 93n.32
Campbell, John 161n.27
carelessness, intellectual 153–4
cataleptic impressions 160, 162–3
character traits 6–7, 12–13, 31–3, 42–3,
    126–7
    behavioural dimension of 31–2
    high-fidelity vs. low-fidelity 32, 34,
      45, 57–8
    local 57
    robust 31n.6, 43–4, 57
character vice 30, 38–9, 50–1, 56, 58–60,
    98–9, 128–9, 132–3, 137, 179–80,
    182–3, 185–6
Cheney, Vice-President Dick 1–2
Clarke, Richard 175n.16
Clegg, Nick 93n.32
Clinton, President Bill 175–6
closed-mindedness 3–5, 12n.25, 16–17,
    29–31, 34–43, 56, 100–1, 106, 109,
    128–9, 151–7, 159–60, 165, 183–4
    behavioural component of 33
    consistency requirement on 34
    epistemological benefits of 35–8
    ethical component of 33–4
    impact on knowledge 35–8
    psychological component of 33
Coady, C. A. J. 156n.20
Coates, Justin 17n.30
Cockburn, Andrew 2n.5, 3
cognitive behaviour therapy (CBT)
    170–1
cognitive bias 23–7, 65–6, 140, 178–9;
    see also implicit bias
cognitive closure, need for 28–9, 33
confidence, as a condition of
    knowledge 10–11, 67–8, 95–6, 115
confirmation bias 24–6